PSYCHOLOGY & YOU
An informal introduction

PSYCHOLOGY & YOU

An informal introduction

JULIA C. BERRYMAN
David J. Hargreaves
Clive R. Hollin
Kevin Howells

Departments of Adult Education and Psychology,
University of Leicester
and Department of Psychology, University of Birmingham

Published by The British Psychological Society
and Routledge

First published in 1987 by The British Psychological Society, St Andrews House, 48 Princess Road East, Leicester LE1 7DR, in association with Methuen & Co. Ltd, 11 New Fetter Lane, London EC4P 4EE.

Reprinted 1991, 1993

British Library Cataloguing in Publication Data

Berryman, Julia C.
Psychology and you: an informal introduction.
1. Psychology
I. Title   II. British Psychological Society
150   BF121

ISBN 0-901715-72-7
ISBN 0-901715-71-9 Pbk

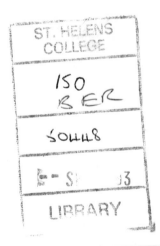
Set in Garamond
by Prestige Filmsetters, James House, 43–51 Welford Road, Leicester LE2 7AE
Printed and bound in Great Britain by Biddles Ltd, Guildford and King's Lynn

CONTENTS

Start reading this book at the point, chapter or sub-heading that interests you most. Each chapter is self-contained but refers you to other related chapters as appropriate. A glossary at the end defines all the technical terms. We hope that by dipping in here and there you will soon find that you have read the whole book.

LIST OF EXERCISES

LIST OF FIGURES

PREFACE AND ACKNOWLEDGEMENTS

Psychology & You is written for all those who would like to find out how psychology relates to their everyday experiences. As a psychologist teaching all sorts of people in 'Adult Education' I became aware of a need for a broad-based introduction to this subject. Adult education students of psychology are people of all ages and backgrounds from school students to retired people; they are keen to increase their knowledge of an area that is, for the most part, not covered in school. Most of us have a grounding in subjects such as history, geography, mathematics and the sciences but psychology, a subject of immediate relevance to us all, rarely forms part of the school curriculum. As a result most people glean their knowledge from TV, radio, magazines and popular books. However, it is surprisingly difficult to find a book that introduces the subject in an up-to-date manner whilst also starting at the point that interests you. A-level and undergraduate textbooks are necessary for students who must cover a particular syllabus and take an exam. My aim is to bring together all the topics which my own and my co-authors' teaching experience has shown are intriguing and relevant to everyday life. We hope that this book may be the beginning of a life-long interest in psychology for you. With this in mind, we have included recommended reading and references. We also hope that all teachers of psychology will find this book a lively introduction to the subject for their students.

All chapters, except the last, include exercises, the aim of which is to stimulate interest in the topic in a practical way. Psychology is about people and, as such, is concerned with exploring every aspect of human behaviour, thoughts and feelings. Psychologists have certainly not found all the answers, but we hope that you, the reader, will feel that the topics which we have considered will enhance your understanding of yourself and others.

The following people have played a vital part in the preparation of this book: the students whose questions and comments have been the major stimulus for producing this book; Ruby and Eric Berryman, Philip Drew, Linda Hargreaves and Liz Pratt for reading drafts of the text and making helpful comments; Sue Cavendish for providing some information on research material; Lesley Ralston, Vivienne Doughty and Barbara Hudson for typing drafts of the chapters; and Sue Lloyd for preparing with great care and efficiency the final version of the manuscript. Our thanks to them all.

Introduction: Beginning to Understand You

▽ *What is psychology? – Was Freud a psychologist?*
▽ *Three different approaches.*
▽ *The psychologist's approach.*
▽ *Are psychologists devious experimenters?*
▽ *The importance of objectivity.*
▽ *What we expect affects what we see.*
▽ *Experiments are not enough.*

'Why did you do it?'

'What were you thinking?'

'How did you feel?'

These three questions are crucial in any attempt we make to understand another person; they are also crucial questions in psychology. Like the psychologist we have all asked such questions when another's behaviour, thoughts and feelings have baffled us; if we know someone well we expect to be able to predict what they will do, think or feel in everyday situations.

If someone in your family is slow to wake in the morning, and is bright-eyed at midnight, you soon learn not to discuss important topics at breakfast but to save them for late night consideration. You come to expect him or her to eat little at breakfast, nod rather than talk, and through the experience of many mornings together you are able to predict a whole host of other things about that person's behaviour. In a sense we are all amateur psychologists because we observe our friends' and partner's behaviour carefully and discover rules by which they seem to act. This ability is not unique to adults. In a family it is likely that the children and the dog have also learned to make these predictions about other family members.

1

Perhaps, you are saying, this is all just common sense. But we hope that this book shows that psychology goes well beyond what can be answered by common sense. It is a subject which has developed a variety of methods to assist in answering questions about human behaviour, thoughts and feelings. These methods are illustrated by examples throughout this book.

WHAT IS PSYCHOLOGY?

What does psychology mean to you? When people who have not studied the subject are asked to say what comes into their mind when the words 'psychology' or 'psychologists' are mentioned a whole rag-bag of answers is given:

'Psychologists can read your mind.'

'They analyse you – like Freud did.'

'They measure I.Q. and personality.'

'Psychologists deal with problems like phobias and depression.'

'They use lie detectors.'

'They do devious experiments.'

The commonest answers deal with uncovering the hidden aspects of people and their psychological problems and, as these answers show, there is often more than a certain wariness about psychologists and their profession. Sigmund Freud's name is often mentioned in connection with psychology and his ideas have certainly influenced psychologists, but what did he actually do?

Was Freud a psychologist?

Freud, often referred to as 'the father of psychoanalysis' was not a psychologist. Freud (1856-1939) was a Viennese physician who became interested in the role of unconscious mental processes in influencing people's behaviour and, in particular, their psychological problems. He was interested in exploring human behaviour, feelings and thoughts, but his ideas were based on his clinical work. He built up a view of what makes humans 'tick' from his deductions about the causes of the problems he saw in his patients. Thus his view of human nature was shaped by observing and trying to help those who had problems; he was not concerned wih the 'normal' or average person but just a small number of rather unhappy people.

Essentially Freud believed that a large part of the mind was unconscious, and that our behaviour was 'driven' by instincts housed in this unconscious area of mind. The expression of these instincts was, he suggested, shaped by our early life experiences: thus, for example, a person who was deprived of adequate breast feeding, or mother love, might later show neutrotic patterns of behaviour such as a craving for comfort, food or love.

In attempting to find the causes of psychological problems, Freud's approach, in psychoanalytic therapy, was to use a variety of techniques which were intended to give insights into a person's unconscious mental processes. Two of these techniques were free-association and dream analysis. In the former, a patient would lie on a couch and be asked to report freely whatever thoughts or feelings came to mind; in dream analysis the content of the patient's dreams were explored using free association with a dream event as the initial stimulus. Freud believed that these techniques led him to the source of a patient's problems and, by bringing that source out into the open into conscious awareness, the emotional release (or catharsis) induced would assist in helping the patient towards a solution of the problem.

But being based on clinical evidence, which is open to a variety of interpretations, Freud's ideas cannot be easily tested or verified in the way that modern psychologists believe to be essential. And so although Freud's views of the human mind and behaviour have influenced psychological thinking, they are not, as we shall see, central to it.

Three different approaches

The distinction between psychoanalysis, psychiatry and psychology needs to be clarified, because it is not a simple one. Psychiatry is a branch of medicine and, as such, psychiatrists are concerned largely with the treatment of mental *illness* and psychological *problems.* Any qualified physician may choose to specialize and take a further qualification in psychiatry, just as he or she might select gynaecology or surgery. Psychiatrists, like physicians (or general practitioners), may use drugs in the treatment of mental illness, or they may use other methods such as behaviour therapy – a technique also used by psychologists.

Psychologists train by taking a degree course in psychology in which all aspects of behaviour and its underlying causes – in both humans and other animals – are studied. One distinction between psychologists, psychiatrists and psychoanalysts is that the former are concerned with all people, the latter two are concerned solely with those who cannot cope, and who are unwell. Clinical psychologists however also make the *patient* the main focus of their work, but the treatment methods used by them involve therapies which do not rely on the prescription of drugs.

Psychoanalysts have their own training which is quite separate from that of both psychologists and psychiatrists. This training usually involves the would-be analyst first undergoing psychoanalysis to gain increased insight. Psychologists and psychiatrists sometimes undergo further training in order to become psychoanalysts and thus it is perhaps not surprising that there is sometimes confusion, in the minds of the public, about these three professions.

In this book we are concerned with psychology which has developed its own rigorous methods for studying humans. These are quite distinct from the techniques of psychoanalysis. Indeed at the height of Freud's influence, at the turn of the century, psychologists showed a marked disregard for subjective reports of mental processes (introspection) as the major source of data. Overt behaviour became the focus of attention and psychology became known as the 'science of behaviour'; thoughts and feelings were largely ignored because they are intangible and unobservable. Speculations about the causes of human behaviour based on introspection were thought to be unhelpful and misleading.

What do you know about dreams?

Dreaming is used as an important source of information in *psychoanalysis,* but let us look at the *psychologist's* approach to studying it. If we use common sense, or introspection, what can we find out about it? Before you read on answer the following questions:

- [ ] Does everyone dream?
- [ ] How long does a typical dream last – seconds, minutes, hours?
- [ ] How often do you dream – several times, once a night, occasionally, rarely, never?
- [ ] Does sleep walking occur during dreaming?

If you simply ask people about dreams, some will tell you that they never dream, others that they have dreams that last just a second, whilst others last hours, and most people believe that sleep walking occurs whilst dreaming.

Psychological research using other techniques, as well as introspection, gives us different and more reliable answers:

- [ ] A typical dream lasts about twenty minutes.

- [ ] All people dream several times in an average length night of sleep (whether or not they recall these dreams).

- [ ] Sleep walking is highly unlikely when dreaming since the body's muscles are in a state where walking is virtually impossible.

Dream researchers made these discoveries whilst studying sleepers and recording their brain waves by sticking tiny electrodes on to their heads. The electrodes reveal characteristic patterns of electrical activity in the brain during dream sleep. Dreaming coincides with this brain activity (sleepers woken during this brain activity report dreams), with:

- [ ] rapid eye movements beneath closed eye-lids (REM sleep),

- [ ] in men, dreams are associated with penile erection, and

- [ ] dream events appear to last about as long as the same events in waking life.

Repeated studies of many people (or subjects as psychologists call the people whom they study) have demonstrated the universality of dreaming, in a way that introspection alone could not.

THE PSYCHOLOGIST'S APPROACH

Today psychologists base their conclusions about humans on both observations of the behaviour of many subjects, and reports from those subjects themselves. It is more than the *science of behaviour* because people's own unique experiences also form part of the data.

Psychologists use a wide range of equipment to measure both easily observable and unobservable bodily changes. The well-known lie detector or polygraph is one example: this measures a variety of physiological changes, including heart rate and skin moistness, but psychologists would rarely use this to detect lies. Indeed most psychologists are well aware of its fallibility in this respect. What is fascinating about the polygraph, is that it can reveal minute changes in emotional arousal.

Read the following words:

CHAIR, TEAPOT, CROSS, MOTHER, PAGE, SEX, CLOCK, DAISY, BABY.

Did you detect any change in emotional level in yourself as you read them? Probably not. But a polygraph would reveal that certain words are more emotionally-loaded for some people than are others. Mother, baby, and sex might *mean* much more to you than the other words because they obviously stand for things about which many people are emotional. But if you have a friend called 'Daisy', and if you are a Christian, *DAISY* and *CROSS* might also be emotionally-loaded words for you, and this would show on the polygraph reading. Thus the polygraph can give us more information about someone's emotions than they can themselves. Chapter 8 tells us more about this.

Years of study of human behaviour, thoughts and emotions have enabled psychologists to see how certain psychological problems may arise, and how they may be cured; by charting human behaviour, patterns emerge which enable predictions to be made about the frequency with which one event may follow on another. Whilst there is also much to learn, there is already quite a lot that psychologists can predict about human behaviour and hence the measurement of personality and intelligence in part, if not in total, is a reality, as Chapters 2 and 10 will show.

Are psychologists devious experimenters?

Psychologists are sometimes charged with doing rather devious experiments. In the past this assertion is probably quite fair in relation to a small proportion of psychological studies and, later in this book, in Chapter 4 for example, one or two such examples are given. However a certain degree of control over events under study is necessary in the initial stages of studying people, and there are good reasons for this.

Most of us are aware that we behave differently when we know that we are under scrutiny. Have you ever felt uncomfortable going through Customs even though you had nothing to declare? Do you get flustered when your boss stands over you? Or, do you work better when someone is watching you? If you answer 'yes' to any of these, then you are already aware that behaviour and performance is changed by being observed. Psychologists have to ensure that this effect does not distort the results in their studies of people. Thus if psychologists studying anxiety want to find out if a particular drug reduces anxiety then they must test it in such a way that their subjects do not know whether or not they are receiving this particular drug.

The importance of objectivity

Having selected a particular sample of people to act as subjects, and having decided how anxiety is to be measured, the aim would be to compare individuals who receive a given dose of the drug with those who receive no dose. The problem is to ensure that the people do not know whether they are receiving the drug despite the fact that the subject must of course consent to take part in a study, and be aware that drugs might be used. There are numerous regulations concerning these latter points which we need not consider here.

Psychologists solve this problem by using a *placebo,* an inert substance which can be administered in exactly the same way as the drug under investigation. Thus, in our hypothetical study, the placebo might be a sweet-tasting tablet which can be given alone or into which the drug can be mixed without being detectable.

Subjects in the experiment would be assigned at random to a drug, or non-drug condition, and each would receive what appeared to be identical tablets prior to the measurement of anxiety. It is just as important that the psychologists are protected from any bias, as the subjects. A further control in such a study would be that the psychologist measuring anxiety would not know which subjects receive the drug (the subjects in the *experimental* condition) and which did not (those in the *control* condition). To do this a second psychologist might be used who was 'blind' to the diagnostic category of each subject.

A subject who is told that a drug is being tested in order to find if it has anxiety-reducing properties may immediately feel less anxious, a sceptical subject on the other hand may be convinced of the ineffectiveness of such a drug and be concerned to demonstrate its ineffectiveness. If they do not know whether a drug is being used, or precisely with what aim, their expectations cannot interfere with the true effects. Similarly the psychologist who is sure that the drug *is* effective may be less than objective in handling the subjects, and in measuring anxiety levels.

In fact, in such a study we may well find that anxiety levels in our placebo group are actually reduced compared with another set of subjects who took no tablet at all.. Thus the very act of taking a tablet may have a measurable effect even though the tablet itself contained no active substances.

In our view it is not devious to operate these systems of 'control' whilst running experiments, but it is vital that once an experiment is complete those taking part are given a full account of what was done and the reasons for it, so that they can see exactly what part they played in the research. And because subjects do not know all in advance they must be given the option to drop out at any point, during the procedure, should they wish to.

What we expect affects what we see

Our beliefs about things can have quite dramatic effects on us and everyday experience can confirm this. There are no scientifically-proven aphrodisiacs, for instance, and yet many people firmly believe that they know of such substances. Providing that their belief is not disturbed it is likely that the substance will 'work' for them. The psychologist must always be aware that if he or she seeks to investigate any aspect of humans the expectations of those humans must be taken into account and, if necessary, *controlled for* in a study such as the drug study just described.

Perhaps all this control seems ludicrously contrived – but another example may serve to show how necessary such procedures are.

Many parents assert that they have always treated their babies in the same way – regardless of their sex. Yet, psychological research has shown that parents' treatment, or descriptions, of babies vary greatly as a function of the infant's sex.

In a study which we carried out a 9-month-old baby was filmed with its mother. We showed the film to groups of people who were asked to make an assessment of the baby (its behaviour, appearance, healthiness and so on) but to some groups we said 'this baby is a little girl called Mary', and to others we said 'this baby is a little boy called John'. We found that on measures such as activity, fidgetiness, appearance and weight estimates the 'boy' baby and 'girl' baby were consistently seen differently. (Don't forget the baby was the same throughout.) For example, the 'boy' was seen as more active and more fidgety. Other studies show similar findings, and they reveal how easy it is for our judgements to be shaped by our pre-conceptions.

Experiments are not enough

The studies described above indicate just one way in which psychologists can control events in order to study human behaviour, but there are many other methods which psychologists use. Perhaps you will have realised already that the experimental method cannot be applied to just any area which we want to investigate. Indeed our discussion of the differences which parents report in boy and girl babies is a case in point. We cannot assign sex to one group and not another in order to investigate how 'sex' influences behaviour. We all have a biological sex, no one is truly neutral, and thus in exploring sex differences all we can do is *correlate* observed behaviour with one sex or the other. If we observe that males have shorter hair than females (that is, short hair and maleness are positively correlated) or that males cry less or fight more than females we are *not* justified in saying that biological sex per se *caused* these differences.

Correlational studies provide much useful information for the psychologist, as we shall see, but these studies and experiments are only two of a number of techniques which psychologists have for investigating feelings, thoughts and emotions and these methods are covered in the final chapter.

Many people find methodology difficult to understand fully until they have more idea of the questions and problems which psychologists are seeking to understand. For this reason we have given you lots of examples of the psychologist's work first and then, when you have these examples in mind, you can look more closely at methodology at the end of the book.

What next?

The following chapters cover a range of topics which have been found to be of particular interest to those seeking to understand more about *behaviour, emotion* and *cognition.* The first chapter looks at behaviour of which we are all very aware – body language.

Recommended Reading

Colman, A.M. (1981). *What is Psychology?* London: Kogan Page.

1. *Body Language*

We might think of ourselves as very sophisticated animals, able to communicate highly complex and abstract ideas through language, but our bodies are equally sophisticated in conveying subtle changes in emotions without the need for language. This form of nonverbal communication is called *body language,* and the signals include facial expressions, postures, nonverbal sounds, touch, as well as dress and hair style.

Many people believe that nonverbal signals may be a more reliable indicator of how people feel than are their words; and in evolutionary terms, many body language signals evolved long before verbal language. When we sense that another person's words do not 'ring true' our intuition is often, we believe, based on our unconscious awareness of signals from the body which contradict the verbal messages. Psychologists have found that where there is a conflict between words and body language we are five times more likely to rely on the latter.

Of course body language can be used to deceive, just as words can, but because so many messages are available from different parts of the body, at any one time, total deception of the perceptive observer is virtually impossible. You may put on a happy face but your postures and gestures can convey a very different emotion.

DOES BODY LANGUAGE COME NATURALLY?

Body language comprises both learned and innate patterns of behaviour. For example: the nature of a smile is built into the human species as a way of expressing pleasure and friendly non-aggression. Desmond Morris suggests that it is derived from an appeasement gesture and thus it can also include a fearful element – as in the nervous smile. Babies do not have to learn to smile. Deaf/blind babies smile in the same way as normal babies, and true smiles occur at about six weeks of age in all babies responding to social (rather than gastric) signals. Similarly crying is an innate response and is shown by all babies, including deaf/blind ones, in an instantly recognizable form. Nevertheless we learn culturally acceptable ways of where and when to express these patterns. In Western society girls are permitted to cry more than boys. The extent to which the smile is used publicly also varies: Japanese smile little in public whereas Arabs do so much more freely.

'Involuntary' reactions are often real give-aways in the body language vocabulary. Turning pale, blushing, cold moist hands, prickling at the back of the neck, and a dry mouth all occur involuntarily and are controlled by the sympathetic part of the autonomic nervous system over which we have no conscious control. The pallor and the prickling neck (due to the hairs standing on end) are a result of the automatic flight or fight reaction of the body in which blood is redirected to the muscles from the surface capillaries through the action of the hormone adrenalin. A dry mouth and cold moist hands are also caused by this reaction.

Reddening of the face is a sign of anger, embarrassment or sexual awareness. In anger this occurs as a back-lash to the white-faced stage when the parasympathetic part of the autonomic nervous system counteracts the effects of the sympathetic nervous system in order to restore equilibrium. At this stage we feel hot and uncomfortable and probably get a strong urge to go to the lavatory. Many an interviewee has entered the interview in the former state, and left it in the latter – the 'fight' for a job is won or lost and the body then restores its emotional and physical equilibrium in the second stage.

Blushing in children may extend all over the face and ears and it can be a very conspicuous signal. Research on children has indicated that this reddening is associated with the desire to attack, when no overt attack is made. After puberty blushing is associated with sexual signalling. Girls, rather more than boys according to Desmond

Morris, may blush involuntarily, and this, Morris claims, is a sexual attractant to the opposite sex despite the embarrassment caused to the one who blushes.

Voluntary signals include those which we learn, without being aware of it, probably very early in life, together with those which we actively choose to display. An example of the first might be the use of touch in social interactions, and of the second our use of the head nod to say 'yes'. Many of these signals are culturally specific – in Greece nodding the head means 'no' – and to understand other cultures fully we need to learn both their verbal and their body language.

Edward Hall compared the body language of Arabs, Japanese and Americans. He found that Arabs touch each other much more and stand closer to friends than Americans do, and that even when Americans were made aware of this difference they found it difficult to adapt to the Arab style of interacting. These 'rules' of social interaction appear to be learned early in life and are very resistant to change.

Our first experience of cultural differences in body language is likely to be when we first meet a foreigner. Michael Argyle illustrates some of the differences in forms of greeting in his book *Bodily Communication.* On greeting the Lapps smell each other's cheeks and rub noses, Polynesians stroke each other's faces, Arabs embrace, Japanese bow, and the British may just make a slight nod or jerk of the head. Without knowing these forms of greeting, it is clear that the scope for spoiling a potential friendship, or causing offence, is enormous.

The topic of body language is a very large and well researched one and thus this chapter can only cover selected areas. In general, people tend to be most aware of their use of visual signals and for this reason we shall concentrate on these in most detail; touch and smell are discussed briefly, and the signs of deception are also considered. The final part of the chapter explores ways in which people can learn to improve their social skills.

THE FACE

The face is the chief part of the body which we look at in order to collect information about another person's emotions. The face contains a complex musculature which permits a wide range of expressions and yet relatively few emotions are recognized consistently by the onlooker if the context in which an expression occurs is not known.

Figure 1.1: What do you consider the child on the left is feeling? Horror, disgust, revulsion? *(From Philip Jones-Griffiths (Magnum).)*

Look at the two children in *Figure 1.1*. You probably have little difficulty in identifying the feelings of the child on the left but would you be so certain of this if the context was removed? Michael Argyle found that studies of the human face (using photographs) show that only about seven emotions can be identified unambiguously by adults. Look at *Figure 1.2* to see if you can identify and name these seven emotions correctly. The answers are printed on page 17. How successful were you? Mistakes are commonly made between emotions depicted by photographs adjacent to each other in terms of number order – such as surprise and fear.

One study which explored teachers' ability to recognize, through facial expressions, whether a child had understood a problem in class revealed that experienced teachers were *no* better than beginners. However this skill can be readily learned once people have been shown the relevant body language cues.

Careful observations of both adults and children have shown that certain expressive facial patterns have specific meanings, for instance, those accompanying fear and the desire to escape (flight), or aggression. Flight signals include the mouth drawn back with lips either apart or together (the oblong mouth), chewing and licking of the lips, and swallowing; the latter are all signs of a dry mouth caused by the body's flight reaction described earlier. The chin may be held in (withholding the face from the situation) and a sharp head movement may be made away from the other person. Ethologists describe these two movements as *intention movements* of flight, that is, when a small fragment of the desire to escape is displayed in a tiny movement. In general these patterns reflect increased anxiety and signs that the person is trying to withdraw from the situation. When aggression is felt the exact opposite of the flight responses is shown, with the person pushing forward towards the other. The lips may be apart and pushed forward; the chin is pushed out and the head may be held forward often for long periods. In physical aggression the mouth is made small and tight.

THE EYES

The eyes – 'the windows of the soul' – are felt by many to be highly expressive. If we ask people to identify emotions from the eyes alone, however, there is real difficulty in getting them to agree. Only *surprise, anger* and *pleasure,* or *pairs of these,* are easily identified

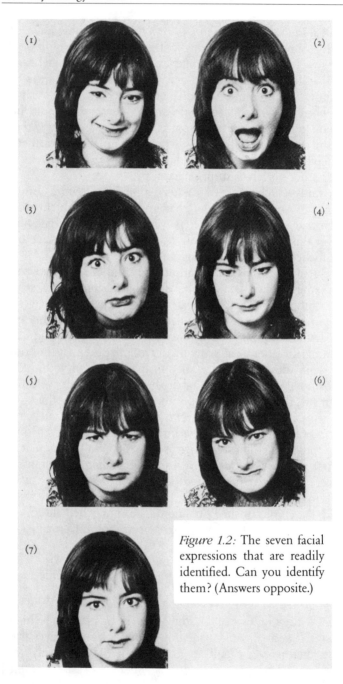

Figure 1.2: The seven facial expressions that are readily identified. Can you identify them? (Answers opposite.)

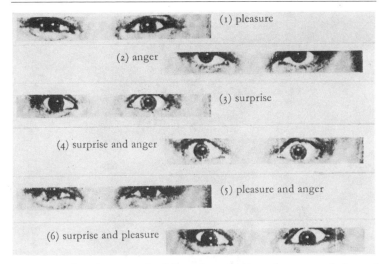

(1) pleasure

(2) anger

(3) surprise

(4) surprise and anger

(5) pleasure and anger

(6) surprise and pleasure

Figure 1.3: Emotions perceived from the eyes alone. *(From Argyle (1975.) (After Nummenmaa).)*

(see *Figure 1.3*). However, eyes *can* give us more information in at least two other ways: through changes in pupil dilation and the use of gaze in social interactions.

Signs of attraction

Pupil size can change from as little as 2mm to as much as 8mm and can be seen in *Figure 1.4.* A face seen with dilated pupils is preferred to an identical one with smaller pupils, and indeed momentary pupil dilation occurs when we like or find attractive the thing that we look at. Thus a face looking at us with dilated pupils tells us that we are liked. This brief dilation occurs independently of the level of illumination and it happens whether we look at a person, a painting, or a plate of fish and chips – so long as we like them. The constriction of pupils does *not* occur when we dislike or hate someone, as was once thought. Most of us are unaware of pupil dilation in others, although we may respond to it unconsciously. However Arabs are well aware of its significance and might screen their eyes when trading so as not to show too much interest in the goods they wish to purchase.

(From Argyle (1975.)

Answers for *Figure 1.2:*
(1) happiness (2) surprise (3) fear (4) sadness (5) anger (6) disgust (7) interest.

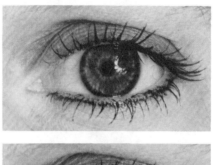

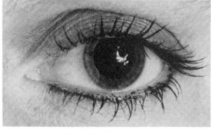

Figure 1.4: Pupil size variations. *(From Eric Crighton.)*

Telling looks

Observations on how people use their eyes in conversation with others have produced some intriguing findings. People talking on a fairly neutral topic probably spend about two thirds of the time looking at each other, but *mutual gaze* (that is, simultaneous looking by both) rarely lasts for more than a second or so. In general, talkers look at listeners for about 40 per cent of the time whilst listeners look at talkers for about 75 per cent of the time. Thus looking depends on what we are doing in the interaction.

Moreover, status or dominance and gaze behaviour (looking at the other) are linked. People who feel themselves to be in the presence of their superiors look more often than more dominant people. Extraverts (the more sociable, outgoing personalities) look more than introverts (the quieter, more reflective personalities): and women look more than men. These generalizations only hold when all other factors are held constant. Perhaps the sex difference noted here reflects more about a woman's feeling concerning her status than about gender as such. As you would expect, gaze behaviour is also influenced by the topic under discussion: the more personal or intimate the topic the less gaze behaviour occurs amongst friends and acquaintances, but again it increases between those who like each other, and is greatest between those in love.

Michael Argyle suggests that the reduction of gaze behaviour, or the termination of each gaze, is probably performed to reduce arousal or anxiety. Thus, as arousal becomes uncomfortable gaze is reduced. This also helps us to understand the personality differences noted earlier since it is thought that extraverts are at a lower level of arousal than introverts, and are thus more able to take the increased arousal caused by gaze behaviour before needing to look away. The reduction of illumination in places where people hope to find new friends, at parties for instance, may well help to reduce arousal and anxiety inherent in a situation where people feel themselves to be under close scrutiny by others.

Disturbances in gaze behaviour, and very reduced eye contact, is often shown by highly disturbed or anxious people, and is common in people with certain psychological problems, for example, child-hood autism. A colleague of ours found that when he was working with highly disturbed patients they felt more at ease when he wore reflecting sunglasses. Presumably this reduced their feelings of being watched. Most people find that being stared at makes them feel un-comfortable and it is common to put up barriers in order to counter-act such behaviour: the commuter typically 'hides' behind a newspaper to minimize eye contact with fellow travellers.

Cultural differences in the degree of eye contact are marked. Japanese look less at each other than people in the West and, for them, the polite place to rest your eyes when in conversation is on the other person's neck, and not on the eyes or mouth. Indeed a high level of eye contact is seen as aggressive in Japan, whereas Westerners see it as essential in establishing an honest relationship. Arabs use greater levels of eye contact than we do, and it is not unusual to see an Arab man walking backwards in front of the person with whom he is talking in order to maintain the required level of direct eye contact.

GESTURE AND POSTURE

So far only facial signals have been considered, but other parts of the body also signal our emotions and attitudes; the term *emotional leakage* has been used to describe these signals which are found below head level. This term implies, of course, that emotions not revealed in the face may leak out elsewhere. Those in public life often

Table 1.1: (a) Postures, gestures and their meaning

Motivation	Posture or gesture
☐ FLIGHT	shoulder forward (one or both) chin in and hunch crouch (head to knees in seated person) rocking of head or body immobility
☐ AGGRESSION	'beating' postures fist clench hand to neck expand chest
☐ AMBIVALENCE	fumble head groom/scratch finger sucking

(b) Some common forms of emotional leakage

Posture or gesture	Motivation
Rubbing/stroking	self assurance
Rubbing arm of chair (when sitting)	emotional, restless
Making a fist	aggression
Foot flex and extend	aggressive/defensive
Hand to nose	fear
Fingers to lips	shame
Hand covering eyes	shame
Face picking/scratching	self blame or attack

have large lecterns or desks in front of them as much for protection and security as for their notes since these barriers also conceal any leaked signs of their public speaking nerves.

Showing your feelings

A number of gestures and postures have been found frequently to accompany particular emotional states and these are summarized in *Table 1.1(a)*. Again it is clear that the person wishing to escape may hold back from a situation. This is shown clearly in children who, like frightened rabbits, may show total immobility and thus hold back any overt response. The foot flex can be seen as an intention movement of escape (or walking away). Aggressive signals are signs of the readiness for combat (verbal or physical) and, in some cases, they are clearly ritualized physical aggression as in the 'beating' postures.

Maurice Krout, from the Chicago Psychological Institute, studied the meaning of signals which he felt were not intended as communication but were used instead of language, either when the person was prevented from speaking or when alone. He contrived experimentally to arouse strong emotions in his subjects by putting them in rather awkward, uncomfortable or controversial situations. For example, in one of the 15 contrived situations Krout led each of his subjects to believe that he or she was to receive a prize for an excellent performance, only then to discover 'accidentally' that through an error no prize was forthcoming. The person was at this point prevented from saying anything until given a signal to do so. This signal was given only after the subject's body language including gestures of all kinds had been noted. The results of this and many other studies of posture and gesture have shown the frequent occurrence of the following signals (see *Table 1.1(b)*).

In general, touching of the head or face by the hand indicates negative feelings about oneself and these signs are so common that our police and customs officers watch for them when questioning people. It should be noted however that feeling negative about oneself is not equivalent to having actually done something wrong or illegal. Indeed, there is some evidence that the more honest you are the more uncomfortable you feel when under suspicion.

The orientation of our bodies towards those with whom we associate can reveal our attitudes and feelings towards them. If we like a person we orient our bodies towards them for most of the time. We lean forward, stand closer, look more, touch more, and show a relaxed

Figure 1.5: Examples of posture mimicry.
(From Zefa Picture Library (UK) Ltd.)

posture. Mixed feelings about a person are revealed in ambivalent postures: for example, when sitting we might have our knees pointing away, whilst our trunk is oriented towards that person; tightly folded arms or high, tight leg crossing might reveal a withdrawal or protection of ourselves from the other. Postures of course are changed from moment to moment so that a snapshot glance will not necessarily reveal anything significant. It is the postures which we adopt most of the time which are important and revealing. Another sign of friendship is *posture mimicry* – the adoption, perhaps without realizing it, of a posture shown by someone we like or love (see *Figure 1.5*).

The close similarity that is frequently commented on in long and happily married couples, or between long-term friends, may well stem from posture mimicry because the long use of similar expressions, gestures and postures ultimately shapes or leaves marks on our bodies.

TOUCHING

Very little research has been carried out on this form of behaviour although, as Argyle points out, this form of contact is 'basic social behaviour' since many other forms of communication lead to 'tactile' events as for example in caring, sexual and aggressive situations. The vital importance of touch is clear from the following example. In the early part of this century very high mortality was found amongst orphaned American infants living in institutions. Evidently these infants were deprived of adequate physical contact because mortality was dramatically reduced by the introduction of cuddling.

Who touches whom?

The British are known for their rather standoffish behaviour relative to some Mediterranean and Arab people, but in all cultures there are rules for who touches whom and on what part of the body. Mark Knapp has summarized the findings of this research and he suggests that in general females are touched more and themselves touch others more than males, mothers touch more than fathers, and opposite sex friends touch more than same sex friends. *Figure 1.6(a)* on page 24 depicts these differences and *Figure 1.6(b)* on page 25 shows a cross-cultural comparison in which it is clear that Americans permit more touching than do Japanese.

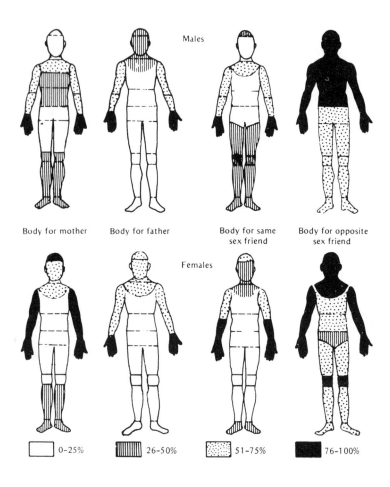

Figure 1.6 (a): Areas of the body involved in bodily contact. The top row indicates which part of a male's body may be touched by the person indicated beneath each figure. The bottom row indicates which part of a female's body may be touched by the person indicated above. Percentages show the relative amount of touching for each area.

(From: Nonverbal Communication in Human Interaction, 2nd ed. by Mark L. Knapp (1978) Eastbourne: Holt, (Rinehart & Winston. *Reproduced by permission of CBS College Publishing.)*

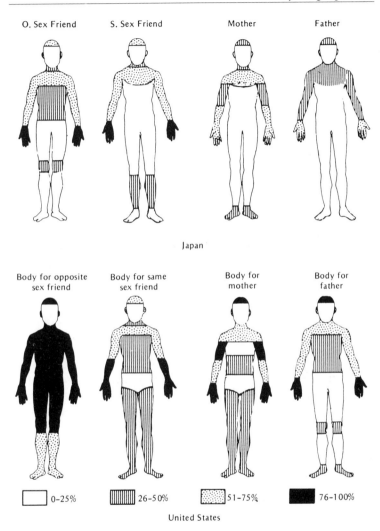

O. Sex Friend   S. Sex Friend   Mother   Father

Japan

Body for opposite sex friend   Body for same sex friend   Body for mother   Body for father

☐ 0–25%   ▥ 26–50%   ▦ 51–75%   ■ 76–100%

United States

Figure 1.6 (b): Physical contact patterns in Japan. The top row shows the amount of a person's body that can be touched (the percentages reveal the extent of touching) by a friend of the opposite sex (extreme left), by a friend of the same sex (left of centre), by the mother (right of centre) and by the father (extreme right). The bottom row indicates the same data for contact patterns in the United States.

(From: Nonverbal Communication in Human Interaction, 2nd ed. by Mark L. Knapp (1978) Eastbourne: Holt, Rinehart & Winston. *(Reproduced by permission of CBS College Publishing.)*

Touching effects

Being touched, however, even without being aware of it, might greatly alter our perception of a situation, as an experiment in America revealed. This study, at Purdue University in 1976, showed that when a woman at the library desk 'accidentally' touched students (male or female) when handing back their library cards, they later described her very differently from students who had not been 'accidentally' touched, but had otherwise been treated similarly. This difference occurred whether or not the student recalled being touched by the woman, who was later described in such terms as trustful, warm and sensitive when she had touched them, but as distant, formal and insensitive when she had not.

More recent research using geriatric patients showed that when a 'programme' of touching them by a staff member was introduced, patients began to show a number of improvements in health and well-being.

SMELLS AS SIGNALS

Because we are very visual creatures the bulk of this chapter has concentrated on visual cues. However a few paragraphs on odours are important because research is beginning to show their significance in social interactions. The words 'smell' or 'odour' are embarrassing words for many people; they are virtually synonymous with bad smell or bad odour, and our language has few words to describe the great range of odours which people can distinguish. We rarely discuss natural odours or smells and if someone were to tell us we smell nasty we are quite likely to feel mortified; whereas if we are told that we have a black smudge on our cheek we would probably be glad of the information.

This excessive sensitivity to smells is not universal. The Arab appears to be more at ease with smells, whether nice or nasty, than we are. An Arab man would not baulk at telling a friend about his bad breath, and likewise he might comment on the pleasantness of someone's body smell. Indeed, in conversation, Arabs both like and expect to feel the breath of friends on them and if this is withheld they will feel that the friend is behaving as if ashamed of something. British people place great value on people looking each other in the eye during conversation, but breath contact is just as important to the Arab.

Smells and sex

Smells may well play a larger part in regulating our behaviour than we are aware. Research on other mammals shows that odours from one sex can have prolonged and dramatic effects on the other. In the mouse, for instance, a pregnancy can be terminated in its early stages if the female is exposed to odours from a strange male mouse. There is no equivalent of this in humans but odours from human females do affect other females. Michael Russell showed recently that a human female exposed daily to the odour of a small amount of underarm secretion from another female will show synchrony of her menstrual cycle with that of the donor's cycle, even though the females have never met. This could explain why girls and women living in close proximity often show synchrony, or near synchrony, in their menstrual cycles.

Why deodorize?

Smells probably play an important part in human sexual behaviour. It is known that females of reproductive age show increased sensitivity, relative to males, to certain 'male' odours (for example boar taint), and this may be enhanced around ovulation. Many perfumes include musk, a secretion from a species of deer which is used by deer in sexual attraction. Thus we deodorize our own bodies but apply another mammal's sexual signals which are in fact very similar to some of our own. Not all humans reject the use of natural body odours as a sexual attractant. In some Mediterranean areas, Iranaus Eibl-Eibesfeldt notes that odour is used in a courtship dance to stimulate the woman. The man carries a handkerchief in his armpit, and then during the dance uses it to wave in front of the woman of his choice. The smelly cloth is supposed to arouse the passions of the woman he has selected.

It is interesting to speculate on why some of the human race has neglected the smellier side of life, whilst others appear to use and enjoy it. Since our bodies have a number of sites which produce odoriferous secretions it seems unlikely that these have totally lost their signal value in modern life, especially as we direct so much of our attention to removing natural odours and replacing them with 'socially desirable' ones.

ARE THERE SIGNS OF DECEPTION?

Body language and deception has been mentioned several times already and so it is appropriate to explore in more detail the ways in which people may reveal through body language that their words are untrue.

Experiments on lying have obvious ethical difficulties. However one study which simulated a real-life situation overcomes the problem to a great extent. American researchers Paul Ekman and Wallace Friesen reasoned that nurses may sometimes find themselves in a situation in which they must conceal from their patients the true facts of their illness. They arranged for student nurses to see films of patients undergoing various treatments. Subsequently the nurses were asked to describe what they had seen sometimes truthfully, and sometimes untruthfully (that is, concealing the true seriousness of the problem), as if they were actually telling the patient. Whilst doing this their body language was recorded on film so that truthful and untruthful explanations could be compared.

When 'lying', nurses showed nonverbal give-aways. Hand-to-face contacts increased relative to those shown in true reports and, in lying, most hand gesticulations were reduced with the exception of the shrug of the hand which was increased. Body shifts also increased. The results showed that there were consistent differences in the use of gestures used in true and untrue reports by the nurses, consistent with earlier research findings. Face touching is associated with negative feelings about oneself. Lying makes most of us feel bad, even when we have to lie in order to give another the will to fight for their life. So once we know how a person acts when being honest we may be able to detect in them the signs that they are deceiving us.

If you would like to explore further how dishonesty reveals itself in body language, try Exercise 1.1 on pages 35 − 37.

BODY LANGUAGE AND A NEW TECHNIQUE

Much of the research which led to an awareness of the importance of body language in social relationships took place in the 1960s. However, two other seemingly unconnected developments were taking place at the same time which combined to provide *Social Skills Training (SST)*, a major new technique in psychology.

The first took place in the United States, with research being carried out into schizophrenia by a team including Edward Zigler and Leslie Phillips. These investigators showed a clear link between recovery from schizophrenia and 'social competence', such as employment history, type of occupation and marital status. The better the social competence before the onset of the disorder, the lower were the chances of rehospitalization after return to the community. There is, obviously, nothing that can be done to increase social competence prior to hospitalization – unless *at risk* screening for schizophrenia were conducted. But could something be done to increase social competence whilst the schrizophrenic person is in hospital? With increased social competence, perhaps more successful rehabilitation could be achieved. A clear need was established but the technique was lacking.

The second development arose from the work of the clinician Joseph Wolpe in South Africa. Joseph Wolpe did not work with schizophrenics, but with people who are excessively anxious and passive – the neutrotic type of disorder. The traditional treatment for such disorders was psychotherapy in which people are encouraged to talk about their difficulties. Joseph Wolpe was concerned to develop a therapy based not only on discussion but on training new behaviours as well. A good example of this is *Assertion Training*. He reasoned that if people are anxious about not being able to stand up for themselves, then if they could be trained to become assertive their anxiety could be removed, or *counterconditioned*.

This technique for training in assertion was the first to analyse and describe appropriate assertive behaviour, and then to teach these behaviours to the anxious person. By using methods such as role-play, which you tried out in Exercise 1.1, the anxious person enacts the situations which are causing difficulty, and a therapist offers comment and advice. Gradually the anxious person's ability to be assertive is improved. (In Chapter 4 you have an opportunity to try out one exercise in becoming assertive.)

For training of this type to be successful a detailed understanding of assertive behaviour is obviously required, which brings us back to the research on social communication. The three strands were being drawn together: the link between social competence and schizophrenia; the beginnings of a training method to improve social behaviour as a therapy for anxiety; and the growing understanding of bodily communication.

The final, vital contribution to the development of *SST* came from the contention by Michael Argyle and his colleagues that social

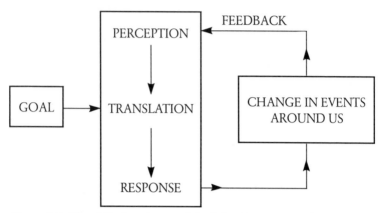

Figure 1.7: The skills learning model. *(After Trower, Bryant & Argyle, 1978.)*

behaviour is acquired in the same way as any other behaviour. They argued strongly that we have to learn social behaviour in the same way we learn, say, to drive a car or to use a typewriter. Such behaviours are referred to as *motor skills,* and so it was suggested that to interact successfully with other people what we need are *social skills.*

Learning social skills

Having said that skills need to be *learnt,* we must then ask how this learning takes place. Based on the understanding of how motor skills are learnt, Argyle and his co-workers suggested a similar model for learning social skills.

Our aim in any social interaction is to achieve some particular goal; this might be friendship, company, stimulation, and so on. In order to achieve this goal we must be able to perceive our social world: what people are doing, what relationships are being formed, and all the complexities of verbal and nonverbal behaviour or body language. The next step is to translate our perceptions to understand what is happening, and to decide what course of action we should take. Having made this decision we make our response: examples of this might be to talk or just listen, or show approval or disapproval.

Our actions will, of course, have an effect on those around us, changing events as a direct result. We perceive these changes taking place, giving us feedback on the results of our actions. Depending on the feedback we will be able to see if we have achieved our goal: if we are successful we might well behave in a similar way in the future; if unsuccessful we might decide to adopt a modified, or even totally different, approach next time the same situation arises.

Let's look at a simple example. Suppose your goal is to talk with an acquaintance whom you see talking with another person. Your first decision is whether or not to interrupt and, let's say, you decide you will. You approach, smile, say 'hello', and begin a conversation. This will have an effect on the two people you have approached; you may be greeted warmly, or you may be rebuffed. The changes you have caused in their behaviour will come to your attention – the feedback – and you will remember what happened for the future.

Learning of social skills is a process which begins at a very early age and continues throughout life. Like any skill there are some people who are very good at it. We all know someone who is never at a loss for words and can carry off any social situation, whilst most of us are of average ability and get along quite nicely. However, there are also those who fail to learn, to a greater or lesser degree, the social skills required for living, and when this happens, problems almost invariably follow.

Social skills training

The exact contents of a SST programme will, of course, vary according to the level of ability of the trainees and their particular difficulties. However, there are certain essential components which are shown in Table 1.2.

Included in Table 1.2 are the cognitive skills of planning and problem solving. However, there is considerable debate amongst clinicians concerning whether such skills should form part of SST or whether they should be the focus of separate training perhaps using cognitive behaviour modification techniques, that is, helping people to change their ways of thinking about a problem. A solution to an individual's social difficulties which emphasizes thought rather than action clearly has different implications for training, and it is here that the disagreement lies between clinicians. The present mood is that rather than one or the other, thought and action should be taken together in training programmes as vital components of human functioning.

The methods used in SST, like assertion training, are those which would be used by an instructor teaching any new skill and include modelling, practice, and feedback.

Modelling is the demonstration of the correct behaviour, for

Table 1.2: The basic components of social skills training *(After Trower, Bryant and Argyle, 1978.)*

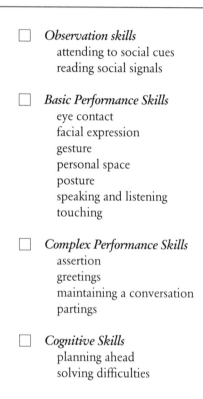

☐ *Observation skills*
    attending to social cues
    reading social signals

☐ *Basic Performance Skills*
    eye contact
    facial expression
    gesture
    personal space
    posture
    speaking and listening
    touching

☐ *Complex Performance Skills*
    assertion
    greetings
    maintaining a conversation
    partings

☐ *Cognitive Skills*
    planning ahead
    solving difficulties

instance, good eye contact, by someone proficient in the particular skill. The people being trained are able to observe the model and then practice the skills for themselves. The practice is carried out using role-play during training sessions, with additional 'homework' tasks between sessions. As the trainee practises the individual skill or some more complex situation, such as starting a conversation, the trainer is able to give feedback on performance.

It is, of course, important that the newly learned skills transfer, or *generalize,* to real life. A way of encouraging generalization is to include as many 'real life' people as possible, such as parents or friends, in the actual training.

The first use of *SST* was mainly with psychiatric inpatients and anxious or neurotic clients, usually on an outpatient basis. However, over a short time the (deceptive) simplicity of the technique led to an explosion in its use. *SST* programmes were devised for other clinical groups such as those with depression and the mentally handicapped. The technique was applied to childhood disorders, adolescent disorders, and adult problems such as marriage difficulties. Delinquency, alcoholism, violent and sexual crime, and drug abuse are further examples of areas to which *SST* has been applied.

In addition, *SST* has now moved away from its clinical foundations, and is used in the training of many professional groups such as teachers, nurses, and police officers. Indeed, there are *SST* programmes for people whose work brings them into contact with other cultures where, as we saw earlier, different social rules apply. Finally, the basic skills model has been applied to those skills we all need at various times, such as training in job interview skills, to give the related technique of *Life Skills Training*.

Research seeking to assess and refine the effectiveness of social skills training is very much a part of contemporary psychology, providing a perfect example of how apparently unrelated areas of 'academic' research can be applied to advantage to influence for the better the lives of many people.

Recommended Reading

Hollin, C.R. & Trower, P. (eds) (1986). *Handbook of Social Skills Training, Volume 1: Applications Across the Life-span*. Oxford: Pergamon Books.

Hollin, C.R. & Trower, P. (eds) (1986). *Handbook of Social Skills Training, Volume 2: Clinical Applications and New Directions*. Oxford: Pergamon Books.

Knapp, M.L. (1978). *Non-verbal Communication in Human Interaction*. New York: Holt, Rinehart & Winston.

Morris, D. (1977). *Manwatching: A Field Guide to Human Behaviour*. London: Jonathan Cape.

References

Argyle, M. (1975). *Bodily Communication*. London: Methuen. [A detailed study of body language.]

Argyle, M. & Kenden, A. (1967). The experimental analysis of social performance. In L. Berkowitz (ed.), *Advances in Experimental Social Psychology, 3*, 55–98. [The study of performance in social situations.]

Eibl-Eibesfeldt, I. (1970). *Ethology: The Biology of Behaviour.* New York: Holt, Rinehart and Winston. [Facial expressions of deaf-blind children; odours and Mediterranean people.]

Ekman, P. & Friesen, W.V. (1974). Detecting deception from the body or face. *Journal of Personality & Social Psychology, 29*, 288–294. [Experiment on deception.]

Hall, E.T. (1969). *The Hidden Dimension.* New York: Anchor Books. [Body language in Arabs, Japanese and Americans.]

Krout, M.H. (1954). An experimental attempt to determine the significance of unconscious manual symbolic movements. *Journal of General Psychology, 51*, 121–152. [A study of blocked emotions.]

Russell, M.J., Switz, G.M. & Thompson, K. (1980). Olfactory influence on the human menstrual cycle. *Pharmacology, Biochemistry & Behaviour, 13*, 737–38. [Odours and the human menstrual cycle.]

Trower, P., Bryant, B. & Argyle, M. (1978). *Social Skills and Mental Health.* London: Methuen. [Gives an introduction to theory and practice in social skills.]

Wolpe, J. (1958). *Psychotherapy by Reciprocal Inhibition.* Stanford, California: Stanford University Press. [The beginnings of assertion training.]

Zigler, E. & Phillips, L. (1961). Social competence and outcome in psychiatric disorder. *Journal of Abnormal & Social Psychology, 63*, 264–271. [Schizophrenia and social competence.]

Exercise 1.1
BODY LANGUAGE AND LYING

This exercise is an interview role-play in which your general conversational and social skills are tested by the interviewer. Two people are needed for this exercise but if a group is available choose pairs to work together who do not know each other well. Before starting, the interview pairs select 10 questions which the interviewee is prepared to answer on important or personal topics, but to which the pair do not know each other's answers. The reader of this book acts as interviewee and the partner is the interviewer. *It is important that the interviewer does not read these instructions.*

For interviewees only: The interviewee now chooses any 10 questions which he or she is prepared to answer. The following list may give you some ideas:

1. Where were you born?
2. Did you enjoy your school days?
3. Are all your grandparents still living?
4. Do you get on well with your brother(s) and sister(s)?
5. Do you think your personality is most like your father's or your mother's?
6. Do you believe that capital punishment is ever justifiable?
7. Who is your favourite TV personality?
8. Do you really enjoy your job?
9. Are you married? How long have you been married?
10. What is your favourite hobby?

Write down the questions so that you can give this list to the interviewer. You, the interviewee, explain to the interviewer that s/he must simply go through the list of questions, asking you each one and then as you give your answer the interviewer records your body language in the categories listed on p.36. Write the 'interviewer checklist' out on a piece of paper and allow plenty of space so that for each question asked the body language can be recorded. The interviewer only proceeds to the next question when s/he has noted down all the body language signals observed.

continued over page

─── Exercise 1.1 continued ───

INTERVIEWER CHECK LIST

Body language	Response to question	Things to look for
Eye contact	....	reduced, increased, maintained
Tone of voice	....	husky, raised/lowered
Hand to face contacts	....	note type (e.g. picks nose)
Bodily movements	....	note type (shuffle, jump, etc.)
Leg/foot movements	....	note type (leg flex, cross/uncross)
Hand movements	....	note type (clench, shake)
Other	....	Anything else of note (e.g. swallowing, blink rate)

BODY LANGUAGE AND LYING

The crucial part of this experiment is that the interviewee *chooses to lie* in answer to 5 of the 10 questions. S/he selects at random 5 questions from the list (do not simply alternate) and plans the answer — this part of the exercise must not be revealed to the interviewer until afterwards.
The interviewer must not know the exercise is concerned with deception.

To start the interview. The interviewer asks several 'practice' questions (other than the 10 selected) to get used to recording body language.

On completion of the interview, honest and lying responses are compared. Are there consistent differences? Discuss with the interviewer exactly what was happening. Had s/he any sense of being misled? How did you feel, were you aware that you gave yourself away?

For those working in groups compare answers. Are people consistent on how they 'show' dishonesty or is it very individual?

One common response is that when lying a person tries to simulate being honest. In Britain honesty is linked with eye contact and often people increase their eye contact to abnormally high levels when lying.

2. *Your Personality*

Many of us first take an interest in psychology because we have become intrigued by some characteristic or behaviour of our own or of another person and become curious about it. Arthur, a colleague at work, may often act in an aggressive way. Another, Estelle, is quiet and withdrawn, while Amy is sociable, friendly and outgoing.

Curiosity is increased when two people differ markedly despite the fact that they have been exposed to apparently similar circumstances. Brian and Danny have both been exposed to the stress and turmoil of suddenly being made redundant. Their financial, domestic and general life circumstances are much the same and yet they react in different ways. Brian becomes increasingly anxious, dejected and apathetic while Danny recovers quickly from his initial disappointment and remains undented by the blow, maintaining a steadfast, if unrealistic, cheerfulness. In trying to understand these differences between people we are concerned with the study of *personality.*

EVERYONE HAS PERSONALITY

Beyond the assertion that personality concerns individual differences it is very difficult to give a more detailed definition of personality with which psychologists of different persuasions will agree. It must also be borne in mind that the man or woman in the street may use the term 'personality' in a different way. They might, for example, refer to someone as having 'lots of personality' or 'not much personality'. Personality, here, refers to the possession of attractive or salient social qualities. For the psychologist, everyone has a personality and the person of low social attractiveness is of as much interest, as much in need of explanation, as the opposite type.

IT DEPENDS ON YOUR POINT OF VIEW

The field of personality is one of the most perplexing to the reader new to psychology. This perplexity may be shared by full-time students and psychologists themselves. One of the authors of this book who has taught psychology to medical students for some time understands well why personality theories cause problems. Medical training involves the learning of many (apparent) *facts*. Medical students starting to learn about the psychology of personality are alarmed to discover that what appear to be simple human behaviours can be viewed in radically different ways, depending on the theoretical orientation of the person studying the behaviour. For example, in discussing 'difficult', uncontrollable behaviour in a child (refusing to comply with parents, tantrums, aggression) they would be startled to find that the typical psychology textbook might give four or five different explanations. One might emphasize the child's general temperament and its biological foundations; another might suggest that difficult behaviour is learned or conditioned because the parents rewarded (reinforced) the child's problem behaviour by giving in to his or her wishes; yet another that the unacceptable behaviour was merely a symptom of underlying unconscious conflict stemming from relationships in infancy . . . and more.

Not only is there a multiplicity of explanatory theories but they suggest radically different ways in which the child and family should be assessed and treated ranging from treating the child with drugs to behaviour modification and family therapy. A common reaction to this quandary is to ask 'which theory is correct?' But this proves to be a question without a clear-cut answer. In this chapter we sketch a few contemporary approaches to personality and personality problems and some of their strengths and limitations.

THE TRAIT APPROACH

We are all trait theorists to some degree. In describing the 'nature' or behaviour of a person we like, we might describe them as 'friendly', 'interested in people', 'intelligent' or 'perceptive'; and conversely, the villains in our lives are 'distant', 'uninterested in people', 'stupid' and 'unperceptive'. Individuals may be idiosyncratic in terms of the relative importance of particular traits in their judgements of themselves and others, as we shall see when we discuss *Personal Construct Theory,* but we all have a vast number of terms available to us to describe the attributes and dispositions of people. It has been estimated that there are 18,000 or more 'trait' descriptions of this sort in the dictionary.

Naming is not the same as explaining

A trait description is no more than a summary of some consistencies in the behaviour of the person we are judging but it is easy for people to believe that, in attributing a trait to someone, we have somehow *explained* their behaviour. Thus they act in an *unfriendly way* because they are *unfriendly people.* The evidence for their being *unfriendly* is that they act in an *unfriendly way!* This is, of course, entirely circular. It is important to bear in mind, therefore, that traits are no more than summary descriptions of people.

It's all a matter of degree

There have been many studies in psychology of single traits. The most common approach is to view a trait as a *dimension* in terms of which people vary. Thus on a dimension of 'dominance' there will be individuals who obtain extremely high scores, others who obtain very low scores because of their submissive behaviour, with the majority of the population near the middle of the range.

Most trait researchers attempt to create reliable, objective tests of the particular dimension they are interested in and then use such tests to discover how other aspects of behaviour can be predicted from test scores. For example, the researcher might speculate that 'dominance' is an important requirement for being an effective leader and go on to compare successful and unsuccessful leaders on a measure of dominance to see if this particular prediction is upheld. A vast number of single trait tests of this sort now exist and are widely used in work, educational and medical settings.

Just how many traits are required to account for differences between people is a matter of some debate. Some of the best known and most influential personality theorists have brought a particular statistical technique, factor analysis, to bear on this question. Perhaps the most famous and enthusiastic exponent of the factor analytic approach has been the British psychologist, Hans Eysenck.

EYSENCK'S THEORY: THREE CRITICAL DIMENSIONS

Factor analysis is a mathematical method for investigating the degree of association ('correlation') between different behaviours or between different traits. It reduces the complex patterns of association found to a small number of underlying clusters or 'factors'. It is a way, then, of revealing the underlying structure; a structure not likely to be easily visible to anyone who simply scans the scores of a large number of people on a whole range of tests or observations.

Eysenck has used and advocated the factor analytic method for more than 40 years, studying very diverse groups of people and using a wide range of measures – scores from questionnaires, ratings of the person by others, scores on psychological tests or even biographical information (for example, whether or not the person ever received psychiatric treatment). He claims that throughout this work three underlying factors have been revealed with considerable consistency. The two long-standing factors he has described are: *Extraversion – Introversion* and *Neuroticism – Stability*. To these he added a third in the 1970s – the dimension of *Psychoticism – Impulse control*. Eysenck calls these 'types', each type being composed of a cluster of traits which together define the type.

Extraversion – Introversion

The associated traits which make up Extraversion include sociability, liveliness, activity, assertiveness, the tendency to be sensation-seeking, carefreeness and dominance. The implication is that individuals high on any one of these traits will tend to be high on the others.

Neuroticism – Stability

Neuroticism, on the other hand, comprises traits of anxiety-proneness, depression-proneness, guilt feelings, low self-esteem, tension, moodiness and emotionality.

Psychoticism – Impulse Control

Psychoticism, in turn, includes aggressiveness, coldness, lack of empathy and a divergent kind of creativity.

The distribution of each of Eysenck's types in the population is a 'normal' one, meaning that both extremes of each dimension are relatively rare, with most people scoring near the mid-point of the continuum, showing, for example, a balance of introverted and extraverted tendencies.

FROM DESCRIPTION TO EXPLANATION

What distinguishes Eysenck from a number of other trait and factor analysis researchers is his attempt to move beyond description of how traits and behaviours cluster together (the taxonomy of behaviour) to the 'dynamics' of behaviour: the attempt to explain *why* humans differ on these three dimensions. The specifics of his explanatory theory have changed over the years as it has been reformulated to accommodate new findings. We shall look here, however, at some of the more enduring aspects of the theory, concentrating particularly on the Extraversion – Introversion dimension.

It's mainly in the genes

Eysenck sees individual differences as firmly rooted in biology. For him, the cause of extraverted patterns of behaviour is firmly located within differences in the nervous system, and the type of nervous system a person has is genetically determined. This is not to say that Eysenck rules out environmental factors. Social factors also contribute to whether a person is extraverted or introverted in behaviour, but Eysenck clearly sees himself as a crusader against over-enthusiastic environmentalists who have entirely ruled out biological predispositions.

The Extravert is inhibited?

The Extraversion – Introversion dimension is identified with differences in the level of *arousal* in the cerebral cortex. The level of arousal is, in turn, a product of the activity of a 'cortico-reticular loop' involving a part of the mid-brain called the ascending reticular activating system, one of whose functions is to alert and activate the parts of the brain responsible for 'higher' psychological functions. In simple terms, the introvert's cortex is more aroused and more arousable than the cortex of the extravert, which is more prone to 'inhibition'. The cortex is responsible for many of the higher level 'control' functions of the brain and thus, paradoxically, a high level of arousal in this structure is associated with controlled, rather than excited, behaviour. Similarly alcohol, which generally has an 'inhibiting' effect on brain function, will reduce arousal in the cortex and produce less controlled, more extraverted, social behaviour.

From explanation to practical prediction

Eysenck suggests that these individual differences in arousal affect a range of basic psychological processes which produce the extraverted or introverted pattern of behaviour that we actually observe, and he made predictions about how extraverts and introverts would differ on a wide range of tasks. Attempts to verify or refute these predictions have generated an enormous number of studies and experiments over many years. Hans and Michael Eysenck (his son) have recently attempted to draw conclusions from such work and to defend the theory against the criticisms that have been made of it.

Amongst the predictions of the theory are that extraverts (E's) and introverts (I's) will differ in their 'vigilance'. Vigilance refers to a state of readiness to detect and respond to small or infrequent changes occurring in the environment, as in scanning a radar screen to detect a 'blip'. Eysenck predicts poor vigilance in extraverts because, in everyday language, they have poor concentration and become easily bored.

Another important prediction was that E's and I's differ in their *conditionability*, I's being more easily conditioned and hence more likely to be socially conforming. In his early work Eysenck made this idea the basis of a theory of criminality and it has, therefore, attracted much attention. In general, there has been little evidence to support the idea that a general factor of conditionability exists. There may also be important differences between 'aversive' conditioning (for example, learning to associate fear with a neutral stimulus) and 'appetitive' conditioning (learning to associate gratification or pleasure with a neutral stimulus). Eysenck has recently reformulated the theory to suggest that it is the impulsivity component of extraversion, rather than the sociability aspect, which is related to low conditionability. It remains to be seen how this new prediction will fare.

Are introverts more sensitive?

One of the more interesting predictions from the theory is that E's and I's differ in their *sensory thresholds;* the introvert's aroused cortex is more alert and hence efficient at detecting low levels of stimulation. As introverts are more aroused by stimulation so they will react more to stimuli.

It is not difficult to see how differences in sensitivity to stimulation might have consequences for medicine and related areas. One of the authors recently had some painful dental treatment, in the middle of which the dentist asked why individuals vary in their pain sensitivity. He was able to suggest that 'Git gall gepends gone gether gou gare gan gintrovert gor gextravert'. At least, according to Eysenck's theory, if introverts are more sensitive to stimulation we would expect them to feel pain more acutely. Eysenck sees pain as part of a continuum of sensory stimulation. Both very low levels (sitting in the dark in a quiet house) and high levels of stimulation (a crowded, noisy party) may be perceived as unpleasant, while stimulation in the intermediate range is pleasant or neutral. If introverts generally 'amplify' stimulation because of the nature of their nervous system, we would expect them to be *less* troubled by low levels of stimulation but to be made uncomfortable by high levels of stimulation *sooner* (at a lower point on the continuum). Extraverts, conversely, will find low levels of stimulation more unpleasant but will be more tolerant of high levels of stimulation. Eysenck labels the introvert as *stimulus aversive* and the extravert as *stimulus hungry.* So at a noisy party we might expect the introverts to be the first to complain about the music being played too loudly, though this assumes that they will be bold enough to voice their irritation and also that they would have attended the party in the first place. For a discussion of developments and findings for this aspect of Eysenck's theory, the reader should consult the relevant sections of Hans and Michael Eysenck's book.

CRITICISMS OF THE FACTOR-ANALYTIC APPROACH

The factor-analytic method has not been without its critics, some saying that the apparent objectivity of these statistical methods is illusory. There is certainly a subjective element in that what is derived from factor analysis depends in part on the nature of the items included in the first place, and the mathematical patterns derived need to be labelled and interpreted by the researcher. Moreover, a number of different factor analytic methods exist, making it possible to derive quite different factors from the same test results.

Cattell's 16 dimensions

One check, therefore, on the validity of any assertion that core personality dimensions have been isolated (as claimed by Eysenck) is to compare the findings with those of other researchers using different methods. One such, Raymond Cattell, concluded that there are 16 major personality factors, rather than three. Closer inspection of Cattell's work, however, reveals many similarities with the conclusions of Eysenck. Cattell was not concerned to establish *independent* factors and his 16 dimensions are correlated with each other. If an attempt is made to derive 'second order' or more general factors from Cattell's work the two major factors produced are strikingly similar to Eysenck's Extraversion–Introversion and Neuroticism–Stability. There does indeed seem to be an emerging consistency of findings.

It would appear that some progress has been made in mapping the broad temperamental dimensions on which individuals vary. Few would claim that knowledge of a person's position on two or three dimensions would tell the complete story about their personality. But controversial though Eysenck's theory may be, few theories can have generated so many testable hypotheses across so many areas of psychological enquiry.

'AM I ME OR AM I THE SITUATION?' THE PROBLEM OF CONSISTENCY

The American psychologst, Lawrence Pervin, has encapsulated in this question a debate which has rumbled on for about 20 years amongst personality researchers. What is at issue is easily demonstrated. Ask a person who knows you well to name one of your most undesirable personality traits.

One of the authors of this book was bold enough to try this experiment and was told that he was 'obsessionally tidy' by a colleague who had clearly found this characteristic to be rather tiresome. The immediate response to this label was to become aware of how unfair and over-generalized it was. Admittedly he kept his office very tidy and was fussy about clearing his desk before leaving but, on the other hand, his wife complained he was appallingly messy when working in the kitchen. Had his daughter not opined that he was the scruffiest dad in the playground when picking her up from school? Anyway, his pattern of tidiness in the office had not been present in his previous job. The amount of paper work in his current job meant he had to be tidy to prevent being overwhelmed.

It all depends?

How can we maintain the notion of a trait of tidiness, with the implications of consistency over time and across situation, in the light of such apparent inconsistencies? Does the concept of a fixed personality not collapse and need to be replaced by the notion that particular responses have been learned to particular situations?

These questions and a range of related ones were raised by Walter Mischel in a book in 1968 which burst like a bombshell at the heart of personality theory, which until that time had emphasized the importance of the stable characteristics of individuals. Mischel produced evidence which, he suggested, demonstrated that intellectual skills apart, traits and dispositions showed little evidence of stability over time or across situations. Where consistency was present, he argued, it was because of similarities in the situation. According to Mischel, although the attribution of trait characteristics ('sociability', 'aggression', 'shyness') appears to be a useful way of organizing our perceptions of other people, traits do not reflect the actual patterning of behaviour in the real world. Perceived consistency may be simply a matter of the 'halo' or stereotyping effect whereby the perception of a characteristic in one setting leads one to expect and perceive it in other settings.

Mischel's criticisms had some major implications for the assessment of personality. The vast majority of personality tests assume consistency of personality, and at the time Mischel's book appeared, personality testing was a major industry in the United States. Established tests such as the Thematic Apperception Test (TAT), the Cattell Sixteen Personality Factor Inventory (16PF) and the California Psychological Inventory (CPI) all assume consistency. If Mischel was correct it would be expected that any test of a trait or disposition would be poor at predicting actual behaviour in a specific real-life setting. To return to the earlier example, our author's score on a test of 'obsessional tidiness' would not be very useful in predicting how neat and clipped he kept the edge of his garden lawn. Mischel found that correlations between trait score and actual behaviour were indeed very low. Given that the whole purpose of personality testing is often to make *specific* predictions (for example, using personality tests to predict who will or will not be a good salesperson, who will or will not be readmitted after discharge from a psychiatric hospital) Mischel's conclusions were of considerable practical importance.

Mischel's critique was particularly influential because it also suggested an alternative approach to personality and its assessment. This was to focus on external factors, the environmental situation itself, as a cause of behaviour. Such a focus was consistent with the behavioural or 'social learning' approach to problems which was becoming well established in clinical and other areas of applied psychology in the 1960s and 1970s. From this viewpoint the best predictions about a person's future behaviour in a particular situation can be made by assessing how he or she has behaved in similar situations in the past.

Assessing the person or the situation

It is not difficult to see how 'situationism' of this sort suggests very different techniques for assessing a person's suitability for a job, for instance, or for assessing the problems of a patient on discharge from a psychiatric hospital. The situationist would try to define the specific tasks the person might meet in the job (or living outside the hospital), and then assess how the person would behave or has behaved in situations of this sort. It might even be desirable to devise a similar situation for the person to respond to at interview. The traditional trait approach to assessment would be to assess dispositions of a very general sort through personality tests or interview assessment. As we shall see, there is something to be said for combining both person and situation factors in assessment.

As might be expected, Mischel's book stimulated some forceful and cogent defences of trait theory and attacks on the new situationism. The counter-attack has been of two kinds: first criticisms of the kinds of methodology used in the studies quoted by Mischel, and, second, theoretical criticisms. Kenneth Bowers and Jack Block in the United States are amongst those who have written in defence of the trait approach. Bowers has concentrated on some of the logical inconsistencies of the extreme situationist position. Block argues that many of the studies reported by Mischel were badly carried out, and that many were done with children, who would be expected to be less consistent than adults. Block's own work, studying individuals long-term over a period of 20 years, found evidence of considerable consistency over time in personality ratings. Individuals rated as 'dependable' and 'responsible' at school tended to be rated in the same way some 20 years later. A similar consistency over time has been reported for aggressive boys by the Norwegian psychologist Dan Olweus.

THE PERSON and THE SITUATION: THE INTERACTION

Mischel perhaps overstated the case against trait consistency. It was a necessary corrective at the time and it has been productive in bringing traditional personality theory back to a consideration of the effects of settings and situations. Lawrence Pervin suggests that psychology in general undergoes periods of shifts of emphasis. There are periods when theories emphasize *internal* determinants of behaviour and periods when *external* factors are stronger. The effect of Mischel's early work was to produce some shift towards an appreciation of the external situation. Contemporary thinking about personality tends to be increasingly *interactionist,* accommodating both internal and external factors.

Mischel now acknowledges some stability of personality over time and setting, while at the same time recognizing that people show what he calls 'a great discriminativeness' in their behaviour, depending on the situation they are in:

> Complex behaviour is regulated by interactions that depend ultimately on situational variables, as well as on dispositions. Humans are capable of extraordinary adaptiveness and discrimination as they cope with a continuously changing environment. *(1981, pages 517–18).*

Consistency may be more evident for some individuals than for others and more evident for some traits than for others.

The world is largely what we make it

The word 'interaction' used in the heading to this section signifies not only that *both* person and situation are important but also that the effect of situations will vary with the nature of the persons exposed to them and, conversely, that the effect of personality traits will vary with the situation. Life changes – changing job, moving house – may overall be associated with stress and anxiety but there will be some individuals who thrive on such changes while others suffer. It might not be possible to separate personality and situation. Particular personalities may *create* life changes while others minimize them. In this sense, the environments to which we are exposed are, in part, an expression of our personality.

PREDICTING DANGEROUSNESS: THEORIES IN ACTION

So far the person/situation debate may seem largely academic and of little real social importance. This is far from being the case. Many important decisions are made on the basis of predictions about future behaviour and attempts to make such predictions inevitably involve consideration of the relative importance of person and situation.

One of the most difficult areas of social decision-making is that of whether or not to detain offenders who have been extremely violent. Is the person still 'dangerous' and likely to act in a violent way in the future? Judges, doctors, psychologists, social workers and others are called upon to make such assessments. The traditional approach has been to investigate internal characteristics of the person. Does he or she have an aggressive personality? Is he or she lacking in impulse control? Or is the person suffering from mental illness?

Attempts to predict future dangerous behaviour in this way have been largely unsuccessful, few tests or interview methods being able to predict who will or will not reoffend violently should they be discharged. Ronald Blackburn, a clinical psychologist involved in such decisions, has reviewed the problems of making predictions in this way. The situationist argument would be that violence is highly specific to particular environmental conditions. To predict violence we need to know the situations and confrontations to which the person will be exposed. Estimates of present aggressiveness will, at best, have only very weak associations with future violence. From this point of view, attempts to predict violence are doomed to failure because we have little information about the situations to which the person will be exposed.

Blackburn himself concludes that violent behaviour *does* show some consistency across situations and over time and that aggressive dispositions are therefore worth assessing. Once again, the inter-actionist account would suggest both situational and dispositional factors need consideration. We need to know whether the person has an aggressive personality and also the particular situations to which he or she is likely to respond with violence. These situations, of course, may be very idiosyncratic. There will be violence-prone people who respond violently only in reaction to domestic disputes (arguments with a spouse), while others react mainly to abuse in a work setting, and others again only to pressures in violent gangs.

COGNITIVE PERSPECTIVES: IT DEPENDS ON HOW YOU LOOK AT IT

Views about personality have always, inevitably, reflected accepted general psychological theories and methods of the time. One of the striking features of much of psychology in the 1970s and 1980s has been its 'cognitive' flavour and this has permeated thinking about personality and personality problems. The meanings of 'cognitive' and 'cognition' are various, but the terms usually refer to mental representations of events: to the processes of interpreting, predicting and evaluating the environment, as well as to beliefs, thoughts and expectations. What the cognitive theorist brings to the study of individual differences in behaviour is summed up in the oft-quoted maxim of the philosopher Epictetus, that 'Men are not moved by things, but the views which they take of them'. Cognitive theory, then, leads us to try to understand, assess and, in a clinical context, change mental representations of the world, including the self and the external environment.

There is no one cognitive approach to personality. We describe here two areas of research which share a cognitive perspective.

PERSONAL CONSTRUCT THEORY

The American psychologist George Kelly proposed an elaborate theory of personal constructs in the 1950s which was some 20 years or more ahead of its time, anticipating many later developments in cognitive theorizing, though Kelly himself would reject the term 'cognitive' as being too narrow to characterize the theory. Kelly's starting point is a view of the person as a scientist engaged in the task of interpreting and theorizing about the world and using these theories to predict the future. Kelly's theory is rooted in the philosophical position of constructive alternativism which states that the world can be construed in infinitely varied ways. Individuals construe the world in terms of *personal constructs* which are bi-polar descriptions, these personal constructs being organized into systems. Thus a person may view his or her relationships with other people in terms of the bi-polar construct 'a relationship in which I am dominant' versus 'a relationship in which I am submissive'. Any one important construct will have implications for other constructs in the system. A relationship in which 'I am submissive', for example, might imply for that person 'an uncomfortable relationship'. The importance of constructs will vary for different individuals (constructs are *personal*) as will the implications of the construct within the system. For some people submissiveness may be associated with comfort and relaxation.

The nature of the personal construct approach to personality is best shown by exploring your own construct system. Kelly devised a method for doing this – the *Repertory Grid* – which has been widely used in a range of applied settings including hospitals, prisons and education. Instructions for completing a grid on yourself are given in Exercise 2.1 on pages 59 and 60. You might wish to try this exercise before reading the next section which describes the use of the repertory grid with a psychiatric patient seen by one of the authors.

James was a man in his early 30s who worked for an insurance company doing what most people would consider 'a good job'. He had applied for promotion some months previously but had been unsuccessful. He was upset by this for a few weeks but eventually regained his equilibrium. Shortly afterwards an important relationship with a girlfriend broke up. He reported good relationships with his parents and his two brothers. In the period before coming to see a psychologist he had been moody, irritable and prone to bouts of depression. He was pessimistic about his future and about the world in general.

The repertory grid technique was used to explore his view of significant people in his life and of himself and to elicit the constructs actually important to James. An interview estabished that the major people in his life at the time were his father, his mother, a brother whom he saw frequently, a friend at work, his boss at work and his recent girlfriend. Constructs elicited from James are shown in *Table 2.1*. James was asked to think about each of his important people and

Table 2.1: James' personal constructs

1.	'respected by others'	versus	'looked down on by others'
2.	'educated'	versus	'poor education'
3.	'warm, open people'	versus	'cold'
4.	'over-emotional'	versus	'stable'
5.	'relates easily to others'	versus	'has difficulties in relating'
6.	'successful in work'	versus	'a failure'
7.	'confident with other people'	versus	'unsure of themselves'
8.	'did well at school'	versus	'did poorly at school'

to decide where he would place them on each construct.

There are a number of mathematical methods for assessing which constructs were the most important for James. These suggested, and he was able to confirm this himself, that the construct relating to 'respect' (1) was a vital one. There was an association between this construct and constructs (2) 'educated' and (6) 'successful'. A second important construct was that relating to 'confidence' (7), which was also associated with constructs (3) and (5). These two groups of constructs cluster together then, suggesting they reflect two important dimensions for James in judging himself and others. Another way to demonstrate this is to plot the location of significant people on important dimensions. This is illustrated in Figure 2.1.

Perhaps the most striking thing about this map of James' world is the great distance between himself as he is and how he would like to be. He falls short on both the 'respect' and 'confidence' dimensions. Despite his good job, he clearly has major doubts about his achievements and his status in relation to other people. The other males in his family, his father and brother, approximate to his ideal. It is not difficult to see how many lines of further enquiry a repertory grid of this sort opens up and we shall leave it to you to think further about what sort of help James might need, given his view of the world.

[A further use of the repertory grid is considered in Chapter 11.]

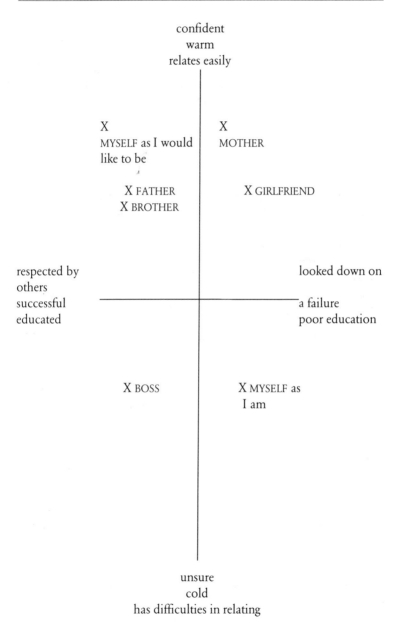

Figure 2.1: James' view of important people

ATTRIBUTION:
ANSWERING THE QUESTION 'WHY?'

George Kelly has not been the only psychologist to stress that people create theories about themselves, others and the world in general, and that understanding personal theories is crucial to understanding their behaviour. Over the same period that Kelly's theory was beginning to influence the thinking of many clinical psychologists, a line of research was gathering pace within experimental social psychology, which has become known as *Attribution Theory*. Attribution theory concerns itself with one particular form of construing the world, namely with the perception of *causality*. From an attributional perspective, people are viewed as engaged in the task of explaining *why* events happen.

Laying the blame

Arriving at an attribution for a particular action involves the use of complex information about the *context* of the action. If you see, for example, a stranger *(A)* assault another person *(B)* in the street, in order to arrive at an attribution for why this has happened, you would need to consider:

Is *A* violent in general or is his or her violence specific to *B?* This is called 'distinctiveness' information.

You might also need to consider whether *B* is often the victim of assaults by other people ('consensus' information).

Finally, has *A* hit *B* before or is this the only occasion? ('consistency' information).

Contextual information of this sort will play a part in determining whether we isolate *A, B,* or some temporary factor in the situation as the *cause* of what happened. It is obvious that on many occasions in everyday life we fail to make rational use of such information. If a stranger acts in an unfriendly way towards you, you might assume that you have offended him or her in some way without attempting to find out whether he or she acts in this way towards everyone (failing to use 'distinctiveness' information). Similarly, you might explain some problems you have in terms of your 'inadequacy' without stopping to

Exercise 2.2

YOUR ATTRIBUTIONAL STYLE

1. Think about the two worst things that have happened to you in the past year. Write 200–300 words describing each event.

2. Consider the two events again. For each event write a few sentences explaining *why* the event happened.

3. Complete *1* and *2* before turning over the page.

   Seeing the point of the exercise might bias how you carry it out.

consider that many other people have an identical problem ('consensus' information). If you would like to find out a bit more about your own attributional style try out Exercise 2.2.

Psychologists have asked whether, when we try to explain behaviour, we evaluate the situation rationally or whether we are biased towards arriving at particular sorts of attribution. One particular form of bias has been suggested in studies. People in general often show a 'positivity' bias, that is a tendency to explain things in such a way as to maintain self-esteem. Many of us tend to explain successes in terms of our own qualities and failures in terms of factors outside ourselves. As we shall see later, people vary markedly in this. People with psychological difficulties often show a reversed positivity bias, habitually explaining bad events in ways that are highly damaging to their self-esteem.

ATTRIBUTIONS AND PSYCHOLOGICAL DISTRESS

Bias in the attribution process has been reported in a number of groups who present with psychological problems. Distress may be generated, for example, by the tendency to attribute some difficulty or problem behaviour to a *negative internal disposition*. Suppose, for example, that Michael is gauche in social situations. He attributes this gaucheness to his 'social inadequacy' which, in turn, makes him even more anxious and gauche in subsequent situations. A sexual failure with a member of the opposite sex may be attributed, quite falsely, as indicating that 'I must be a homosexual' and the effect of this is to further impair confidence in heterosexual situations. 'Exacerbation cycles', as they have been called, have been reported in relation to a range of neurotic problems.

One of the most important applications of attributional ideas has been to depression. Christopher Peterson and Martin Seligman have argued, and amassed much evidence to support their view, that there is an habitual way of construing causality – an *attributional style* – which predisposes people to become depressed, should they experience unpleasant and stressful life events.

The person prone to depression explains 'bad' events that happen in particular ways. First, they attribute the event 'internally' rather than 'externally'; and second, the internal cause is 'stable' rather than 'unstable'. Finally the internal cause is 'global' rather than 'specific'. Let us illustrate this by an example quoted by Seligman himself.

If the event which you are trying to explain is a rejection by a girlfriend, and you are predisposed to depression, you explain this occurrence in terms of something about you rather than something about her ('I am unattractive' rather than 'she was cruel'). You may make depression even more likely if your explanation is stable and unlikely to change ('I am unattractive' rather than 'I had been acting strangely'). Finally, you may explain the rejection in terms of a very general quality of yourself which extends beyond the particular situation ('I am useless as a person' rather than 'I have difficulty in sexual relationships').

Depressed people have been shown in some studies to think in this way, but the question must then be asked whether the attributional style is a consequence of the depression rather than a cause of it. Ideally, to prove Seligman's theory, it needs to be demonstrated that bad attributional styles *precede* depression. To assess people's attributional style prior to them meeting stressful life events and becoming depressed is no easy task.

As we suggested earlier, the cognitive approach to personality and personality problems is currently still in the ascendant, reflecting the general influence of the cognitive perspective within psychology. Some of the weaknesses of cognitive theories will undoubtedly have occurred to the reader. The reading suggested for this chapter at the end of the book will provide the opportunity to explore this and other matters in greater depth.

─ ── ── ─Exercise 2.2 continued ── ── ── ─

YOUR ATTRIBUTIONAL STYLE

4. Attribution theory would suggest that you would spontaneously try to *explain* the two events. Look through your two original accounts. Are there any phrases that suggest an explanation ('because', 'therefore', 'as a result', 'since' etc.)

5. Look through both your spontaneous accounts and the explanations asked for under 2, and try to classify your explanations in terms of Peterson and Seligman's depressive attributional style (see text).
Did you explain the bad events in terms of (a) internal, (b) stable, (c) global factors?

6.. How similar were the explanations for event 1 and event 2?

7. What might be your own attributional style for bad events?

Recommended Reading

Cook, M. (1984). *Levels of Personality*. London: Holt Rinehart & Winston.
Fransella, F. (ed.) (1981). *Personality: Theory, Measurement and Research*. London: Methuen.
Mischel, W. (3rd edn. 1981). *Introduction to Personality*. New York: Holt Rinehart & Winston.

References

Antaki, C. & Brewin, C. (eds.) (1982). *Attributions and Psychological Change*. London: Academic Press. [A good introduction to attribution theory and its applications.]

Blackburn, R. (1983). Psychometrics and personality theory in relation to dangerousness. In J. Hinton (ed.) *Dangerousness: Problems of Assessment and Prediction*. London: George Allen & Unwin. [This chapter illustrates the relevance of theoretical disputes to a real-world social problem.]

Block, J. (1971). *Lives Through Time*. Berkeley, California: Barcroft Books. [A longitudinal study of stability of personality over time.]

Bowers, K. (1973). Situationism in psychology: an analysis and critique. *Psychological Review, 80*, 307–336. [An influential critique of the extreme situationist position.]

Eysenck, H.J. & Eysenck, M.W. (1981). *Personality and Individual Differences: A Natural Science Approach*. New York: Plenum. [Explains Eysenck's theory and also his attempt to update his thinking in the light of research.]

Gray, J.A. (1981). A critique of Eysenck's theory of personality. In H.J. Eysenck (ed.), *A Model for Personality.* Berlin: Springer. [An appraisal of the theory by someone who has been influenced by it but who has also reformulated some aspects of it.]

Kelly, G. (1955). *The Psychology of Personal Constructs, Vols. 1 and 2.* New York: W.W. Norton. [The 'classic' and original book on personal construct theory.]

Kline, P. (1981). Recent research into the factor analysis of personality. In F. Fransella (ed.), *Personality: Theory, Measurement and Research.* London: Methuen. [Gives a good account of what factor analysis is and of its use by workers such as Cattell and Eysenck.]

Mischel, W. (1968). *Personality Assessment.* New York: Wiley. [A classic in personality theory.]

Olweus, D. (1979). Stability of aggressive reaction patterns in males: a review. *Psychological Bulletin, 86,* 852–875. [Looks at stability of one particular kind of behaviour.]

Pervin, L.A. (2nd edn. 1984). *Current Controversies and Issues in Personality.* New York: Wiley. [A readable account of important theoretical issues.]

Peterson, C. & Seligman, M.E.P. (1984). Causal explanations as a risk factor for depression: theory and evidence. *Psychological Review, 91,* 495–512. [A summary of research on attributional style as a predictor of depression.]

EXPLORE YOUR OWN CONSTRUCT SYSTEM

In recent years some very complex ways of analysing repertory grids have been developed, most of them requiring the assistance of a microcomputer. Nevertheless, it is not difficult to evaluate your own grid in a very simple way. You will need to allow about one hour to complete this exercise.

a) MOTHER

1.   Prepare 10 pieces of blank card, each about the size of a filing card. Mark each card in the top left-hand corner from 'a' to 'j'.
2.   On card 'a' write 'Mother', on 'b' 'Father', on 'c' the name of your spouse/girl/boyfriend, on 'd' the name of someone you dislike, on 'e' the name of someone you consider successful, on 'f' the name of a friend, on 'g' the name of your immediate 'boss' or employer, on 'h' the name of any other family member. On 'i' write 'Myself as I am', on 'j' write 'Myself as I would like to be'.
3.   Put card 'i' on the table in front of you. Shuffle the other cards and randomly select two cards from the pack and put them on the table with 'i'.
4.   Think about the three people whose cards are in front of you. Try to identify some important way in which two of these people are similar and different from the third. For example, both my father and myself are 'sympathetic', while my boss is 'unsympathetic'. Record this 'construct' on a separate sheet of paper.
5.   Keep card 'i' on the table. Put the other two cards back in the pack and shuffle. Randomly select two others.
6.   Repeat 4 above.
7.   Continue doing this until you have a list of 8 constructs.
8.   On a separate sheet of paper construct a Repertory Grid like that shown over page, using your own eight constructs across the top. The 'people' whom we have used are termed 'elements' in the repertory grid.
9.   Think about Construct 1. Think about each person from 'a' to 'j' in turn, and apply the construct to them. If they are like the first end of the construct ('sympathetic') put a '1' opposite their name. If they are like the other end of the construct 'unsympathetic' put a '0'.
10.   Repeat 9 for constructs 2 to 8.

Continued over page

EXPLORE YOUR OWN CONSTRUCT SYSTEM

LAY-OUT FOR YOUR GRID

People (Elements)	Personal constructs			
	1. Sympathetic– Unsympathetic	2. Clever– Stupid	3. Assertive– Shy	4. Etc.
a	1	1	1	
b	1	0	1	
c	0	1	0	
d	0	0	0	
e	1	1	0	
f	0	0	1	
g	1	0	1	
h	0	0	0	
i	0	1	0	
j	0	0	0	

Things to ponder

☐ Reflect on the fact that these are *your* personal constructs. Another individual would provide a very different list. Are/were you aware that these are the dimensions you use to structure your world?

☐ How do your constructs associate with each other? Check this by comparing any row of '1's and '0's with the other rows. If the pattern of vertical '1's and '0's match (or nearly match) this suggests overlapping meaning between the two constructs. Does it surprise you that any particular constructs match? What does a match reveal about your way of thinking? Remember that a reversed match (all '1's match with '0's) is equally significant.

☐ How do the people compare with each other? Do any people have identical or similar patterns of '1's and '0's in the horizontal rows? Are the similarities surprising? What do they suggest?

☐ Who is most like 'Myself as I am'? Would you have guessed this?

☐ How similar is 'Myself as I am' to 'Myself as I would like to be'? On what constructs is there a gap between your actual and ideal self?

3. *Your Sex: On Being Male or Female*

It is much easier to identify people as male or female than it is to class them as masculine or feminine. The first distinction refers to *sex,* which is biological; we all come into the world with a certain genetic make-up, internal physiology and bodily structure, which are quite difficult to change. The second refers to *gender;* 'masculine' and 'feminine' are words which summarize different ways of behaving, and these are much more wide-ranging and susceptible to change. The 'masculine' person is typically thought of as tough, ambitious and dominant, and the 'feminine' person as gentle, non-assertive, and concerned for the welfare of others. The question is, how are sex and gender related to one another?

It is quite easy to think of examples of males who could be described as feminine, as well as of masculine females; Frederic Chopin and his companion George Sand provide good historical examples, and there are plenty of current-day equivalents. The qualities admired by some in the leadership of a woman such as Britain's Margaret Thatcher, for example, are precisely those regarded as typically masculine. Such people can be thought of as exceptions to the rule that males are in general likely to be masculine, and that females are likely to be feminine.

SEX OR GENDER?

In other words, sex and gender are not related to one another in a simple, direct manner. Some feminist thinkers would take this argument still further, and challenge the widely-held belief that gender differences are mainly based on sex differences. They would maintain that society's beliefs about what is appropriate behaviour for the sexes are the only really important influence on how men and women actually behave, and that biological differences have virtually nothing to do with it. This argument is actually just another version of one of the oldest debates in psychology, the 'nature-nurture' issue. Psychologists have been debating the question of whether our behaviour is determined by our biological make-up (our 'nature'), or by what we learn (our 'nurture'), for as long as the subject has been in existence.

Happily, something of value has come out of this argument. From the heat of the 'women's liberation' debate in the 1960s and 1970s, psychologists rediscovered the idea of *androgyny;* this comes from the Greek words *andro* and *gyne* meaning man and woman. The idea is that males should no longer confine themselves to masculine behaviour, or females to feminine behaviour, because this effectively means stifling half of one's personality. Instead, the suggestion is that both sexes should endeavour to be *androgynous,* that is, they should be able to act in either a masculine *or* a feminine manner when the situation demands it. Men should not have to 'keep a stiff upper lip' in emotional situations where the natural thing to do is to cry, for example; and women should not have to hold back the desire to win in competitive situations, such as in sports, or indeed in the 'rat race', as it is often described, for careers and employment.

Now this idea is very clearly in tune with the ideals of feminism, and maybe because of this, it has been the subject of a great deal of recent research and investigation. One of the pioneers in the field has been Sandra Bem of Cornell University. She was amongst the first to propose that androgyny is a 'psychologically healthy' state of mind and behaviour, and that it might be correspondingly unhealthy to be too traditionally feminine a female, or too masculine a male.

In order to test her theory, Bem worked out a psychological test which has been extensively used to measure people's masculinity and femininity, called the *Bem Sex Role Inventory (BSRI).* This consists of a list of 60 adjectives, such as 'forceful', 'competitive', 'affectionate', 'gentle', 'adaptable' and 'truthful'. People taking the test are asked to say how well each of the 60 adjectives describes them by giving a score on a scale ranging from 1 ('never or almost never true of me') to 7 ('always or almost always true of me'). Twenty of the adjectives are masculine words, 20 are feminine words, and 20 are neutral words; and so by adding up people's scores on the scales, Bem was able to give people overall assessments of their 'masculinity' and their 'femininity'. This applies to both males and females, and so the test enabled Bem to identify the 'masculine females' and the 'feminine males' that we mentioned earlier.

At Leicester University we have designed a *'Play and Games Inventory'* which is based on the same principles: masculinity and femininity in children are assessed in terms of the activities and games they like to play. You can try this out in Exercise 3.1.

Many researchers have made use of Bem's test since she first brought it out, and it has had various improvements and changes as different people have used it, and as Bem has updated her own ideas. The most common technique, in recent years, has been to use the *BSRI* to classify people into one of four different types.

1. 'Androgynous' people are those who score high on both masculinity and femininity; they are men and women who have achieved the 'psychologically healthy' state of being able to display both types of behaviour in appropriate situations.

2. 'Feminine' people are those who score high on femininity but low on masculinity, and vice versa for people described as 'masculine' on the test. Not many males come out as 'feminine', and not many females as 'masculine', although there may be more of the latter than the former.

3. By far the largest groups of people are of course 'masculine' males and 'feminine' females; and these are the people who Bem would like to move, in an ideal world, towards a state of androgyny.

4. People who score low on both scales are described as 'undifferentiated', neither masculine nor feminine.

How do these four groups fare in various aspects of life? The general conclusion seems to be that 'androgynous' people are better off in a variety of ways. Research studies suggest that they seem to be more effective as parents; to be more mature when making moral judgements and decisions; to have better emotional feelings about themselves; to be more adaptable to new situations; and so on.

Findings like this are very much at one with liberal and feminist sentiments, although one recent review has raised a cautionary note. Before we get carried away with the idea that all the good things of psychological life follow from being androgynous, we should bear in mind the conclusions that Marylee Taylor and Judith Hall drew from their review of the literature. They interpret the research evidence as showing that *masculinity* is just as strongly linked with well-being as is androgyny in both males and females, and so the question remains open for further investigation.

This area of research is a very active and rapidly-changing one, and so it is not surprising that disagreements and new ideas are emerging all the time. One of the most recent views is that we should not be concerned about making people 'androgynous' quite so much as about trying to stop thinking about almost every aspect of behaviour in terms of male and female, masculine and feminine. There can be no doubt that these distinctions have a powerful grip on our current ways of thinking. For most people sex differences begin with biology and so it is to this that we now turn our attention.

BIOLOGICAL INFLUENCES

Our sex is assigned at birth on the basis of our external morphology; in other words, on whether we possess male or female genitals. Our sex, of course, is determined long before birth, and depends on the types of chromosomes we receive from our parents. Humans typically possess 46 chromosomes, two of which are concerned with determining sex: in females these two are called X chromosomes and are represented as XX. In males a single X and a single chromosome called Y are present, represented as XY. Maleness is determined by the presence of the Y and, in its absence, the individual produced is female, even if no second X chromosome is present (as in *Turner's Syndrome*, although she shows various abnormalities). A neutral individual cannot arise because as the embryo grows it develops as a female unless the Y is present. Contrary to the Biblical view that woman was formed from man's spare rib, it is the male that is made out of a form that is essentially female.

The presence of the Y chromosome alters the course of development of the embryo. Its presence speeds up the growth and division of the cells which form the male gonads (or *testes*) and by about 16 weeks after conception, the male is fully, sexually differentiated. In the female this differentiation of the gonads, or *ovaries,* both starts and ends later, being achieved fully at about 20 weeks.

Once the testes and ovaries are formed they begin to secrete sex hormones and the rest of the process of sexual differentiation is under hormonal control. If hormonal secretions are interfered with in some way, development may proceed along different lines and a genetic male may be feminized, or a female masculinized. In other words, the possession of particular sex chromosomes does not in itself mean that a person will develop fully as a male or female. On a more practical note the 'sex test' operated for sportsmen and women at the Olympic Games cannot reveal whether someone has been exposed to hormones of the opposite sex in earlier life. Genetic sex guarantees us neither a male nor a female body, nor a gender identity which makes us feel appropriately masculine or feminine. As we shall see in the next section, various genetic and hormonal abnormalities have helped us to understand more about relationships between sex and gender.

HORMONES AND BEHAVIOUR

Male hormones, the chief one of which is *testosterone,* are collectively called *androgens,* and these have a masculinizing action on the developing body. Androgens are responsible for the production of sperm in the testes, and for the growth of the extra muscle and bone which characterize the body of the adult male.

The female is hormonally more complicated than the male. She has *oestrogens* which, in early development, are concerned with sexual differentiation, and which are concerned later with the growth of the eggs (or ova) in the ovaries, with the maturation of her genitals and breasts, and with the increased deposition of fat during adolescence. *Progesterone* is also present in the female and is concerned with preparing the womb (or uterus) for pregnancy, maintaining the pregnancy after conception, and in nourishing the developing embryo. In adult females the secretion of oestrogens and progesterone is cyclic, and on average the cycle, known as the menstrual cycle, is repeated every 28 days.

In both sexes the appropriate sex hormones are produced by the testes and ovaries, but the gonads are controlled by the *pituitary gland* and the *hypothalamus* of the brain. It should be noted however that apart from the gonads, small quantities of sex hormones may be produced at other sites in the body, for example in the *adrenal glands;* and in both sexes, hormones of the opposite sex are found.

Male and female alike

Sex hormones affect the expression of various types of sexual and non-sexual behaviour; indeed almost all forms of behaviour can be shown by both males and females. This statement will be made clearer by examples from non-human animals although of course we cannot assume that humans function in exactly the same way. We expect that a cow will be quieter and less aggressive than a bull, and that the latter will mount the female for copulation. However cows can be highly aggressive in some circumstances, and when ready to mate, at ovulation, will mount other females. Thus the notion that males and females show quite separate patterns of behaviour appropriate only to their own sex is misleading. This sort of evidence lends some support to Sandra Bem's view that maleness and femaleness are not opposite poles of a single continuum but rather are two dimensions which exist side by side within every individual.

Physiological studies of rodents have shown the impact of sex hormones on development and behaviour. If a male rat is castrated at birth before full sexual differentiation has occurred (unlike humans) and then primed with female hormones in adulthood, its behaviour is like that of a female, although it cannot reproduce. Similarly the removal of ovaries from the infant female rat makes her behaviour more masculine in adulthood and she behaves as a male in the presence of a receptive female. In both these cases genetic sex does not determine the behaviour; the presence or absence of hormones plays the crucial role.

The belief that human males are more aggressive, and that females are more emotional and submissive is by no means universally held. Some evolutionary theories have suggested that early in human history man was the hunter whilst woman cared for the offspring. The link between this view and aggression in males and females is still controversial. Indeed whilst male hormones are typically associated with aggression in many animals – the castration of bulls has been used for thousands of years to quieten them – it should also be noted that female hormones have also been linked with an increase in aggression in some species. Thus generalizations from other animals to humans must be made with caution. In humans the measurement of aggression is problematical chiefly because it can be displayed in so many ways other than through physically violent acts, as in verbal abuse or sarcasm for instance, and so when aggression in males and females is compared there is difficulty in equating different forms of this behaviour. This problem is discussed in more detail in Chapter 5.

PROBLEMS OF SEX AND GENDER

As we have seen, genetic sex does not in itself guarantee appropriate sexual behaviour and its relationship to *gender identity* – the individual's private experience of him- or herself as male or female – is uncertain.

Earlier on in this chapter we said that at birth a sex is assigned to a newborn infant. You might think this would be easy, but there are times when it is not. Occasionally sexual differentiation is ambiguous and a decision must be made as to whether to bring up the infant as male or female.

Male and female in one?

John and Joan Hampson have studied the development and experiences of a large number of so-called *hermaphrodites*. In these individuals there exists a contradiction between their external genitals and various internal structures such as the gonads, chromosomes, and hormones. The Hampsons' research dealt with the experiences of over 100 such people who had been reared as the sex which later medical investigation showed was wrong. Almost all of these people were found to be entirely adjusted to their assigned sex, and felt themselves to be the sex that they had been brought up to believe that they were, even in the face of later contradictory evidence. This research led to the idea that a person's psychosexual orientation is chiefly determined by rearing, and to the suggestion that at birth the infant is psychosexually neutral; or, to put it another way, that gender identity is learned.

Another case supports the view. A surgical accident caused a male identical twin to lose his penis and the child was subsequently reared as a girl. To his parents' surprise 'he' developed typical feminine interests unlike his genetically-identical brother and appeared to be entirely girl-like in behaviour.

Of course these studies do not provide conclusive proof that psychosexual orientation is learned. Neither hermaphrodites, nor identical twins, are representative of the 'normal' population, and in the former case we can hardly imagine that many people, faced with evidence that their idea of their own sex is wrong, would seek to change it. There must be strong pressures on hermaphrodites to retain their original assigned sex and be content with it.

Some psychologists oppose the view that psychosexual orientation is acquired. They suggest that the research shows sex differences at such an early stage in life that these cannot possibly be due to nurture rather than nature. This view is a controversial one, since the evidence for the genetic determination of many observed sex differences is far from established, and there can be no doubt that learning plays a highly important role in the development of men and women.

What can we learn from studies of some forms of less common sexual orientation such as *homosexuality* and *transsexualism?*

Homosexuality

The homosexual is someone whose sexual behaviour is like that of the 'normal' heterosexual but he or she chooses a partner of the same rather than the opposite sex. Until quite recently this behaviour was outside British law, and it is still considered by many to be an abnormality which requires treatment to effect a 'cure' back to heterosexuality. This belief is dying out: in North America homosexuality has now been removed from the *'Diagnostic System of the American Psychiatric Association'* and is thereby recognized as a 'normal variant' of human sexual behaviour rather than as a disorder or illness. The Roman Catholic Church, on the other hand, sees it as unnatural and against God's laws. But what do we actually know about homosexuality?

We know that homosexual behaviour is shown by a significant minority of people. Alfred Kinsey in 1948 reported that over one third of the males whom he studied had displayed some form of homosexual behaviour. Cross-cultural studies have found that in over half of the dozens of primitive societies compared, some form of homosexual behaviour is considered normal and acceptable. Homosexual behaviour is not exclusive to humans; it is displayed by other species. Thus it appears that it is within the range of patterns of behaviour which we might expect in men and women, although it is not present in the majority, just as green eyes or left handedness are not.

What is its cause? Several suggestions have been made. Psychoanalysts have suggested that homosexuality may arise if there is incomplete resolution of the *Oedipus complex* – an idea put forward by Freud to explain how the male comes to identify with his father. Other studies have explored genetic and hormonal imbalances, but attempts to establish a link have so far failed. Homosexuality may not have a single cause. Studies of the backgrounds of male and female homosexuals, relative to heterosexuals, show that both the homosexual and heterosexual groups of females tend to come from backgrounds which are more similar than are those of the homosexual or heterosexual males; thus the causes of this behaviour both within and between the sexes may be multifaceted. At present we do not understand the cause or causes of this behaviour, just as we do not fully understand what determines heterosexual behaviour.

Transsexualism

Transsexuals, unlike homosexuals, choose a member of the opposite sex as a sexual partner, but they feel themselves to be trapped in the wrong body, as a female within a male shell, or vice versa. These individuals have normal bodies and show no abnormality of chromosomes or sexual behaviour, but their gender identity is mismatched. Transsexuality has not been linked with a physical cause but it has been suggested that the child's early learning experiences – such as parents permitting or even encouraging the child to dress as the opposite sex – may play a role here. So where does all this leave us in considering the link between sex and gender?

What is a problem?

It seems that some of the psychosexual problems which occur are greatly exacerbated by our society's narrow view of what constitutes appropriate masculine or feminine behaviour and in future it may be necessary to reconsider our views of what is normal and acceptable. If individuals are allowed to express both the tender and intuitive, as well as the aggressive and competitive sides of their natures regardless of their sex, then we might find that we have individuals who are happier and psychologically-healthier people. Nevertheless there can be no doubt that sex is a major division in our society and to make less of its importance will certainly be a long and very gradual process. The effects on others of being male or female become apparent almost as soon as a child is born, and the ways in which boys and girls are brought up to behave differently and to think about each other differently, are complex and deep-rooted.

BOYS AND GIRLS GROWING UP

Even the most liberal of parents would have to admit that any attempt to bring up children to be unaffected by sex roles is almost certainly doomed to failure. Sex roles are all-pervasive: children see examples of what is regarded as the appropriate behaviour for boys and girls in books and magazines, on television programmes, in advertisements, in the playground, in the classroom, and indeed almost everywhere. The enormous power of these influences is shown by the extremely early age at which sex differences in behaviour start to emerge, as well as by the age at which children become aware of them.

Studies of parents and their young babies have clearly shown that boys and girls are consistently treated differently from birth onwards. One investigation found that fathers rated their newborn sons as more alert, well co-ordinated and strong, and their newborn daughters as more inattentive, soft and delicate, having only looked at them: they had not yet even picked them up.

Are boys more difficult?

In another study of three-week-olds, it was found that baby boys cried and fussed more than did baby girls of the same age and that mothers took longer to comfort them. There are two possible explanations. The first is that boys are inherently more vocal and that their demands for attention are greater than those of girls. Because mothers of young babies lead distraught and hectic lives it is harder for them to satisfy these demands, and so they take longer to do so for boys. The alternative explanation is that mothers somehow unconsciously think of boy babies as being 'tougher' and more resilient than girls and leave them to cry for longer before investigating. This is a 'chicken and egg' argument, of course; it is impossible to determine whether the crying determines the mother's behaviour, or whether the mother's behaviour causes the crying. What *is* certain is that the differences are present very early on; and it seems a reasonable bet that some form of 'stereotyping' may affect the mother's attitude to her baby son or daughter.

As far as children's own awareness of these differences is concerned, it seems likely that there are some early glimmerings at around the age of two. The first sign of this is the child's verbal distinction between 'mummy' and 'daddy' (and also maybe between 'boy' and 'girl'). Early on, these words are likely to be 'labels' that have no consistent reference to sex, but this reference soon becomes apparent. When this happens, children start to classify themselves as members of one sex or the other; in other words they develop a *gender identity*. Quite a lot of research has explored different aspects of gender identity.

Preschoolers have been shown pictures of different toys and games (football, Wendy house, etc.), and have been asked to say which are for boys and which are for girls. Another technique has been to show pictures of adults engaged in characteristic activities – washing the car, putting up shelves, cooking dinner, hanging out washing – and to ask similar questions. This research shows clearly that preschool children have a detailed knowledge of gender roles, and that they judge their own behaviour in terms of them. Gender identity is well established by the age of four or so.

The race to grow up

One interesting aspect of these early sex differences in growing up is the early lead that girls have over boys, and its eventual disappearance. Boys lag behind girls in most areas of early development such as standing, walking, and talking, and this lead carries on into the early school years. Girls are generally ahead of boys in most areas of infant school work. There are two possible reasons for this. The first is that girls mature physically more quickly than boys. The second is that in the preschool world, teachers and childminders are nearly all female, and this may have something to do with girls' early developmental lead.

Another interesting part of this puzzle is trying to explain why girls lose their early advantage after the age of six or so: boys seem to catch up, if not to take over, in many areas. This is very likely to be another manifestation of the powerful influence of society's expectations. The pathway that children travel from school, maybe to higher education, and then into the world of work and careers is much more clearly defined for boys than for girls. Boys stay on this pathway, and they develop a complex of competitive skills and attitudes. Girls are more likely to step on and off at different points in their lives, and consequently they seem not to fulfil their early potential.

Becoming masculine or feminine

Psychologists have tried to explain the process of *socialization* in different ways. Sigmund Freud had a theory of how boys and girls are involved in tense, emotional and sexually-based relationships with their mothers and fathers. Freud used the idea of the 'Oedipus complex' to try to explain how boys eventually take on the masculine characteristics of their fathers, but his account of the equivalent process for girls was much less satisfactorily worked out.

Another more realistic theory is that children learn what behaviour is appropriate for each sex by the rewards and punishments that they receive for imitating the people around them. A little boy might receive praise and encouragement for acting like his father in being successful at sports or games, for example. He would almost certainly be 'punished' (by verbal discouragement, criticism, or worse) if he showed an interest in playing with dolls, or engaged in other 'feminine' pursuits. This theory holds that boys perceive their fathers, and girls their mothers, as the most powerful source of rewards and punishments – and so in order to receive the maximum rewards and the minimum punishments, they *imitate* and *identify with* the same sex parent.

The power of identifying with people we admire is well known to all of us. Our parents provide the first 'models' for behaviour – but very soon we want to be like favourite pop stars, sporting personalities and other figures. Later on we may consciously try to model ourselves on an admired teacher, colleague or friend. This idea implies that our personalities and attitudes are formed of a whole complex of identifications with other people: we take the bits we like from a variety of others and put them together in our own unique way. There can be no doubt that sex is a very important framework around which these 'multiple identifications' are organized.

THE WEAKER SEX?

We have got used to the idea of female political leaders, doctors, and business executives, though we are still unhappy about the idea of female judges, priests, or plumbers. Most people in the West would probably look twice at a female roadmender or building site worker, although these are reasonably common in Eastern Europe or the USSR or Japan. Many people would argue that 'it's not natural' for women to do heavy manual work; they would say that this is more naturally suited to the greater height, weight and strength of men. Are they right or wrong? Such questions about what is or is not 'natural', that is, somehow biologically determined, are very important questions. They are also very difficult questions because society's views about the relative roles of men and women are constantly changing.

What actual differences are there?

A great deal of effort has been devoted in recent years to identifying exactly what are the main psychological differences between the sexes. Although it is virtually impossible to find complete agreement amongst all psychologists, there are some general ideas that many psychologists would accept. Let us consider what suggestions have been made about *physical skills, personality, interests* and *intelligence.*

One aspect of *physical skills* in which sex differences have been sought concerns the sensitivity of some of the sense organs. Women generally have a lower touch and pain threshold than men: this means that they are more sensitive to pain. But there is perhaps a paradox here since women seem able to withstand prolonged pain better than men. Women also seem to be more sensitive to sound and smell. For example, they are superior at distinguishing between two very similar sounds, as well as pinpointing exactly where a very quiet sound is coming from. On the other hand, boy babies seem to do better than girl babies on some visual tasks; in certain respects, they can see better. Another aspect of physical skills, aside from these sensory capabilities, concerns the ways in which males and females are able to carry out more complex everyday tasks. It is fairly well established that boys are better at activities involving gross motor skills, such as kicking a ball or pushing a heavy load. Girls may have a corresponding advantage for fine motor skills, such as using a typewriter or threading a needle, but the evidence for this is less clear-cut.

Many suggestions have been made about how the *personalities* of the sexes differ. As we saw earlier, qualities such as ambition, drive and competitiveness are widely regarded as typically masculine, whereas passivity, nurturance and emotionality are seen as typically feminine. It is extremely difficult for researchers to get any clear answers as to whether or not these views have any foundation. Aggression has frequently been studied in other animals as well as in people, for example, and we looked earlier at some biologically-based theories as to why males might be more aggressive than females.

In studies of preschoolers in the playground, for example, there seems to be no doubt that boys engage in more physical fighting and rought-and-tumble play. When *verbal* aggression such as taunts, shouts and insults are taken into account, however, it is by no means clear that girls are any less aggressive than boys. It may well be the case that the sexes are equally aggressive but that this aggression is channelled in different ways.

Other studies in this vein have suggested that boys tend to be more adventurous, independent and competitive, and that girls are correspondingly more affectionate, socially sensitive and emotional. But even if these personality differences between the sexes *can* be demonstrated, we cannot necessarily conclude that they are biologically rooted.

Another fascinating and unanswered question is this: do the sex differences that we can see in children carry on into adult life? Let us think about this in the context of typical male and female *interests.* One suggestion, for example, has been that males may be more interested in *objects,* or things, whereas females are more interested in *people.* This is clearly true in children's play. Many studies have shown that boys tend to have mechanical and 'scientific' play interests – in machines, construction games and computers – whereas the typical games of girls tend to revolve around other people. Playing with dolls and in Wendy houses, and acting out school, home and hospital scenes all centre on personal relationships. Can we go on from this to suggest that the interests and attitudes of men and women differ in a similar way? The idea would be that women are more social and emotional in their outlook, and that they have a stronger and more detailed interest in personal relationships than men. There is no doubt that men predominate in 'objective', impersonal fields like science and engineering, and that women are much more prevalent in the caring professions (e.g. nursing and social work), so it may not be too far-fetched to suggest that these specializations derive from childhood interests.

When we come to the topic of *intelligence,* there are two prevalent ideas about sex differences. The first is that females tend to do relatively better on intellectual tests involving words, (on *verbal* skills), and that males tend to be correspondingly better at *spatial* and *numerical* tasks – at working with shapes and numbers. This fits in with, and may even partly explain, the characteristic interests in people as distinct from things that we have just mentioned.

The second, more controversial, idea has provocatively been referred to (by a female psychologist) as the 'mediocrity of women'. If we look at the overall spread of scores of large numbers of males and females on certain intelligence tests, it sometimes turns out that a far greater number of females get scores around the average. More males, correspondingly, get scores that are well below the average as well as scores that are well above it. There may be greater variability or *scatter*, in other words, amongst males than females.

One fascinating real-life application of this idea comes from Corinne Hutt's survey of the degree classes obtained by students at Keele University over a ten-year period. She found that more men got first class and upper second degrees (the highest grades), as well as more pass degrees (the lowest); whilst women got lower seconds and thirds, that is, the intermediate grades. However, her finding may reflect the expectations of the university examiners just as much as any real differences in ability. This is not as far fetched as it sounds – a lack of history firsts amongst women graduates at Cambridge University disappeared when the examiners decided on 'blind' marking and removed the names and hence the sex of the candidates from the scripts.

All the findings that have been summarized in this section are intended to be detached, objective descriptions of sex differences that are observable in our society at this time, even though some experts would dispute them. They are not meant to be *prescriptive*, i.e. to indicate what should or should not be the case, and their *demonstration* cannot necessarily throw any light on their *explanation*. In the next section we shall consider some broader questions: can (male and female) psychologists remain scientifically neutral when researching sex differences, and how much *should* we accept that these differences affect our lives? Before reading the next section try out Exercise 3.2 and consider your answers to the questions posed.

SEX DIFFERENCES OR DISCRIMINATION?

Early biologists and psychologists sought to explain differences between the sexes by looking for sites in the brain of the male which were relatively larger than those in the female brain, and hence responsible for men's superiority in virtually every area of life, as

Charles Darwin believed. Their objectivity was highly questionable, and on more than one occasion the researchers had to change their views when a site thought to be larger in the male was found to be as large or larger in the female. Today this form of research has been abandoned.

In the 1980s we have become used to the notion of equal opportunity for both sexes and yet, in practice, males still predominate in jobs thought to be more intellectually demanding, or in positions of greater power. The few women who have power such as Golda Meir, Indira Gandhi, or Margaret Thatcher, are the exceptions which prove the rule. Let us consider the field of education. Most teachers of the young are female, and yet at the top of this profession, at headteacher grade, males are found in increasingly high proportions. As children get older and reach college or university they enter a world dominated by male staff, and this domination is even greater at more senior levels. Even within the field of psychology there is a preponderance of female undergraduates, but a corresponding predominance of males amongst researchers and teaching staff. One explanation of this evidence might be that intellectually males are superior and that this is inevitably reflected in the jobs which they occupy, and their pay.

The fallacy of this argument can be seen when we make cross-cultural comparisons. In North America, for example, the profession of medical doctor is highly prestigious and well paid, and it is dominated by males. In the Soviet Union it is an occupation predominantly staffed by women, with considerably lower status and pay. One cannot justifiably argue that the skills necessary for this profession are any greater in either of these two countries.

Equality in education?

Do we attach different values to the contributions which the two sexes make in education and working life? There is some evidence that we do. Research in the classroom shows that teachers provide more criticism as well as more praise to boy pupils than to girl pupils. This may well have the effect that boys are more actively encouraged to explore a subject and to develop their skills than are girls. Does this mean that boys are being promoted in intellectual terms more than girls? One investigation suggests that the more closely the girl adheres to the traditional feminine stereotype in adolescence the more intellectual decline she shows during these years, whilst the reverse is true for boys, in whom traditional stereotypes foster intellectual growth.

Many psychologists are beginning to recognize that there is a bias in society which favours boys. Research has shown that many girls, unlike boys, both fear and seek to avoid success in academic areas. Indeed there is some evidence that where a woman achieves success by her own ability and skill, *neither* she *nor* the men around her recognize fully her part in it. Women's success is often attributed to luck rather than skill, whilst the reverse is true for men.

These examples suggest that there is a self-fulfilling prophecy in the achievements of men and women. For centuries women have not been thought to be the intellectual equals of men, and recent attempts to disabuse us of this view have not had any obvious practical results. If those who teach, or who run the country, or who have power in any area really believe in the superiority of the male then this will be reflected in how males are treated relative to females. There is no doubt that expecting great things of people greatly enhances their chances of achieving them. It seems likely that, in the intellectual sphere, these expectations have been a major factor in influencing the levels of achievement of males and females.

Psychologists have accumulated a great deal of evidence which has led them to question many long-held beliefs about innate differences between the sexes. Sex roles are socially constructed – they are not simply the inevitable result of biology. If research has shown that one sex has been undervalued – to its detriment in many spheres of life – then the implications of such findings are obvious: the freedom to achieve one's potential in any sphere should be equally available to both women and men.

Recommended Reading

Archer, J. & Lloyd, B. (1985). *Sex and Gender,* rev. ed. Cambridge: Cambridge University Press.

Hargreaves, D.J. & Colley, A.M. (Eds) (1986). *The Psychology of Sex Roles.* London: Harper & Row.

Nicholson, J. (1984). *Men and Women: How Different Are They?* Oxford: Oxford University Press.

References

Archer, J. & Lloyd, B. (1982). *Sex and Gender.* Harmondsworth: Penguin. [A wide coverage, includes evolutionary theories and hormonal factors.]

Bem, S.L. (1975). Sex role adaptability: one consequence of psychological androgyny. *Journal of Personality & Social Psychology, 31,* 634–643. [Sandra Bem's theory of androgyny.]

Davison, G.C. & Neale, M.N. (1978). *Abnormal Psychology.* New York: John Wiley. [Chapters 11 and 12 in this are on abnormalities in sexual behaviour.]

Hampson, J.L. (1965). Determinants of psychosexual orientation. In F.A. Beach (ed.), *Sex and Behaviour.* New York: Wiley. [Research on hermaphrodites.]

Hargreaves, D.J., Stoll, L., Farnworth, S. & Morgan, S. (1981). Psychological androgny and ideational fluency. *British Journal of Social Psychology, 20,* 53–55. [Compares children's scores on a 'Play and Games Inventory' with their creative thinking.]

Hutt, C. (1975). Sex differences: biology and behaviour. In R. Lewin (ed.) *Child Alive.* London: Maurice Temple Smith. [Student degree grades at Keele University.]

Kinsey, A.C., Pomeroy, W.D. & Martin, C.E. (1948). *Sexual Behaviour in the Human Male.* Philadelphia: W.B. Saunders. [Males and Homosexuality.]

Moss, H.A. (1967). Sex, age and state as determinants of mother–infant interaction. *Merrill-Palmer Quarterly, 13,* 19–36. [Mothers' contacts with infant boys and girls.]

Rubin, J., Provenzano, F.J. & Luria, Z. (1974). The eye of the beholder: parents' views on sex of newborns. *American Journal of Orthopsychiatry, 43,* 720–731. [Fathers' initial reactions to their newborns.]

Sayers, J. (1982). *Biological Politics: Feminist and Anti-feminist Perspectives.* London: Tavistock Publications. [Feminism and sex differences.]

Stanworth, M. (1983). *Gender and Schooling: a Study of Sexual Divisions in the Classroom.* London: Hutchinson. [Boys' and girls' treatment in the classroom.]

Taylor, M.C. & Hall, J.A. (1982). Psychological androgyny: theories, methods and conclusions. *Psychological Bulletin, 92,* 347–366. [Masculinity, androgyny, and psychological well-being.]

PLAY AND GAMES INVENTORY

INSTRUCTIONS: Please tick the activities and games that your child likes to play.

1. singing
2. running races
3. building forts and huts
4. hopscotch
5. cops and robbers
6. dressing up
7. skipping
8. sewing
9. playing with cars
10. drawing and painting
11. climbing trees
12. cooking
13. playing on slides
14. playing doctors and nurses
15. playing with kites
16. card games
17. playing with dolls
18. putting on plays
19. building models
20. playing spacemen
21. fishing
22. playing shops
23. knitting
24. throwing snowballs
25. Action Man
26. marbles
27. football
28. jacks
29. dancing
30. working with machines
31. playing house
32. reading
33. cricket
34. playing on swings
35. playing cowboys and indians
36. wrestling
37. darts
38. doing handstands
39. putting on puppet shows
40. clay modelling
41. playing soldiers
42. using tools
43. ballet dancing
44. playing school
45. doing cartwheels
46. playing with toy guns
47. playing with bows and arrows
48. playing with toy trains
49. crochet
50. playing musical instruments

SCORING: Count up the number of ticks given to items 2, 3, 5, 9, 11, 15, 19, 20, 21, 24, 26, 27, 30, 33, 35, 36, 37, 41, 42, 46, 47, 48. This is your child's masculinity (M) score. The equivalent number of ticks given to items 1, 4, 6, 7, 8, 12, 13, 14, 17, 18, 22, 23, 28, 29, 31, 34, 38, 39, 43, 44, 45, 49 is your child's femininity (F) score.

RESULTS: These activities are designated as either 'M' or 'F' on the basis of previous surveys of children's actual play activities. (There are also four 'neutral' items to act as 'fillers'.) It has consistently been found that boys get higher 'M' than 'F' scores and vice versa for girls.

As a comparison, you might like to know that when this inventory was developed on a group of Leicestershire and Durham schoolchildren in 1981, 67 10 to 11-year-old boys scored an average of 14.16 and 3.42 on the 'M' and 'F' items respectively, and the equivalent figures for the 80 same-age girls were 8.03 and 12.90.

A SCHOOL-LEAVER CASE STUDY

A description of a school leaver follows – read this through carefully and then answer the questions below.

Candidate X has the following characteristics:

1. Academically very good – particularly in science (biology, physics and chemistry).

2. A competitive student with plenty of enthusiasm and drive.

3. Enjoys sports especially team games.

4. Is liked by pupils and staff.

5. Is good and popular with the opposite sex.

6. Would like a job involving 'helping' or 'caring' for others.

7. Has been happy at school but looks forward to leaving.

QUESTIONS

(a) What sorts of jobs do you think would suit this candidate? Write down your reasons.

(b) How do you imagine the career of this candidate over the next 20 years?

Note: Invert the page only after completing the exercise.

What sex did you imagine candidate X to be? How do you think this influenced your answers? Now using the same information but assuming X to be the opposite sex to the one which you imagined, reconsider your answers to *(a)* and *(b)*.

N.B. It is often difficult to repeat this exercise once we have a particular image of X in our minds. An alternative approach is to read out the exercises to a friend, telling him or her at the outset that X is Mary Brown. Do the exercise once only with this friend, then repeat it with another friend now telling her or him that X is John Brown. Compare the answers. To what extent did you find that *different* characteristics were highlighted when the sex of the candidate was given?

4. *You and Others*

Humans are *social* beings: we all act, think and talk the way we do in relation to other people. One theory of personality is that our selves are partly formed by our imitating, or 'taking on the role of' other people, who are thought of as *models*. In young children, it is easy to see that the most influential models are other family members: boys tend to imitate the behaviour of their fathers, for example, and girls the behaviour of their mothers. As children get older, these models become more and more varied, including brothers and sisters, friends, teachers, and neighbours, as well as more remote figures such as pop and football stars; adults' models might include great thinkers, social reformers or politicians.

SOCIAL ROLES

The process described above is known as 'role taking' and it shows how, to a considerable degree, we think and act so as to fit in with patterns of behaviour laid down by society. Each person is at the centre of a complex web of interrelated roles. You might, at different times of the day, 'act out' the part of parent, trade union member, ratepayer, churchgoer, teacher, spouse, gardener, and so on: different roles are demanded by different situations. You might like to jot down all the different roles demanded of you. Some of these roles are *internalized:* we perform them automatically and unconsciously. Most doctors would adopt a responsible, caring attitude towards others, for example, whether or not they were on duty. A stage actor in an unsympathetic part, on the other hand, might 'go through the motions' without identifying with the character portrayed: there is no internalization of the role. But can we explain how individuals do or do not fit into the roles that society prescribes?

WHAT WE DO AND WHAT WE THINK

☐ Have you ever gossiped or complained about another person 'behind their back'? Have you ever expressed one view to your boss at work, and then expressed a quite different view to your workmates when the boss was not there?

☐ Suppose that you are a firm believer in the concept of public health care. Your spouse, who is also the family's main breadwinner, contracts a kidney disease which needs urgent attention. You will need to wait in the queue for three months to have the operation carried out in a public hospital, but it could be done next week at a private hospital nearby. What should you do?

Abraham Lincoln-types apart, nearly all of us must truthfully answer 'Yes' to the first set of questions in paragraph one. We all hold different attitudes in public and in private (politicians might indeed have made this into something of an art!). It is not quite so obvious how people would respond to the health problem, however. Some would stick to their social principles, electing the public hospital: others would put their private interests above their publicly-held beliefs. Some might even argue that the two are not incompatible: that it is possible to have an abstract belief which is impossible to uphold in practice.

These dilemmas make it clear that what we say and think is often at variance with what we do: our *attitudes* and our *behaviour* are often inconsistent with each other. The reason for this, once again, is that most of our behaviour is social: it has to take account of conditions, and situations, that are created in relation to other people. The end result is that people sometimes do what seem to be illogical or irrational things, as a result of *social influence.* As social psychologist Elliot Aronson puts it, 'People who do crazy things are not necessarily crazy'.

Social comparison

This idea has been expressed more formally by Aronson's mentor, Leon Festinger, in his theory of *social comparison*. The basis of this is that people have a constant need to validate their opinions by comparing them with the opinions of others.

Suppose Bill, a non-musician, is taken along to a modern jazz concert by his friend John, who is a dedicated jazz fan. Bill finds the music unmelodic, incomprehensible, and indeed boring: but John, whose knowledge and opinion is highly respected by Bill, considers the performance to be one of the finest he has ever heard. Bill, confronted by his friend's delight, is quite likely to express the view that 'I can appreciate that this might be very good, but I'm afraid it's all beyond me': or he might even claim to like it. What he will *not* do is express the opinion that he would were John not present. Festinger's theory suggests that our opinions and beliefs are constantly being shaped by this kind of process.

SAVING FACE

In this fictitious story, there is a fundamental inconsistency in Bill's attitudes. He has a negative attitude towards the music, and a positive attitude towards his friend John: but this is incompatible with John's positive attitude towards the music. He is most likely to resolve this problem by changing his own attitude, thereby 'saving face': but there are other possibilities. He could, for example, 'agree to disagree' with John, considering that his own (albeit inexpert) opinion is equally valid. He could even conclude that John's love of the music is phoney: that John only claims to like it in order to appear to be fashionable, open-minded, and forward thinking.

These different ways of resolving the problem are the province of *cognitive consistency theories* in social psychology, and probably the best-known of these is Leon Festinger's *cognitive dissonance theory*. Festinger proposed that when *dissonance* exists in people's knowledge, opinions and beliefs, such as in the story above, there is always a corresponding pressure to reduce it by changing one's behaviour and/or attitudes. For example, most smokers will readily agree that smoking is bad for them, and that the only rational course of action is simply to stop; yet they continue to spend money on cigarettes, and to risk their health. Their attitudes and behaviour are clearly dissonant with one another, and they try to reduce the dissonance in various ways. They might argue that medical research on the ill-effects of smoking is not conclusive; that Uncle Joe lived to be 96 and smoked all his life; claim to smoke only filter-tipped or low nicotine cigarettes, or a pipe; or even somehow manage to give up altogether. They change their behaviour and/or attitudes in order to *save face.*

What's in it for you?

In one study, Leon Festinger and Merrill Carlsmith asked groups of experimental subjects to carry out some extremely tedious tasks, such as filling trays with spools, then emptying the trays, refilling them, emptying them again, and so on. In an elaborate experimental design, the subjects were divided into three groups. The *control group* were told that they were to rate the dull, boring tasks for 'interest' and 'scientific value' as a check on other experiments being conducted in the psychology department. The *one-dollar group* were paid one dollar for telling new subjects, just about to start on the tasks, that they were 'intriguing', 'enjoyable', and 'a lot of fun'. The *20-dollar group* were paid 20 dollars for misinforming the new subjects in the same way.

Subjects in both of the 'dollar' groups also made their own 'interest' and 'scientific value' ratings after finishing the tasks. There were some clear and surprising differences between the average ratings of the three groups. The control group, predictably, gave low ratings on the two scales (an average of −0.45 on a scale from −5 to +5). The 20-dollar group gave slightly higher ratings than this (−0.05), but the one-dollar group's ratings were considerably higher (1.33). The dissonance theory explanation for this result is based on the fact that subjects in the two paid groups had to deceive the new subjects, that is, to make attitude statements which were inconsistent with their own knowledge of the tasks. The 20-dollar subjects were well paid: they had a good justification for lying, and so they experienced relatively little cognitive dissonance. On the other hand, the one-dollar subjects got a trifling reward for lying, and consequently experienced considerably more dissonance. The latter group apparently reduced this dissonance by upgrading their ratings of the task itself: they 'saved face' by convincing themselves that it was indeed 'interesting' and of 'some scientific value'.

This is a powerful result because it is counter-intuitive. The most obvious common sense prediction would be that people who receive a large reward for saying that the tasks were enjoyable would themselves rate them as such, in comparison with those who only receive a small reward. Exactly the opposite seems to be the case. In this case at least, psychology seems to involve more than just common sense.

STEREOTYPES

☐ Are the Japanese punctual, precise, and pedantic?

☐ Are Americans loud, brash, and extravagant?

☐ Are the British reserved, polite, and eccentric?

☐ Are women more nurturant, caring and submissive than men?

☐ Are bespectacled people intelligent?

☐ Are bearded men untrustworthy?

Some people would answer 'yes' to many of these questions, and would therefore have certain expectations about the behaviour of any new Japanese, American, British, female, bespectacled or bearded person they might encounter. There can be no doubt that these expectations are faulty. Some Japanese are sloppy and imprecise. Some Americans are quiet and reserved. British people can be extravert and sociable, and so on.

Such *stereotypes* about distinguishable groups of people persist nevertheless. They involve *overgeneralization:* people erroneously attribute all the characteristics of the stereotype to individual members of the group, even though only some (if any) of those characteristics are truly applicable. The power of stereotyping is illustrated in Exercise 4.1.

If you are doing this as a class exercise, do not read on until it is completed.

In the exercise, two equivalent groups of people are given descriptions of 'Mr Smith' and 'Mr Brown' respectively. These descriptions are identical in every respect except for occupation: Mr Smith is described as a lawyer, and Mr Brown as a factory worker.

Respondents are asked to assess the personality of one of the two men by ticking either one or the other of 20 pairs of positive and negative statements (for example, 'scrupulously honest' versus 'not averse to petty dishonesty').

Since the descriptions of the two men are identical in every respect but one, and since there is no obvious reason why a lawyer and a factory worker might not have similar personalities, we might reasonably expect the groups' assessments of the two to be very similar. Was this the case? The exercise usually reveals that Mr Smith is seen in a much more favourable light than Mr Brown. This undoubtedly results from (unfounded) beliefs about the typical personalities of lawyers and factory workers – from occupational stereotypes. It would be fairly easy to devise similar demonstrations of other forms of stereotyping, such as those based on sex, social class, or nationality, for instance.

THE ROOTS OF PREJUDICE

Stereotypes are inaccurate and misleading beliefs about groups of people, and they can convey *prejudice* when they imply a negative or hostile attitude towards those groups. A very visible, offensive and divisive example of this is of course racial prejudice: some people believe that blacks are stupid, lazy and oversexed, or that Jews are selfish, grasping and dishonest.

It's only a joke

This forms the basis for a good deal of racist humour: the basis of 'Irish jokes' in England is that the Irish are stupid, and there are similar Polish equivalents in the USA, for example. Do these jokes simply serve to 'let off steam': do we express prejudiced attitudes in a harmless, joking context (such as the revue in the social club) because we do not really hold them? Or is it that the humour itself creates prejudice: that sharing jokes about the Irish, about Jews, or about newly-weds actually reinforces our stereotypes of these groups?

Competition

This is a difficult question to answer, and it leads us to the even knottier problem of explaining the causes of prejudice. One plausible suggestion is that prejudice arises from economic competition between different social groups. With unemployment at an all-time high in Great Britain, for example, there is a good deal of ill-feeling amongst unemployed indigenous whites towards immigrant groups who have jobs, such as the Asian communities in cities like Leicester and Birmingham. One might reasonably expect this to fuel stereotyped and prejudiced attitudes against individual Asians, and these are likely to be elaborated by the effects of social influence described earlier. If one's workmates express prejudiced attitudes against 'the blacks', it is much more uncomfortable to openly disagree than to 'go along' in silence with the conversation.

Authoritarian personalities

Another theory is that prejudice is part of personality: that the thoughts and beliefs of *authoritarian personalities* predispose them towards prejudice in all of their dealings with other people. Alf Garnett, the anti-hero of the popular British TV comedy series *'Till Death Us Do Part'*, is a good example of the archetypal authoritarian personality. Alf sees himself as a 'true blue' patriot, extremely respectful of Queen and country, and deeply suspicious of anyone who is not. By the same token, he demands respect from those he perceives as being lower in the social pecking order than himself (notably non-white immigrants). His beliefs and values are rigid and conventional, and he is intolerant of anyone who fails to come up to these standards. The key to Alf's personality is *respect for authority*: he believes that we must be subservient to those in authority over us, and that we are justified in patronizing those 'beneath' us. Archie Bunker, star of the TV series *'Archie Bunker's Place'*, is the American equivalent of Alf Garnett.

An important book called *The Authoritarian Personality* was published by Theodor Adorno, Else Frenkel-Brunswik and others in 1950, reporting some research which sought to explain the psychological basis of anti-semitism. The Jewish researcher, Else Frenkel-Brunswik, and her husband Egon studied at the University of Vienna during Hitler's rise to power, and subsequently settled in the USA. Their academic quest had powerful social implications which could equally well apply, for example, to racial conflict in South Africa in the 1980s. Adorno and his co-workers devised questionnaire measures of anti-semitism, ethnocentrism (the tendency to view things only from the point of view of one's own group), political and economic conservatism, and fascism, in an attempt to pin down the essence of the authoritarian personality. Although the original study suffered from various methodological problems, subsequent research seems to support the idea that the authoritarian personality exists.

Blind respect for authority implies that one's behaviour is totally dependent on the demands of others: that one's individual feelings and desires can legitimately be overruled by these demands. This is an extreme example of *conforming to social pressure*, and whilst few of us would exhibit it to the extent of the authoritarian, there is overwhelming evidence that we all conform to some degree, in some situations. Conformity has been the subject of several classic experiments in social psychology, as we shall see.

WHEN DO PEOPLE CONFORM?

People often have a strong desire to do what others are doing. To 'behave like sheep' refers to this tendency in human behaviour because sheep, and many other animals which live in groups, are often seen to act in unison, sitting, standing, eating or sleeping all together. Although this use of 'sheep' is derogatory, doing what others do is not necessarily a good or a bad thing. It can be either.

On a national holiday people flock to the seaside in their thousands – indeed for many people the pleasure of a holiday appears to be enhanced by this togetherness. If, whilst on the beach, a large tidal wave rolls in and those who see it run for high ground, those who follow without thinking, like sheep, may well save their lives. The people who stand apart might not live to regret their behaviour. Taking your cue from others without always questioning can sometimes have survival value, but there are circumstances in which conformity, or the desire to 'go along' with the rest may have unexpected and even appalling results.

In Hitler's Germany conformity was essential. Deviations were not permitted, and, as a result, atrocities were committed that seem inhuman by most standards. Those who tried to stand apart, or actively fight against Hitler's views, were simply eliminated. It is in this kind of situation that we must question this human characteristic and ask how is it possible that the desire to conform overrules what we rationally know to be the evidence of our senses, or the direction of our wishes and beliefs? Social psychologists have been intrigued and puzzled by this aspect of human behaviour and they have gone some way towards helping us understand the factors which promote conformity.

When you are in a group, especially when you are a new member of that group, you are conscious of actively trying to find out about the other members. If you like the group and/or its activities, you are likely to agree with what is said and to show a keenness for acceptance by the others. If you like people you tend to predict that they will feel as you do. But, surprisingly perhaps, the mere presence of others – whether or not you like them – can influence your judgements.

In the 1920s Floyd Allport compared judgements made by people working alone or in groups. Subjects were required to represent the pleasantness or unpleasantness of odours by drawing a line whose length was proportional to the pleasantness experienced. Allport found that those working by themselves gave more extreme responses than when they worked together. Other similar experiments confirmed this finding and it was suggested that when in a group people try to avoid deviating from a 'presumed central tendency' (or average response). Allport and others also reported that those working together performed faster than those working alone: this has been called 'social facilitation'. All sports competitors are highly aware of this type of social influence.

Muzafer Sherif also studied the effects of groups on individual judgements. Subjects were asked to estimate the extent of movement of a point of light in a darkened room. In fact the light did not move; its apparent movement was due to the eye's small involuntary movements and the lack of reference points which are needed to localize such a stimulus. (This is referred to as the 'auto-kinetic effect'; you might well have experienced it yourself.) Over a series of trials each subject's responses became more consistent though they varied widely between subjects: some reported a quarter or half inch movement whilst others said as much as 15 inches. The subjects were next grouped in twos or threes and the experiment was repeated. Soon the grouped individuals' judgements converged to an average of the former responses. When later the subjects were tested alone they adhered to this average, to their group 'norm'. An explanation for the dramatic size of these shifts in judgement might be that they were highly subjective. If so, judgements of a more absolute type might not be influenced by the presence of others. Solomon Asch decided to find out.

Is seeing believing?

Asch designed an experiment on visual perception in which subjects were asked to match a standard line with one of three alternatives: this is a task which all people with normal vision can do quite accurately. Tests were run using groups of seven to nine people who were asked to answer aloud. However the experiment was rigged. Asch used only one true naive subject and the others were confederates whose answers had been pre-determined. Each naive subject was placed towards the end of the row so that the majority of the confederates' responses were given first.

Asch determined in advance that on two thirds of the tests confederates would unanimously respond with one of the wrong alternatives. How would the naive subject react when confronted by this? On testing over 100 naive subjects he found that only 25 per cent of them remained independent. Across the whole sample the error rate was 36.8 per cent of judgements, whereas in normal circumstances it would have been less than 1 per cent. Why did the subjects 'give in' or conform to the majority judgement, despite the indisputable evidence before their eyes?

FACTORS WHICH INCREASE CONFORMITY

The extraordinarily high level of conformity found in the Asch study prompted a number of further experiments. Asch found that the size of the group, providing that it was of at least three confederates, did not affect the degree to which a single naive subject conformed. (Later research indicated that conformity increases up to a group size of seven confederates and thereafter does not rise. A larger crowd does not appear to enhance the effect.) The attractiveness of the group, and the confidence of the naive subject in his or her ability, also influence conforming behaviour. Subjects who perceive the group as desirable, and who feel that they are less competent than average will, experiments show, be more likely to follow the lead of the group rather than stick to their own view.

Having an ally

An important factor in enabling a subject to resist group pressure is an ally. If two naive subjects were present in Asch's experiments, conformity dropped to 5.5 per cent of the judgements given. The support of someone else agreeing with the subject's view clearly enabled him or her to resist strong group pressures.

Feeling uncomfortable

The reality of the pressure to conform is shown in another similar study which used measurements of the fatty acid level in the blood of those taking part. Naive subjects showed an increased level of blood fatty acids when they held out against the confederates' wrong response, but this was lower for subjects who conformed and gave wrong responses. Clearly there was a physiological pressure on the subjects which arose when they found themselves alone in their opinions, which was only reduced by conforming, despite the conflict that giving the wrong answer might produce. The discomfort of group pressure evidently outweighs these other considerations.

How did subjects explain their conformity? Asch found that many subjects complied whilst privately rejecting the majority view which was voiced. But they still underestimated the extent to which they conformed and voiced wrong answers. This suggests that their judgement was partly distorted by group pressure.

COMPLIANCE AND OBEDIENCE

If people will go against their private judgement and comply with the majority view, even when this is obviously wrong, then this is an aspect of human behaviour which should concern and alarm us. Let us now consider a situation in which the subject is explicitly asked to comply.

Stanley Milgram carried out some controversial experiments on obedience. His 'teacher' subjects, who thought that they were taking part in an experiment on the effects of punishment on memory, were told to deliver electric shocks of increasing intensity when a 'learner' subject, out of sight in an adjacent room, made an error in a task. Shocks ranged from 15–450 volts and shock buttons were labelled from 'Slight shock' to 'Danger: severe shock' at the top of the scale. The learner, who was actually an actor confederate of the experimenter, behaved as if he actually received the shocks (in fact he did not) and could be heard crying out as they were apparently given. The true aim of the study was to explore the extent of the 'teacher' subject's obedience to the instructions.

All Milgram's subjects in this experiment were men of above average intelligence and yet two-thirds of them obeyed the instructions, delivering shocks up to the danger zone, whilst showing great distress in doing so and even pleading with the experimenter to stop the study. The power of the experimenter was extraordinary. Psychiatrists asked to estimate the level of obedience had predicted that no more than one per cent would obey instructions to this degree. Obedience to authority appeared to override humane considerations.

Milgram's experiment and the subsequent variations which have been carried out have been severely criticised. Many believe that the trust in psychologists, and the health and dignity of the subjects, were greatly at risk. The fact that the subjects were debriefed only goes part of the way towards allaying these ethical objections. Nevertheless the results clearly show that authority is very powerful: it is hard for a single person to resist, though obedience was found to be greatly reduced if two naive 'teacher' subjects were allowed to work together.

RESISTANCE TO AUTHORITY AND PRESSURE FROM OTHERS

It is difficult to act independently of others, especially when there is strong overt or covert group pressure upon us. As we have seen, the desire to conform is marked, especially if we like or admire those whose views we privately reject. Other people can pressurize us even when we do not like them; and that pressure can give rise to physiological changes in our bodies, as we saw earlier.

A truly independent person does not always reject the majority, unlike the anti-conformist who consistently takes the opposite line. (The latter displays behaviour which is just as much shaped by social expectations as is the conformist's behaviour, albeit in the opposite direction.) Independent people decide for themselves but 'go along' with the rest when they are in agreement. Being independent is not easy, as we have seen, and the increasing number of books and courses on 'assertiveness training' (mentioned in Chapter 1) are an aid to those who feel they are 'yes-people': people who cannot, or dare not, speak up against individual or group pressure.

Being assertive in this sense does not mean taking what you want when you want it: it means negotiating with others to reach a fair or equitable solution when a conflict of interests arises. When conflicts arise emotions are involved, and many people are unable to cope when confronted by an angry person, especially when the person is felt to have some power over us e.g. boss, parent, and even spouse or child. The best technique for dealing with such an emotion may be to neutralize it before responding to the factual element of the argument. Exercise 4.2 illustrates one technique for tackling this.

THE INFLUENCE OF THE MASS MEDIA

The size of the group which can influence us has increased dramatically with the growth of the mass media, and today we can observe people in all parts of the world through film and television and learn about people, places and events which are not accessible to us at first hand. Nevertheless, concern has been expressed about the potentially adverse effects of films and TV, in particular. For example, does the portrayal of violence on the screen lead to imitation by the viewers? In North America it has been estimated that children have probably seen 18,000 TV murders by the time they have graduated from high school. A lot of work has been done on the problem of TV violence.

Aggression and TV Violence

One difficulty in this research is the definition of what constitutes aggression (see pages 106 – 107 for a fuller discussion). Researchers must look not only at the incidence of aggression but also at the way in which it is portrayed. A violent event in the cartoon show 'Tom and Jerry' is unlikely to be comparable to one reported in a news programme. Several hypotheses have been put forward about the effects of observing violence. Seymour Feshbach, amongst others, has suggested that it is 'cathartic': that watching screen violence may reduce viewers' likelihood of subsequently displaying violence. Others believe the opposite: that it may *increase* the chances of violence and aggression in the observers.

Columbia Broadcasting System asked Milgram to investigate this topic. Milgram contrived that a TV show broadcast in some areas would include two antisocial acts: breaking a charity box, and making an abusive phone call. A 'control' programme, which did not contain these acts, was shown in parallel broadcasts in other viewing areas. Many people watched the show in viewing studios containing charity boxes and telephones, and although over a million viewers saw the 'anti-social' show, imitation of the violence was minimal. Only four abusive calls were made to a telephone number broadcast after the show by the viewers of the 'anti-social' programme, whereas six such calls were made after the 'control' programme. This result provides no immediate evidence for the large scale imitation of TV violence, and of course it tells us nothing about the longer-term effects of such viewing.

A number of studies which compared children who have observed TV violence with those who have not indicate that there is some evidence for increased aggression in children in the former group. Other research has found positive correlations between the amount of TV violence viewed, and the amount shown in peer interactions.

Although we must be cautious in suggesting that such correlations indicate a causal relationship, some researchers, such as Munroe Lefkowitz and his colleagues, believe that they have found evidence of such a relationship. Their evidence came from a research study involving a 10-year follow-up of school children who were initially interviewed at around 9 years of age. The children had been questioned about their own and their classmates' TV viewing habits, popularity with peers, and their general behaviour including the extent to which they displayed aggression. Almost 50 per cent of the original sample was re-interviewed, at 19 years of age, and from the later interviews the researchers concluded that the 'building of aggressive habits' was promoted in children who prefer watching violent television.

THE POWER OF SOCIAL INFLUENCE

This chapter has spelled out the immense power of other people upon our behaviour as individuals. Social influence shapes what we do, what we think, and indeed most aspects of our personalities. It determines our impressions of other people, and our attitudes and behaviour towards them. The mere presence of others can alter and distort our judgements, even when we disagree violently with those others.

Under certain circumstances, social pressures may force us to do things which we would not otherwise have contemplated, as the survivors of Hitler's Germany would presumably attest. The atrocities of the Nazi era provide a harrowing example of the power of social influence being used for evil purposes, and George Orwell's famous novel *1984* describes another nightmarish vision of the effects of extreme state control over the individual.

Social influence can be used for the good of humankind as well as for its ill, however, as the world-wide 'Live Aid' famine relief appeals clearly showed. Many people feel that Bob Geldof and his co-organizers are to be congratulated for successfully exploiting the power of the mass media in bringing the plight of famine-stricken inhabitants of the Third World to the notice of citizens of the affluent West. Many Westerners who would otherwise have ignored charity appeals have in this case made generous donations to the cause, partly because they are responding to the actions of their friends, neighbours and colleagues.

The power of social influence in the 20th century is becoming ever greater as electronic communication and information storage becomes increasingly efficient, such that the 'global village' becomes effectively smaller and smaller. In this world-wide context, the insights of social psychological knowledge are increasingly important in making national leaders and policymakers aware of the immense responsibilities with which they are faced.

Recommended Reading

Aronson, E. (1976). *The Social Animal.* San Francisco: W.H. Freeman.

Aronson, E. (ed.). (1977) *Readings About the Social Animal.* San Francisco: W.H. Freeman.

Brown, R. (1986). *Social Psychology: The Second Edition.* New York: The Free Press.

Eiser, J.R. (1986). *Social Psychology.* Cambridge: Cambridge University Press.

References

Adorno, T.W., Frenkel-Brunswick, E., Levinson, D.J. & Sanford, R.N. (1950). *The Authoritarian Personality.* New York: Harper. [The original attempt to identify the authoritarian personality.]

Allport, F.H. (1924). *Social Psychology.* Boston: Houghton Mifflin. [Judgements when working alone or in groups.]

Asch, S.E. (1955). Opinions and social pressure. *Scientific American, 193,* 31–35. [Studies of conformity.]

Cater, D. & Strickland, S. (1975). *TV Violence and the Child.* New York: Russell Sage Foundation. [Refers to the building of aggressive habits in children preferring violent TV – quote from Monroe Lefkowitz and colleagues.]

Feshbach, S. (1961). The stimulating versus cathartic effects of a vicarious aggressive activity. *Journal of Abnormal & Social Psychology, 63(2),* 381–385. [The effects of viewing violence.]

Festinger, L. & Carlsmith, J.M. (1959). Cognitive consequences of forced compliance. *Journal of abnormal & Social Psychology, 58,* 203–210. [Compliance and why its occurs: strategies of 'face-saving'.]

Milgram, S. (1974). Conversation. *Psychology Today,* June, 71–80. [TV and its influence on violence.]

Milgram, S. (1963). Behavioral study of obedience. *Journal of Abnormal & Social Psychology, 67(4),* 371–378. [Experiment on obedience to authority.]

Sherif, M. (1936). *The Psychology of Social Norms.* New York: Harper. [Includes discussion of the autokinetic effect.]

Sherif, M. (1935). A study of some social factors in perception. *Archives of Psychology, 27,* 187. [Research on the autokinetic effect.]

STEREOTYPES

INSTRUCTIONS: *Mr Smith* and *Mr Brown* are described below. Read the description of Mr Smith to one group of people, and ask them to assess his personality by selecting one of each of the 20 pairs of statements appearing in the 'Questionnaire' below. Carry out the same procedure for Mr Brown with a separate, equivalent group of people.

Mr Smith is a 39-year-old lawyer, who has a wife and two children. He was brought up in the town where his family now lives, and is active in local politics. He is keen on sport and the theatre.

Mr Brown is a 39-year-old factory worker, who has a wife and two children. He was brought up in the town where his family now lives, and is active in local politics. He is keen on sport and the theatre.

QUESTIONNAIRE

1.	Mainly an optimist.	Mainly a pessimist.
2.	Regards his work lightly.	Conscientious in his work.
3.	Spends much time with his children.	Usually leaves his children to their own devices.
4.	Tends to be thrifty.	Rather reckless with money.
5.	Rarely helps with the housework.	Often helps in the house.
6.	Lives mainly in the present.	Plans for the future.
7.	Attentive to his wife.	Apt to take his wife for granted.
8.	Quite fond of gambling.	Opposed to gambling.
9.	Self-reliant.	Dependent on others.
10.	Somewhat untidy.	Meticulous in his habits.
11.	Largely self-centred.	Great concern for others.
12.	Active church member.	Not bothered about religion.
13.	Loud and boisterous.	Quiet and reserved.
14.	Shares his wife's interests.	He and his wife go their own ways.
15.	Left in politics.	Right in politics.
16.	Slow and deliberate.	Quick and impulsive.
17.	Somewhat ambitious.	Has few ambitions.
18.	Rather patriotic.	Not very patriotic.
19.	On friendly terms with his neighbours.	Tends to remain aloof from his neighbours.
20.	Scrupulously honest.	Not averse to petty dishonesty.

RESULTS: How did your two groups of people differ in their descriptions? Is your result surprising, given the similarity between the two men in all respects but one?

(Adapted from Brown, Cherrington and Cohen, 1975)

ASSERTIVENESS

Recall an incident in which you were faced with an emotional outburst from someone: perhaps an argument or a situation in which someone was angry with you, or was putting pressure on you. The first step is to analyse what happened. Consider both what was said, and how it was said to you.

ANALYSING THE SITUATION
1. Identify the EMOTIONS of the other person. (What did their body language reveal?)
2. Note the FACTS being stated. (What did they actually say?)
3. Identify the NEEDS of the other person. (Note: facts and needs may be different; needs may not be expressed directly.)
4. What response did you make, and what response would you like to have made?

ASSERTIVE HANDLING OF THE SITUATION
We cannot use your situation but let us take as an example, a situation where someone has angrily demanded that you do 'X', which you think is unreasonable. (This can be used as a general illustration.) Having analysed the situation you should now state points *(1)* to *(4)*. Role play this situation with a friend: your friend should take the role of the other person, and you should try to respond with planned assertive answers first by 'reflecting back' your reading of what was happening:

1. 'I can see that you are angry . . .' (Emotion)
2. ' . . . because I will not do X on my day off . . .' (Fact)
3. ' . . . and you cannot get anyone else to do it' (Need)

By making responses *(1)–(3)* you have clarified the situation, gained time in planning your final response and, by recognizing the other person's emotion, defused it somewhat. You are now ready to give your reply:

4. ' . . . but I am not prepared to do X.'
   [Don't make any excuses here, or you give the other person room to negotiate.]

WHY IT WORKS
By sorting out the emotions first you can often defuse the situation. For example, you may find that the other person explains his or her emotion (e.g. the train was late this morning). This often calms the situation, and takes the pressure off you. Role play other examples from your own experience with a friend and try to sort out the three important elements – EMOTIONS, FACTS and NEEDS. Then act out your example as shown above. Did your response sound reasonable to your friend? Many people are surprised to find that the responses outlined above do not sound impertinent; indeed, they often sound firm and fair, whereas making poor excuses simply makes the other person more angry at your refusal.

5. *Your Emotions*

When we meet someone for the first time we may know very quickly how we feel about that person. It is as if we don't have to think about it, we just know how we feel. Thus, we fall in love, or feel angry, annoyed, irritated, sad, bored or any of a multitude of feelings, or mixture of feelings apparently without any conscious effort. Our emotions can seem to be separate from the thinking part of our mind.

However emotions are not separate from the rational, thinking side of our natures, as we shall see. In general, emotion and cognition are bound up together, and although we can identify our emotion as 'a state of agitation' which has measurable physiological changes, emotional experience is linked with an attribution process. [For a fuller explanation of 'attribution process' see Chapter 2, pp. 54–56.] We actively seek an explanation for our feelings; the physiological changes are not a sufficient condition for the occurrence of an emotional experience. A rapidly beating heart may be due to love, anger or even vigorous exercise; the emotional experience depends on various cognitions that enable us to determine which.

At one time psychologists thought that certain emotions were instinctive – a term used to describe both the inbuilt drive (or motivation) underlying behaviour and/or the unlearned behaviour patterns themselves. In essence it was supposed that instincts were in major part inbuilt into the individual and this led to speculation as to which emotions were fundamental. Needs, or drives, for the satisfaction of physiological needs such as hunger and thirst, were felt to be fundamental motives, but an emotion such as love, for instance, was often described as a secondary drive. Such a drive, it was said, arose through association with a primary drive. A baby's love for its mother was considered by some to fit this category, because the mother, by feeding her baby, satisfied the primary drive of hunger, and thus a need or love for mother was derived by association. Research on love and attachment in infants throws some light on the truth of this.

There are many words to describe human emotions and a small book such as this cannot hope to do justice to so many. We have therefore decided to concentrate on just two areas of emotional experience: 'attachment and love' and 'anger and aggression'.

LOVE AND ATTACHMENT

There is no simple way to describe or define love; we are all aware that it takes many different forms. We use the word in relation to people, other animals and things. We love our parents, our partner, our children, our relatives and friends, out pets and we probably use love in relation to our home, our work and quite specific tastes – from sausages to smoked salmon. If we confine this discussion here to love of other animate, rather than inanimate, objects then we are aware that it still has many shades of meaning.

Psychologists have suggested that love or attachment is 'an affectional tie that binds one individual to another' and that such an emotion is likely to be manifest in certain types of behaviour. Thus attachment behaviour is designed to promote proximity and physical contact with the object of that attachment. This makes it possible to identify patterns of behaviour which are signs of an attachment and thus for the emotion to be measured.

FIRST LOVE

There have been two major influences on the thinking about the importance of the first loving relationship that the human baby experiences. The first influence is that of Sigmund Freud and psychoanalysis, and the second is the research on non-human animals.

Freud stressed the importance of childhood in shaping the individual and suggested that attachment between mother and baby was essential for the socialization of the child. He believed that if this relationship was impaired or damaged, long-term ill effects on the individual were not only likely, but virtually inescapable. This view was to strengthen the universally accepted ideas that mothers, rather than fathers, were vitally important for infant well-being. In studying the essential importance of mothers, it is clear that one obvious way to examine their impact on children would be to study children without mothers. There are natural examples where this occurs – as in children whose mothers die in childhood – but in order to study mother-absence systematically in families which are otherwise comparable one would need to separate babies from their mothers. Fortunately we are not prepared to tolerate such human experiments, but rightly or wrongly (and this is discussed in Chapter 11) we have been prepared to do this with other animals.

Konrad Lorenz is widely known for his work on attachment in various bird species. His approach, as an ethologist, was to study animals in their natural setting and in so doing he observed that young goslings rapidly form strong attachments for their mothers. Lorenz showed that if goslings were separated from their mothers at hatching they would follow, and become attached to, almost any reasonably large object, or animal, to which they were exposed. Indeed the attachment formed was so strong that he likened it to a pathological fixation and termed it 'imprinting'. Imprinting seemed to have long-term effects on behaviour – in particular sexual behaviour – and Lorenz found that his hand-reared goslings later chose him as their mate.

In a series of studies Lorenz showed that imprinting occurred in a variety of bird species. It occurred in the absence of any obvious reward such as food, and it formed most readily in a particularly sensitive period early in development. These findings help to explain why many solitary zoo animals fail to breed when presented with a mate – an unlikely example was observed in Berlin zoo where a peacock housed with giant tortoises spent his time in the unsuccessful courtship of the tortoises.

It would of course be unwise to suggest that humans and these bird species become attached in exactly the way way, but other animal research has shown similar results in animals rather more like us.

Harry Harlow and his associates carried out deprivation experiments on infant rhesus monkeys. They studied separated infant monkeys reared with two model surrogate 'mothers'; one 'mother' was made of wire and the other was covered, to make her more comforting, in a towelling cloth.

All the infants showed a strong preference for the towelling 'mother' and cuddled up to her even in conditions where the only food was to be found on the wire mother. Clearly food was not a vital factor in the formation of their attachment. Infants reared with surrogates, or in total isolation, were very disturbed when six or twelve months later they were placed with other monkeys. They were excessively withdrawn or aggressive and were unable to form normal social or sexual relationships.

Later studies showed, however, that infants reared with siblings, but without their mothers, were much more 'normal' in behaviour, and even isolates could be helped to adjust by being given careful and gradual exposure to other monkeys. Such research shows that whilst maternal deprivation can have marked and long-term effects on behaviour, these effects can be ameliorated in great part by other types of social experience, and thus the mother herself may not be essential to survival.

ATTACHMENT AND LOVE IN HUMAN INFANTS

The findings from research on other animals raise a number of questions for human behaviour. Do babies become attached during a critical or sensitive period? Does attachment only occur because the loved-one is a source of food? To whom is the baby most likely to become attached? And finally, what happens if the baby fails to become attached? John Bowlby, a psychiatrist, and Rudolph Schaffer, a psychologist, have both spent many years exploring the relationship between infants and their parents, in particular their mothers.

In the 1940s John Bowlby was asked by the World Health Organization to study the effects of maternal deprivation on children. He reviewed all the available evidence, studied 'separated' children in hospitals and orphanages and, in a report in the early 1950s, noted that a warm, intimate and continuous relationship with the mother (or permanent substitute) was essential for mental health. The work led him to conclude that children formed a specific attachment for their mother in the second half of the first year, and those who are deprived of such an attachment suffer long-term adverse effects.

Rudolph Schaffer demonstrated that love for the mother (or caretaker) does not develop rapidly. It takes months for a specific attachment to be formed. Signs of attachment between babies and specific individuals include smiling, following with the eyes, crying in the absence of, and greeting responses such as lifting the arms. Although these may occur in the first months of life when the baby is quite sociable, such patterns are typically shown only in relation to particular individuals after six months of age. Schaffer found that by studying babies in the home and during short and longer separations from the mother, specific attachments form between six to nine months of age, and this can be described as the sensitive period for attachment in human babies.

We can see the evidence of this in the behaviour of babies. At four months a baby may smile at a stranger, but at eight months such a smile is unlikely to be forthcoming. The younger baby can be comforted by a variety of individuals, whilst the older one wants comfort from the person (or persons) to whom it is attached, and may seem to be particularly 'clinging' at this stage. Once attached, both short and long-term separations are distressing for babies and they are especially vulnerable during the sensitive period (when they have only just become attached) to separation from the attachment figure(s).

Since babies are almost always reared by the mother, or a female mother-substitute who feeds them, the issue of whether they love because the person they love supplies the food is hard to ascertain. However Schaffer showed that the person who feeds the baby need not be the object of its affections. It is the nature of the interaction between people and the baby that matters. A person who responds quickly to the baby will be the focus of attachment in preference to an indifferent person who does the feeding.

Multiple mothering

Bowlby stressed the role of the mother in infant well-being, but whether a mother, or indeed females in general are the ideal child-rearers is a controversial point. Schaffer's work shows that the mother may not necessarily be first in the infant's affections – babies can be more attached to fathers, in preference to mothers, or the strength of the attachment may be about equal. Indeed the suggestion that the baby needs a special and unique relationship with one person – the mother – is not supported by the evidence available. So long as babies have regular and consistent care, from several people sharing the care, there is no reason to think that this multiple mothering (or parenting) is in any way less satisfactory than care by a 'single' mother. This finding is reassuring for many working mothers.

Both Freud and Lorenz indicated that the first relationship has long-term implications for the well-being of the individual – whether in humans or other animals – and that without a satisfactory early relationship problems were likely to follow.

Fortunately there are few people who have been without any opportunity to become attached to someone in infancy or childhood but the evidence available suggests that, for those who have not loved or been loved, the effects are marked. Such a person develops into the so-called 'affectionless character' – unable to feel any attachment for others in later life and unable to form loving relationships with other people. For those who have been orphaned in childhood, or have been separated from those they love, the long-term effects are much less serious. Loving in adult life appears to be built on early experiences of loving in childhood. It is undoubtedly better for babies and children to have loved and lost than never to have loved – in terms of the long-term effects of this on adult relationships.

LOVE BETWEEN ADULTS

Psychologists have spent relatively little time studying the nature of love between adults. There is no obvious reason why, because it is a topic of great concern to most people. Perhaps it is seen as such a private and personal area of inquiry that few psychologists have dared to tackle it. From the intrepid few who have dared to probe the subject some intriguing findings have emerged.

Love or attachment between adults takes various forms. We may feel affection for people of the same sex as us, or for the opposite sex, and there may or may not be sexual attraction included in our feelings. The definition of attachment given earlier makes no distinction between sexual love and love without this component; nor does it give clues as to whether liking is merely love of lesser intensity, or an entirely different emotion altogether.

In order to distinguish between love and liking Zick Rubin asked a large sample of students to answer various questions about their relationships with a lover and a platonic friend. Careful statistical analysis of the answers revealed that love is made up of at least four components: these are *needing, caring, trust,* and *tolerance.* Later research showed that for any individual the amount of each of the components in their own conception of love may vary.

Liking, in Rubin's terms, emerged as an emotion that is quite different from love. It is characterized by a person recognizing someone as mature and competent. Respect for a person seems to be central to the concept of liking. However, liking and love can go hand in hand, and a relationship described as one of liking or friendship may well contain loving elements. So far as Rubin's work is concerned, in friendship the trust component of love is of greater importance than the need component, whereas in a loving relationship the sexual or passionate element in love is shown by the need component. And, as one might expect, a passionate or sexual relationship can exist in the absence of the other components of love.

From the research described so far it is clear that in common parlance when we say we love someone, the meaning of this word for different individuals varies greatly. Love means different things to different people, and in loving relationships what a person needs to do is to find a partner to whom love means the same.

PERSONAL STYLES OF LOVING

Another large scale survey of loving relationships in people of all ages confirms the view that loving styles vary. John Lee investigated Canadian and British people's loving relationships by asking them to complete a lengthy questionnaire on all aspects of that relationship. From this research he identified three primary styles of loving.

Eros, Ludus and Storge

The first type of love is *Eros*. This is a love based on physical attraction and a quest for the lover's ideal beauty. *Ludus,* the second type, is a playful love unconcerned with commitment and skilled at the tactics of the game. The final primary love is *Storge,* a love that is compassionate rather than passionate. Lee found that few love affairs are pure examples of one type, and the primary 'colours' of love blend to give a new type with its own unique properties. Thus three blends of love were identified: *Mania, Pragma* and *Agape.*

Mania, Pragma and Agape

A blend of eros and ludus produces mania. The manic lover swings from ecstasy to despair, unlike erotic lovers who do not suffer pains with their pleasure. Some people describe this as a neurotic type of love. Pragma is a blend of ludus and storge, or as Lee describes it, 'love with a shopping list; a love that seeks compatability on practical criteria'. The last blend, agape, is less common than the others. This is the classical Christian view of love: an altruistic love lacking in jealousy or impatience. This love is a mix of storge and eros. Lee studied people of all ages, classes and educational background and he found that his classification of loving styles fitted all his groups. He also studied homosexual males and again the typology fitted their styles of loving. It should be emphasized however that this analysis has not been applied to other cultures, nor to non-whites in Western societies, so we do not know whether it accurately reflects women's and men's love around the world.

If you would like to identify your own style of loving try out the questionnaire in Exercise 5.1. This is a short version of Lee's longer questionnaire which he himself produced.

Just as it is possible to identify signs of attachment in a baby, so can this be shown in adults who love one another. Research has confirmed what we might have expected in that typical signs include: displaying love verbally, and physically in hugging and kissing, in being more relaxed in the presence of the loved one, in giving material evidence of love in gifts and helping behaviour, in showing emotional and moral support, and quite simply by increased mutual gaze. These different measures of the behaviour of love reflect what we might expect from the four components in Rubin's study. Finally, is it possible to make predictions about how long love lasts; and whether a relationship can survive a long-term commitment such as marriage? John Lee believes that a lasting relationship is more likely if a couple share the same style of loving, but of the various types the storgic lovers are most likely to survive together longest. Liking for the lover also seems to predict a longer-lasting relationship.

The conception of love in Western culture is that it precedes a long-term commitment, it is perceived as something that is not under full rational control and thus it is common to hear people worrying over whether they love enough to make such a commitment as marriage. In other cultures love is expected to follow rather than precede marriage: this shows us how entirely different are these two views of love, for clearly here what is thought influences and shapes the loving which follows.

Let us now turn to an entirely different emotional experience: anger and aggression.

ANGER AND AGGRESSION

Psychologists are often accused of having little to say about what the man or woman in the street regards as the 'real' issues and concerns of everyday life. This certainly applies to our topic of 'love between adults' but, happily, there are many areas of psychological research which do not support this generalization, and few more so than human aggression.

Aggression, anger and hostility feature prominently on many people's lists of important concerns and have been widely researched. Most of the major schools of thought in psychology have had something to say about this form of behaviour, and some of these ideas have sprung directly from personal concern about the extent of human suffering caused by aggressive behaviour and from fears for the future of the species.

Once again, the first major difficulty lies in defining the term 'aggression'. A useful starting point is to distinguish aggression from the related concepts of anger and hostility. Anger refers to a state of emotional arousal, typically accompanied by activation of the autonomic nervous system and by characteristic patterns of facial expression (described in Chapter 1). It is clear that a person may be angry without being physically destructive. Equally, aggressive behaviour might occur without the aggressor feeling angry prior to the action. Hostility refers to negative appraisals or evaluations of people or events. Psychologists frequently use the term 'cognitive' to describe this aspect of aggression. It would, of course, be possible to appraise a particular group in society (capitalists or communists, for instance) in very negative terms without feeling anger or behaving aggressively, though, as we noted earlier, as a rule cognitive and emotional processes are intricately linked.

Aggression, then, refers to overt or observable behaviour, though precisely what sort of behaviour may be deemed to be aggressive is controversial. Albert Bandura, a leading American psychologist, suggests that the term 'aggression' is restricted to acts resulting in personal injury or destruction of property, while accepting that injury may be psychological as well as physical. Even this apparently simple definition meets some difficulties. Are we to class as aggressive an injurious act that was 'accidental' (for example, shooting a person unintentionally) or an act that was intended to injure but 'failed' (attempting to shoot another, but missing)? In general the definition of an act as aggressive involves a value judgement on the part of the observer. Injurious acts may not be labelled as aggressive when they are socially prescribed or approved – thus capital punishment or beating a child to improve its character are often not construed as acts of aggression. In this sense, labelling a behaviour as aggressive *always* has a social and political dimension to it.

AGGRESSION HOT AND COLD

It is useful to make a distinction between two kinds of aggression – *angry* and *instrumental,* or what some have called *annoyance-motivated* and *incentive-motivated* aggression. The former is preceded by strong feelings. The person is in an aroused, physiologically activated state, often induced by environmental frustration of some sort. This is *hot* aggression. In instrumental aggression, on the other hand, the aggressive act is used as a way of obtaining some environmental reward and heightened emotion may not be present, as in the case of someone using violence to rob a bank. There is a clear difference between a *cold* act of this sort and someone assaulting a neighbour following an angry argument. The two classes are, of course, not entirely independent in that angry aggression is also intended to some extent to secure a 'reward' from the environment, though in this case the reward obtained is likely to be that of inflicting pain or injury itself.

Learning to survive

The many sources of instrumental aggression have been well documented in psychological research. That some aggressive behaviour is indeed learned socially because it is effective in securing environmental rewards or because aggressive models for imitation exist is now widely accepted. The rewards for aggression are many and powerful. Young children may learn to become physically aggressive because initial attempts at fighting off a bully by 'hitting back' proved to be effective. The reward in this case is the alleviation of pain. Similarly, the marked differences between societies in the levels of violent crime are probably attributable in part to the differing extent to which violent behaviour is rewarded and punished. There exist cultures, and also sub-cultures within societies, in which violence is so strongly reinforced that it is pervasive. In such circumstances aggression may be necessary for success and even essential for survival.

Anger in society

Of late there has been increased interest in the study of angry forms of aggression and it is on this emotion that we shall focus for the rest of this chapter. It is striking that anger is an important feature of much of the violence which causes social concern. Studies of homicide, for example, suggest that this violent act is often a response to intense anger. The violent person is often described as in a 'fury' or a 'rage', directed in many cases at a person with whom they have an intimate relationship (a wife or husband). Anger may also be involved in less obvious ways. There is evidence, for example, that many rapes show features of angry aggression. Nicholas Groth interviewed a large number of rapists and found that a substantial number of them were in an angry/frustrated state prior to the assault and appeared to be motivated to hurt and degrade the victim rather than to obtain sexual relief.

THE NATURE OF ANGER

Most people have experienced intense anger at some time, yet it is an emotion that we rarely analyse in any rational and objective way. We asked a group of students to recall and write in detail about a recent experience of anger in their everyday lives. Here are two representative incidents recalled.

    ❞ *The house we had just moved into was promised to be ready for the start of term by the landlady. But the downstairs was still undecorated and this was causing us a lot of inconvenience. What made me angry was the fact that the things we had been promised had not occurred. The landlady always had some poor excuse as to why things were going wrong. I got fed up with her excuses. I felt my blood boiling. It didn't last long because I started to laugh and then I calmed down. I thought to myself it's no use getting annoyed over the situation because that wouldn't help matters and I cooled down.* **❞**

    ❞ *I was sitting in a bus, while the bus-driver was collecting the tickets. When he came to the back seat there were three black guys and one white sitting there. They couldn't find their tickets straight away, and fooled around a bit while looking for them.*

Suddenly the bus-driver stated that he had had enough of their fooling around and ordered them off the coach, threatening them with the police if they refused. I couldn't believe my ears at first. Then I started getting really upset – I was almost on the point of physically showing my anger. 》

What does psychology have to say about experiences of this sort? It is possible to identify four components in the experience of anger: the environment, cognition, emotional/physiological arousal and aggressive behaviour itself. That these components have very complex inter-relationships is now clear (see the account by Raymond Navaco, 1978). All four are likely to be involved in the incidents just described. The first two of these elements, in particular, have been the focus for recent experimental investigation.

WHAT IS A PROVOCATION?

Anger and angry aggression are generally preceded by a triggering environmental event. In the incidents above, for example, they are the landlady's failure to carry out her promises and the unjust treatment of the passengers. There are a number of theories concerning the nature of the event that is likely to be important. The *frustration – aggression* theory, for example, suggests that the blocking of activities directed towards an important goal for the person is likely to be crucial. This is more obvious in the first incident than in the second. In a recent discussion Leonard Berkowitz has argued persuasively that environmental events elicit aggression to the extent that they are 'aversive' for the person or animal. Thus the absence of an expected reward (as in incident 1) or the blocking of goal-directed activity produce aggression because they are unpleasant. Experiencing failure, being insulted, unjustly treated, or attacked, share the property of aversiveness and are capable, therefore, of producing anger and aggression. Leonard Berkowitz suggests that humans and other animals are born with a readiness to flee or to fight when confronted by an aversive stimulus. Which reaction will occur depends on previous learning experiences (flight, for example, may have been found previously to be more effective) and on the nature of the particular situation (a situation where the person has a sense of being 'in control' may make fight more likely). A number of laboratory and naturalistic studies give support to this theory, showing, for example, that pain is a powerful elicitor of angry aggression. Unpleasant smells, 'disgusting' visual stimuli (for example, pictures of diseased and suffering animals), and high temperatures have also been found to lower the threshold for aggression, though in the latter case the effect is curvilinear: that is, fairly high temperatures make us more irritable, but very high temperatures may actually reduce aggression, perhaps because of their tendency to make us sleepy and lethargic.

ANGER DIARY

In recent years psychologists such as James Averill have conducted diary studies of anger and aggression with a view to finding out what we report as making us angry in everyday life, rather than relying on rather unnatural laboratory studies. If you would like to keep an 'Anger Diary' see Exercise 5.2.

Diaries tend to confirm the importance of aversive/frustrating events for anger but also suggest a feature of anger not always apparent in the laboratory – that it is predominantly elicited by *interpersonal events*. Other people, rather than things or impersonal occurrences, make us angry. James Averill reports that people become mildly to moderately angry in the range of several times a day to several times a week, and that only 6 per cent of incidents are elicited by a non-animate object. The frustrating person in over half the episodes was someone known and liked – friends and loved ones are common sources of aversive experiences.

The second component of anger, the cognitive aspect, is concerned with the way in which we appraise, interpret and construct the social environment. Attribution theory has been a major force in cognitive theorizing and attributions are now widely believed by psychologists to be relevant to anger and aggression. Attributions are best viewed as the person's attempt to explain *why* an aversive or frustrating event has happened. The nature of the explanation a person arrives at determines in part how they will feel and what they will do. An everyday example may make this clearer.

Suppose that you are knocked off your bicycle by a car while travelling home from work. This painful and aversive event may be attributed by you to your own inadequacies ('I failed to look where I was going') or to chance ('given the number of cars and bicycles on the road, it is inevitable that accidents will occur'). Neither of these attributions is likely to produce anger or aggression. If you made the attribution, however, that the car driver deliberately intended to knock you off your bicycle, or was driving carelessly, your threshold for anger and aggression is likely to be considerably lowered. Attributions of 'malevolent intent' of this sort have been shown to be important in understanding human aggression.

Psychologists have tried to tease out the factors which determine whether hostile attributions are made. Social judgements of this sort prove to have complex origins. Studies suggest that to assess the actor's responsibility for the harmful event the perceiver attempts first to estabish whether the act was intended or unintended. If unintended, a decision is made as to whether the harmful consequences were foreseeable or unforeseeable. If intended, the action may be construed as malevolently or non-malevolently motivated. It may be the case, of course, that particular individuals are biased in their appraisals. The person who is generally more angry and aggressive than others may habitually see the worst in other people's intentions and motivations and fail to undertake a rational evaluation of what caused a particular event to occur.

The third and fourth components of anger are physiological arousal and the aggressive act itself, which may or may not follow anger arousal. 'I felt my blood boiling', in the anger incident recalled above, probably refers to the effects of the autonomic activation (increase in blood pressure, heart rate, respiration, muscle tension and so on) which we know accompanies the angry state. The precise role of physiological changes in the genesis of emotion is still controversial as is the question of whether the pattern of physiological arousal that accompanies anger can be discriminated from that occurring with other strong emotions such as fear or anxiety. In particular individuals the physiological component of anger can be strong and even overwhelming. One of the authors of this book currently has in therapy a client whose main problem is his inability to control his temper in a range of situations. He reports intense physical symptoms (sweating, muscle tension) for up to two days following an angry upsetting incident. A reaction of this intensity is probably rare but it does highlight the importance of physiological events.

Most experiences of anger in everyday life are not followed by physical aggression as we saw in the two incidents described. James Averill found that less than ten per cent of angry episodes induced physical aggression. What he called 'contrary reactions', activities opposite to the instigation of anger, such as being friendly to the instigator, were twice as frequent as physical aggression. Anger may produce a range of other reactions – the previous learning experiences of the individual are clearly important in determining whether frustration and anger are responded to with withdrawal, help-seeking, constructive problem-solving or what Albert Bandura has called 'self-anaesthetization through drugs and alcohol'.

As suggested above, there are likely to be complex and bi-directional relationships between the environmental, cognitive, physiological and behavioural components of anger. Ways of thinking and appraising may induce anger but equally the emotional state of anger may make it more likely that we will think angry thoughts. Environmental frustration may cause aggression, but behaving aggressively may also expose the person to even more frustration (being disliked by others or even becoming subject to a retaliatory attack from them). Untangling these complex inter-relationships will be a major task for psychologists in the future.

Recommended Reading

Aronson, E. (4th ed., 1984). *The Social Animal,* San Francisco: W.H. Freeman.

Bandura, A. (1973). *Aggression: A Social Learning Analysis.* New York: Prentice Hall.

Duck, S. (1983). *Friends for Life: The Psychology of Close Relationships.* Brighton: The Harvester Press.

Sluckin, W., Herbert, M. & Sluckin, A. (1983). *Maternal Bonding.* Oxford: Basil Blackwell.

References

Averill, J.R. (1982). *Anger and Aggression: An Essay on Emotion.* New York: Springer-Verlag. [A stimulating book, discussing many psychological, physiological and cultural aspects of anger.]

Berkowitz, L. (1982). Aversive conditions as stimuli to aggression, In L. Berkowitz (ed.), *Advances in Experimental Social Psychology, 15.* New York: Academic Press. [Develops the idea that aversive stimulation precedes angry aggression.]

Bowlby, J. (1971). *Attachment and Loss. Volume 1: Attachment.* Harmondsworth: Penguin. [Attachment in infants and maternal deprivation.]

Ferguson, T.J. & Rule, B.G. (1983). An attributional perspective on anger and aggression. In R.G. Green & E.L. Donnerstein (eds). *Aggression. Theoretical and Empirical Reviews, 1.* New York: Academic Press. [A theoretical essay which tries to integrate what is known about the attributional and cognitive components of anger.]

Groth, A.N. (1979). *Men Who Rape.* New York: Plenum. [A clinical account of sexual aggression.]

Harlow, H.F. (1958). The nature of love. *American Psychologist, 13,* 673–685. [Love in infant monkeys.]

Lee, J.A. (1976). *Lovestyles*. London: J.M. Dent & Sons. [Love in adults.]

Novaco, R.W. (1978). Anger and coping with stress. In J.P. Foreyt & D.P. Rathjen (eds). *Cognitive Behaviour Therapy*. New York: Plenum. [An overview of anger with particular emphasis on clinical intervention.]

Rubin, Z.. (1970). Measurement of romantic love. *Journal of Personality & Social Psychology, 16(2)*, 265–273. [Love and liking.]

Schaffer, H.R. (1971). *The Growth of Sociability*. Harmondsworth: Penguin. [Attachment in human infants.]

Schaffer, R. (1977). *Mothering*. London: Fontana. [Mother–infant attachment: includes comment on Freud.]

Sluckin, W. (1972). *Imprinting and Early Learning*. London: Methuen. [Imprinting; includes comment on Lorenz.]

STYLES OF LOVING

(adapted from John Lee (1976) *Lovestyles*. Dent: London)

Which ten of the following thirty 'opinions' correspond most closely with your view of a relationship with a lover (girl/boyfriend, spouse, etc.) Circle the number of the opinions of your choice. (N.B. there are no 'correct' answers.)

1. Lasting love must be based on a decision of the mind or will, not on a feeling or emotion.
2. When two people are truly in love, sex becomes a pure and beautiful way of showing their love and they never do it simply for pleasure.
3. Each lover must find his 'other half', the soul to match his own and make his life complete.
4. True lovers must share every secret, and hide nothing from each other, even though telling may hurt their love.
5. If your love is true, you can overcome every obstacle. Love will find a way.
6. If necessary, lovers should take strong action, even threats of violence or suicide, to prove how deeply they love.
7. If you find your one true love, and it fails, life is no longer worth living.
8. In true love, you feel a strong, unexplainable attraction. If there isn't there, or it goes away after a while, there's nothing you can do to make yourself feel in love with the other person.
9. True lovers 'just can't get enough of each other'. They will never tire of making love with each other.
10. True lovers always enjoy the touch, smell and voice of each other.
11. Love is stronger than us; it cannot be denied or resisted, even when the person involved is already married to someone else.
12. Two people can love each other truly, even when they know they have only a short time before they must part, never to meet again.
13. No one expects a lover to mean sincerely everything he or she says while in love.
14. There's nothing wrong with pretending you are in love, as long as you do the other person no harm.
15. Two people who would never make good friends could still be truly in love with each other.
16. It is possible to fall in and out of love quite a few times without getting badly hurt.
17. If a break-up is coming anyway, it is better to drop the other person than be dropped.
18. There's nothing wrong with playing the field, and having your choice from several persons who love you.
19. It can be very annoying to have someone fall in love with you when all you want from him or her is some good times together.
20. The best cure for heartache is to find someone new.
21. There are other things in life just as important as finding true love.
22. There may be good reasons for people to marry even when both know that they are *not* in love.
23. Lovers should be prepared for a certain amount of letdown and disappointment after marriage.
24. Love between people of similar background and common interests is the only kind likely to last long.
25. The need for someone you have grown accustomed to depending on can grow into true love.
26. It's more important to find someone you'll always enjoy being with than to find someone good-looking and exciting.
27. The test of time is the only sure way to know if your love is real.
28. Physical (sexual) attraction is not an important part of love.
29. True love ripens slowly out of friendship; it does not happen suddenly or dramatically.
30. True lovers respect and admire each other, and each feels that the other is somehow the 'better' person.

Answers: On next page.

STYLES OF LOVING

Answers:
AGREEMENT ON THE FOLLOWING:
Items 1–5 and 26–30 AGAPE;
Items 3–10 and 30 MANIA;
Items 8–15, 18 and 19 EROS;
Items 12–21 LUDUS;
Items 18–27 PRAGMA;
Items 21–30 STORGE.
If the majority of your answer falls into one of these six
categories then your love style is as indicated. *See text for
details.*

COMMENT: This exercise is a set of opinions about love, not a set of statements about *behaviour*. We often think one thing and do another, so agreement with an opinion does not prove what would actually make you happy in a love affair. Also, many people have the habit of believing contradictory opinions, applying now one and now another to specific situations. So don't rely heavily on the results of your selection in this exercise.

Professor Lee's complete assessment of an individual's lovestyle requires an interview of several hours, with choices among some 1,500 statements. There are only 30 statements above. If you think you have a fever, you might feel your forehead, but that is not a very reliable test. Better to use an exact thermometer. In the same way, this exercise is just a hand on the forehead of love. For a more accurate assessment see Chapter 11 of Professor Lee's book, *Lovestyles*.

ANALYSING YOUR OWN ANGER

Your own experience may be a rich source of ideas about the nature of anger and aggression. An 'Anger Diary' is simple to keep and often revealing. Keep a diary over a period of two weeks. This should be filled in at the same time every evening. Write an account of the experiences of anger that have arisen in the course of the day. For each experience try to answer the following questions:

1. What was the precise event that elicited my anger? What irritated me most?

2. Was the source of my anger another person? Myself? An object or thing?

3. What interpretations did I put on the frustrating event? Are there other interpretations I did not consider? What sorts of things did I say to myself following the frustration that made me more angry?

4. What physical sensations accompanied the anger experience?

5. What behavioural reaction did I show? Was my response verbal aggression? Physical aggression? Withdrawal from the situation?

COMMENT: A series of incidents analysed in this way will reveal the patterns of your own experience of anger and may encourage you to formulate your own ideas and to compare them with those discussed in this chapter and in the further reading that is recommended at the end.

6. *Growing Up*

▽ *Training children to be good?* ▽ *Preschool play.*
▽ *Studying development.* ▽ *Children's drawings.*
▽ *The world of the infant.* ▽ *Logical thinking.*
▽ *Social development in babies.* ▽ *Adolescence and beyond.*
▽ *Language development.*

'Spare the rod and spoil the child'.

'Children should be seen and not heard'.

'Children learn through play'.

'Children should be encouraged to express themselves'.

These four sayings come from the wealth of 'folk wisdom' that exists about how children should be brought up. The first two, which might well have been current in the nineteenth century, have more recently been replaced by ideas along the lines of the third and fourth. Ideas about bringing up children are often very clearly and firmly held: parents and others tend to have surprisingly strong views on the subject. Nevertheless, every parent knows that there are many difficult choices and dilemmas that are posed daily by a lively five-year-old. It is often *not* obvious where the dividing line falls between healthy self-expression and disobedience, for example. At what point should parents intervene and/or punish the child?

TRAINING CHILDREN TO BE GOOD?

Child psychologists try to give answers to practical questions such as these, and their recommendations are put into practice by playgroup leaders, schoolteachers, nurses, social workers and other professionals as well as by parents themselves. The study of children, and the practical advice given about their upbringing, has shown some pronounced changes over the course of this century. The harsh view of the nineteenth century was that the parents' (or Nanny's) job was essentially to stamp out the undesirable, antisocial behaviour to which they believed young children were naturally predisposed, and to 'train' them towards social acceptability by a kind of military-style 'drilling' process, involving restrictions and punishments.

Since those days, there has been a general increase in permissiveness towards children; they have been given more freedom to develop at their own pace in areas such as feeding and weaning, toilet training, and in developing self-control. There has been a marked decline in the use of physical punishment, such that, in Sweden, it is actually illegal to strike your child; and pressure groups such as STOPP (Society of Teachers Opposed to Physical Punishment) are campaigning for its abolition in schools in the UK.

STUDYING DEVELOPMENT

These changes in attitudes to the upbringing of children are paralleled by changes in psychologists' views of the course and process of human development, and there have been some very significant advances over the last two decades. The field of *developmental psychology* has changed from being a fairly quiet backwater of the discipline into one of its most vigorous and rapidly-expanding areas. In Great Britain, for example, The British Psychological Society's Developmental Psychology Section is one of the youngest as well as one of the biggest Sections of the Society.

1. Training children; training parents

Let us pick out three features of the 'new-look' developmental psychology to show how things have changed. Perhaps the most significant is the growing realization that 'children train their parents' just as much as the reverse. Early ideas about 'child-rearing' saw it as a one-way process in which the child was something like a shapeless blob of clay, to be gradually moulded and shaped by parents, teachers and others. Recent research on babies' smiling, crying, babbling and gazing makes it quite clear that the relationship between parent and child is *reciprocal:* the infant takes the lead in interactions and non-verbal 'conversations' just as much as, if not more than, the parent. In other words, far from being passive blobs of clay, babies exert a considerable influence over their own upbringing. This reciprocity is at the heart of the interaction between biological and social influences on the developing child.

2. When does 'growing up' stop?

The second feature is what has become known as the *life-span* approach. Quite simply, this is that human development should be studied across the full age span, from conception right through to old age and death. Until quite recently, developmental psychologists devoted most of their attention to children aged between about 2 and 11. Early infancy was neglected – perhaps because babies are unpredictable and difficult to manage – but recent technological developments in videorecording and computing have meant that detailed information about babies can now be collected, stored and analysed with relative ease, and fairly inexpensively. This has meant that the study of the origins of behaviour in infancy has become a prominent feature of the subject. The age of adolescence has also been neglected, perhaps because it is a period of transition between childhood and adulthood, but the worst neglect of all has been of virtually the whole of adult life. With the exception of some studies of old age, hardly any attention has been paid to the changes that take place in people's lives between the ages of about 15 and 60. This may be partly because the study of marriage, careers, family patterns and so on has taken place in related disciplines such as sociology and anthropology, but the life-span developmental approach is now, at last, beginning to fill some of these gaps.

3. Mothers and fathers, brothers and sisters

Patterns of child care have changed dramatically in recent years. For a variety of social and economic reasons the traditional family pattern, in which father is the sole breadwinner and mother stays at home to look after the children and do the housework, is becoming much less common. The number of one-parent families is increasing, and many more mothers now have some form of full-time or part-time work. These factors have led to a much greater demand for nursery provision, childminders, and other forms of day care than existed in the past. Furthermore, present-day fathers are more likely to take an active part in childcare than were their predecessors.

These changes are reflected in the new *ecological* approach to the study of development, which proposes that all of the different influences upon the child should be taken into account. Psychologists have tended to concentrate almost exclusively on the mother-child relationship; indeed the well-known early work of John Bowlby stressed the overwhelming importance of this bond (see pages 101 – 102).

Now that mothers are no longer automatically their children's primary daytime caregivers, ecological research has begun to look more closely at the influence of fathers, siblings, other relatives, baby sitters, childminders, and so on. An important aspect of this research is the recognition that all the relationships within the family system are interdependent. For example, when the first baby arrives, the parent–child bonds that are formed inevitably affect the existing relationship between mother and father. The arrival of the second-born, similarly, has effects upon the existing relationships between father, mother and first-born, apart from all the new bonds that are formed. We are just beginning to grapple with some of these questions.

THE WORLD OF THE INFANT

It used to be thought that newborns come into the world with very few capabilities and skills other than a few basic physical reflexes. The infant's *learning experiences* were seen as crucial for development. In recent years, psychologists have moved away from this view, and current research is uncovering more and more abilities that seem somehow to be 'built into' babies, or 'prewired', at birth. Along with this change in attitude, paradoxically, goes the realization that babies' learning experiences probably have an even more powerful effect upon their development than was originally thought. The study of infants is one of the most active areas of contemporary child psychology.

One of the first people to try and map out the changes that take place in infancy was the Swiss psychologist Jean Piaget, and his account formed part of his well-known, influential and controversial *stage* theory of child development, which we will return to later. Piaget proposed that, from birth until the age of about 2 years, all children pass through six *substages,* moving from a rudimentary use of simple physical reflexes through to the beginnings of *symbolism.* Piaget proposed that in the first three of these substages (that is, up to the age of 8 months or so), 'thought is action'. What babies do to toys and other objects *is* what they think about them, such that objects possess what might be called 'motor meaning', and a consequence of this is that objects have no 'permanence'. A baby's taps on a rattle, for example, represent his or her thoughts about the rattle at this early stage. If the rattle goes out of sight, it effectively ceases to exist.

This is what is meant by the well-known expression 'out of sight is out of mind'. Piaget proposed that *object permanence* – the recognition that objects do not cease to exist when they are out of sight – gradually develops over the fourth, fifth and sixth substages of infancy. This represents a fundamental kind of 'liberation': no longer is the infant's thinking tied to the 'here and now', that is, to given situations at given points in time, because he or she can form *symbols,* or *internal representations,* of objects; hence toys are not always out of mind when out of sight.

As with many parts of Piaget's theory, the idea that 'out of sight is out of mind' has been hotly disputed by experimental researchers, and the map of perceptual development in infancy turns out to be more complicated than Piaget first proposed. Nevertheless, there is no argument that the acquisition of symbols is one of the major achievements of the first two years of life.

SOCIAL DEVELOPMENT IN BABIES

Alongside the investigation of perceptual abilities, psychologists have also recently discovered that babies are much better equipped for social interaction than was originally thought. As we said earlier, there can be no doubt that the relationship between parent and child is a reciprocal one in which parent responds to child just as much as the reverse. This has been clearly demonstrated in several areas of research.

In one study by Glyn Collis and Rudolph Schaffer, mother–infant pairs were videotaped whilst playing together with several toys in a novel situation. Analysis of the tapes showed a typical pattern of *turn-taking* in the phasing of the actions of mother and child. For example, a sequence of actions might be started by the child looking at one particular toy. The mother might then look at the same toy and 'elaborate' upon the child's attention towards it by talking, pointing, or maybe touching. This response by the mother in turn stimulates the child to explore the toy further, and so a kind of 'chain' of actions is built up by means of turn-taking.

A key feature of this 'chain' is that mother and infant work together, as a team, with their actions very precisely phased in time with one another. This *synchronization* has been demonstrated in vocalizations, as well as in gestures (such as pointing), and in visual gaze. Daniel Stern's research, for example, clearly shows that when mothers respond verbally to (non-verbal) babbling noises by their babies, they tend to time their 'conversational' responses just as they would in a normal verbal conversation with an adult.

Born social

The precision with which this phasing takes place in parents' interactions with even very young babies has led psychologists to conclude that infants are born with a tendency to respond to other human beings, that is, that they are 'born social'. There is a good deal of evidence that babies can distinguish between people and things very early on. They are much more likely to attend to faces than to scrambled pictures of facial features, for example, and to the sounds of speech rather than to the many other sounds they might hear. It has also been suggested that parents and infants 'interpret' each others' actions, and mutually 'construct the meanings' of the chains of action that they build up. The baby's smile, for example, might be interpreted by the mother as meaning that the child likes a certain toy which happens to be present, and so start off a sequence of actions like that described. The chain is built up and kept going by the baby's 'interpretation' of the mother's behaviour, as well as vice versa. This takes us a long way from the view of the baby as a helpless blob of clay.

LANGUAGE DEVELOPMENT

One of the main ways in which we express ourselves and com-municate with one another is through spoken and written language, and so it is hardly surprising that the study of language acquisition in children is a very active one. Psychologists are concerned with the ways in which the speech-like sounds produced in babies' babbling gradually turn into recognizable syllables and words, with how these are put together to form meaningful sentences, and with how the vocabulary and grammatical structures of children's speech develop and change.

The child who says 'I rided my bike' and 'I runned away' presents a fascinating problem. It is only because of the irregular (and ever-changing) nature of the English language that these utterances are considered to be 'wrong'. In adding the past tense ending '-ed' to the verbs, the child is applying a standard grammatical rule in a perfectly logical and consistent manner. Furthermore, the demonstration by Jean Berko that children can apply such rules even to nonsense words which they have never seen before – ('Here is one wug. Here are two . . . ?') – poses some tricky questions for the psychologist, since it seems to show that language rules are somehow stored by children independently of the words to which they are applied. The identification of these rules, and of the part they play in thought as a whole, is one of the central tasks of research in this field.

PRESCHOOL PLAY

We have all seen children playing doctors and nurses, cowboys and indians, teachers and schools, and so on. These *make-believe* games provide very clear examples of symbolism. In make-believe or fantasy play, children often use one object as a symbol for another: an old cardboard box 'becomes' a boat, or a spaceship. Children also use their own bodies to represent something else. One of the authors vividly remembers being awoken each morning by the 'miaows' of his three-year-old son, who crawled into the bedroom on all fours. Play provides an arena in which children can act out any role that they want: in a sense they can actually 'become' their parent, teacher, favourite TV or pop star, and this probably serves two different functions.

First, it has been suggested that play provides a happy, stress-free atmosphere in which children can act out some of their worries or fears. A child who was frightened by a growling dog, for example, might 're-live' the episode in fantasy play, and this might serve to diminish the anxiety associated with it.

Make-believe

Second, make-believe play serves to prepare children for adult life. In acting out the role of a teacher, doctor or nurse the child is working out and getting to grips with the responsibilities of living with other people, and practising or 'rehearsing' behaviour that will eventually become an essential part of social life. This is really what we mean by saying that children 'learn through play'; a philosophy that underlies a good deal of practice in many of today's nursery schools and preschool playgroups. This is a relatively new idea, of course – the Victorians saw 'play' as being the opposite of 'work', that is, as a waste of time.

Today's view is just the opposite. Not only are children thought to learn through play, but 'play' in adults (hobbies, sports, creative work, and other leisure activities) is becoming an increasingly important part of our view of the future.

Playing and learning

Given the educational importance of this idea, it is not surprising that psychologists have tried to find some clear experimental evidence that children *do* learn through play. A typical experiment is to give matched groups of children different types of play and non-play experience, and then to compare their relative performances on independent measures of learning and thinking. In one study, children who were given free play experience with everyday objects such as a paper towel, a screwdriver, a paperclip and a matchbox were able to come up with significantly more creative thinking responses to the question, 'How many uses can you think of for this object?', than those who had observed an adult making conventional uses of the objects, or than those who had no prior experience of the objects. In this case, free play served to promote creative thinking, and similar conclusions have emerged from a variety of studies along the same lines.

A note of caution has been sounded by one of the leading researchers in this field, however. Peter K. Smith, of Sheffield University, suggests that we should guard against the idea that play is a kind of universal route to almost all forms of learning. Smith's analyses of the research literature show that many of the studies suffer from problems of experimental design and methodology. In many cases, the 'play' and 'non-play' experiences given to the different subject groups have differed from one another in other important respects, such as the amount of contact with adult experimenters, so we can't be sure that play *as such* is the key element in the enhanced performances of children who have experienced it. Certain forms of play undoubtedly promote certain types of learning; but we must be precise about the interconnections, and not forget that other processes, such as imitation, are also taking place in what is loosely called 'free play'. Smith concludes that 'play is only one way to learn'.

CHILDREN'S DRAWINGS

Another fascinating part of children's symbolic activity which is receiving a lot of current research attention is the study of their drawings. Drawings provide a unique insight into the child's experience because they often attempt to portray what the outside world is really like; but they also include many images which are 'playful' and which are not intended to bear any relation to reality. Drawings provide a rich mixture of fantasy and reality, and psychologists have studied them for many years. We now have a fairly detailed picture of how children's drawings tend to change with age. Broadly speaking, four main stages can be identified: the first two of these, which fall partly within the preschool period, are illustrated as part of Exercise 6.1.

Scribbling

The first stage is self-explanatory: around the ages of two and three, drawings are more like 'scribbling'. In the earliest scribbles the child simply enjoys making marks on the paper, but these marks gradually get more and more organized, showing evidence of form and pattern (see Exercise 6.1a and 6.1b). During this stage children gradually make the connection between their own motions with the pencil and the marks that appear on the paper. They also begin to name their scribbles, though the name given to any particular one might well change several times over the course of its production. Towards the end of this stage, the earliest *representations* become apparent; and probably the most prominent of these is the well-known 'tadpole figure' (see Exercise 6.1c).

Tadpole figures

All children seem to go through a stage of drawing tadpole figures, and their explanation highlights some interesting problems for child psychologists. Strictly speaking, the tadpole figure represents an 'error' in depicting the world, since arms don't really come out of people's heads. But can we conclude that children think that they do? Do children have 'immature concepts' of people?

Norman Freeman, of Bristol University, has investigated questions such as this by giving children 'completion' tasks in which they are asked, for example, to attach arms and legs to pairs of 'head' and 'body' circles of different relative sizes. Freeman found that children who normally drew tadpole figures were quite happy to attach arms to an outline 'body' circle when this was significantly bigger than the outline 'head'. He concludes from evidence such as this that children do not have peculiar concepts, or immature mental images, of the world around them. His own view is that drawing 'errors' like the tadpole figures arise from the *production strategies* that children adopt, that is, from the ways in which they try and organize themselves to produce a drawing.

Drawing what they know

In spite of this view, the common view of the second 'preschematic' stage of drawing (roughly between four and seven years) is that children 'draw what they know and not what they see'. In Exercise 6.1d and 6.1e, you can see two examples of drawings that fit this description, that is, they display 'intellectual realism'; and you might like to collect some more of your own. In 6.1d, the man's legs are visible through his trousers, presumably because the child 'knows' that they are there, and the potatoes he ate for dinner could equally well be visible. These effects are known as 'transparencies'. The drawing in 6.1e displays 'turning over'. The trees appear to be splayed out perpendicular to the pond, which is something that the child 'knows' about them; but of course the representation is strictly speaking 'wrong'.

Drawing what they see

In the third and fourth stages, which take us beyond the preschool period, drawings gradually become more and more visually realistic. Those in the third stage still possess some of the 'errors' of the previous stage, such as the 'air gap' that is commonly found in landscapes (see 6.1f). But these disappear with the *visual realism* of the fourth stage. By this stage, of course, realism is only one of several criteria according to which children judge their drawings. Art work serves as an expressive medium, rather than merely as a means of representation.

LOGICAL THINKING IN SCHOOLCHILDREN

We referred earlier in this chapter to Jean Piaget's well-known stage theory of child development. The most influential and controversial part of this concerns the changes which take place in children's thinking at around the age of seven. Piaget believed that this age marks the transition between the second, *pre-operational* and the third, *concrete operational* stages. In the UK, the age of seven also marks the transition between infant and junior school – and this is no coincidence. Piaget gave an extremely detailed account of the sudden advances in logical thinking ability that children make around this age, and his theory has formed the basis of various curriculum schemes for mathematics and science in the first school, such as the Fletcher and Nuffield schemes in Great Britain.

Conservation

One of the central concepts in Piaget's account of this transition is that of *conservation.* This is best explained by looking at one of the best-known of his experimental demonstrations, *conservation of volume.* (Exercise 6.2 explains how you can try this out for yourself, if you can find some willing schoolchildren.)

In the first part of the task, the child is shown two identical containers of liquid (we suggest tumblers of orange juice) and asked 'Is there more juice in this one' (experimenter points to A) 'or in this one' (experimenter points to B) 'or is there the same amount in each?' Children of all ages ought to answer that there is the same amount in each. This serves as a check that they are understanding the questions, and co-operating with the experimenter. The experimenter next pours the juice from container B into container C and repeats the question, this time comparing A and C.

According to Piaget, the pre-operational child typically ansers *either* that A contains more, 'because it's higher', *or* that B contains more, 'because it's fatter'. In the third part of the task, the experimenter pours the liquid from C back into B, and again repeats the question comparing A with B. The child typically reverts to the original answer that there is the same amount of juice in each, not appreciating that the volume of liquid remains the same regardless of its shape. In Piaget's terms, s/he cannot conserve volume. The concrete operational child, on the other hand, does conserve volume, maintaining that there is 'the same amount in each' throughout the experiment.

Piaget devised similar tasks in many areas of school mathematics, including number, distance, time, and classification, and the same basic principles underlie his explanation of the acquisition of concrete operational thinking in each case. In essence, he says that the pre-operational child is unable to *decentre:* to recognize that two dimensions of a display can interact to determine a third, higher-order property. In our exercise, the pre-operational child *centres* either on the height or the width of the display, and is unable to combine these to form a conception of volume. Only with concrete operations do children begin to realize that area is determined by length and breadth, that speed is determined by distance and time, and so on. This represents a monumental advance. The same principle also extends into social behaviour, in Piaget's suggestion that pre-operational children are unable to decentre from their own point of view: that their thinking displays *egocentrism*. The British boy of 4 thinks of his continental playmate Pierre as a foreigner, for example, but he is unable to see that he is himself a foreigner to Pierre. He gleefully announces that he has a brother, but cannot understand that his brother likewise has a brother.

Piaget's theory of this transition has been subjected to a considerable amount of critical scrutiny from within as well as from outside psychology, perhaps because it has had such a profound influence upon adults' views of children's capabilities, and upon the practice of teaching. Many experiments have been carried out with the aim of showing that young children are capable of displaying conservation abilities at a much earlier age than the theory would predict. It has been suggested, for example, that Piaget places far too much reliance on children's verbal replies: that he may be tapping the ability to use words correctly rather than thinking ability. In Exercise 6.2, for example, it may be that the (incorrect) response to the second part of the task, 'there's more juice in A' is actually the child's way of saying 'the level in A is higher', and that s/he understands perfectly well that the volumes in A and C are the same. One way round this problem is to obtain non-verbal responses from the children, and researchers are currently pursuing different ways of doing this.

Do children say what YOU want them to say?

Another important recent idea is that the social understandings inherent in test settings exert a strong influence upon the judgements that children make. The child is not only responding literally to the questions, but is also trying to interpret the underlying intentions of the experimenter by making what has been called 'human sense' of the situation. In Exercise 6.2, for example, the experimenter asks questions about the difference between A and C, just having intentionally transformed B into C. Any classroom- or psychologist-wise 5-year-old could quite justifiably reason, 'Well, she must want me to say that

A and C are different now, otherwise she wouldn't have bothered pouring B into C'. The incorrect response would not necessarily arise from the inability to conserve.

An elegant demonstration of this was made in a pioneering study by James McGarrigle and Margaret Donaldson at Edinburgh University. They found that most of the 4 to 6-year-olds in their study failed on standard Piagetian number conservation tasks, in which the experimental transformation was *intentionally* carried out by the experimenter. When they ingeniously made the transformation appear to be *accidental,* however, by means of a 'naughty teddy bear' who 'spoilt the game', the number of children who succeeded on the task more than doubled.

This is a convincing demonstration that pre-operational children can display conservation abilities when the conditions are right, and many other critical studies have found the same. It still does not prove conclusively, however, that children's natural tendency is to conserve. Young children may be able to show concrete operational thinking, but most of the time they tend spontaneously not to do so. In other words, Piaget's theory might be over-general but it does not seem to be completely wrong. Psychologists still spend a lot of time trying to disprove it, which perhaps speaks for itself.

ADOLESCENCE AND BEYOND

Piaget's view is that the *concrete* operations of later childhood are replaced by *formal* operations in adolescence. The adolescent's thinking is not bound by the immediate situation: 'what is' can be seen in relation to 'what might be'. Different *hypotheses* can be proposed about the likely outcomes of situations and events, and the adolescent has the logical skills to test these systematically. These changes in thinking are, of course, underpinned by the abrupt and profound physical changes which occur at puberty.

From the base of the brain, the pituitary gland secretes hormones into the blood stream which give rise to dramatic changes in primary sexual characteristics (the development of the genitals; the onset of ovulation in girls, and of ejaculation in boys) as well as in secondary ones (sudden increases in height and weight and the growth of pubic hair in both sexes; breast development in girls; growth of body hair and a deepening of the voice in boys). These developments start and finish a year or two earlier in girls than in boys.

These physical changes naturally affect the whole of psychological development, and one of the most obvious outcomes is the awakening of sexuality itself. Adolescence is a time of major re-adjustment: the teenager must suddenly come to terms with new-found sexual feelings, and powerful emotional attachments towards others. The whole pattern of social relationships is changed: with parents and family, with peers, and with those in the world of school or work, such as teachers, supervisors and other authority figures. The adolescent is neither a child nor yet an adult, but is in a confusing, embarrassing and often bewildering period of transition. One prom-inent psychological idea is that wrestling with this 'identity problem' creates a great deal of 'storm and stress', and that protest and rebellion are fairly common and natural reactions to this.

These feelings are quite likely to be taken out on the parents since they are usually on the spot, or 'in the firing line'. This is the origin of the so-called 'generation gap' which can clearly be seen in Western society, but which is not necessarily present in all cultural groups. The adolescent is torn between two conflicting sets of values: with the conventional 'social' attitudes represented by parents and school on the one hand, and with 'peer cultures', which are often anti-authority and sometimes completely anti-social, on the other. The mass media play a large part in defining peer cultures such as this. The clothing, hairstyles, music preferences and attitudes of mods, rockers, hippies and skinheads have all in part been created through television, radio, magazines, and pop records. Of course, the media have a considerable financial stake in the considerable spending power of the teenage market; it is in their interests to make sure that fashions change fairly quickly.

Career versus family life

Somehow most of us manage to survive the trials of adolescence, and to adapt to the typical adult roles of our society. The course of development in adulthood is probably best explained in terms of the ways, as individuals, in which we fit into the conventional patterns of work and career, and of parenthood and family life. These explanations seem to be quite different for men and for women. Most men have a clearly-defined career pattern, followed by retirement, with parenting largely as a background or support role. In contrast, the typical female life span is much more disrupted. The relative importance and priority of the roles of worker, housewife and mother varies considerably over adult life, so that many women could be said to experience 'role inconstancy'.

One effect of this is that women tend to report lower levels of life satisfaction than men, and to suffer more from depressive illnesses and problems, according to the findings of many research studies. It has also reliably been found that single and divorced women seem to suffer less in this respect than those who are married. The moral seems to be that it is better for men to be married, and for women to stay single, though this presents some obvious practical problems.

Traditional sex role behaviour seems to be at its strongest in the years of active parenting – in the 20s and 30s. In later life, at least in married couples, 'sex role blurring' occurs: the interests, attitudes, and behaviour of both sexes become less stereotyped. In men, it seems very likely that this is a direct result of retirement. The man gives up his active 'breadwinner' role. He is based at home, where the jobs to be done are domestic, and so it seems fairly natural that he should take on some of the characteristics of the 'homemaker'. In women, the picture is much less clear. One suggestion invokes the so-called 'empty nest syndrome'; that having devoted a considerable amount of time and effort to childrearing and homemaking, women one day find that their 'birds have flown'. The outcome of this could be a shift *away from* the role of homemaker, that is, in the opposite direction to that of men, though these speculations need further investigation.

This explanation is of course restricted to conventional two-parent married families in Western society, and therefore leaves a great deal unexplained. Today's women are much more likely to have full-time or part-time jobs than in the past, which presumably means that they are fulfilling breadwinner as well as homemaker roles, and of course the combination of these two roles is essential in the increasing number of one-parent families. External social and economic conditions, and the patterns of employment and unemployment that they create, exert a strong influence upon our continuous 'growing up'.

Recommended Reading

Donaldson, M. (1978). *Children's Minds.* London: Fontana.

Gardner, H. (1982). *Developmental Psychology,* 2nd ed., Boston: Little, Brown.

Miller, P.H. (1983). *Theories of Developmental Psychology.* San Francisco: W.H. Freeman.

Silva, K. & Lunt, I. (1982). *Child Development: A First Course.* Oxford: Basil Blackwell.

References

Boden, M.A. (1979). *Piaget.* London: Fontana. [A sound, sensible guide to the theory.]

Bowlby, J. (1971). *Attachment.* Harmondsworth: Penguin. [Bowlby's theory of parent-child bonding.]

Berko, J. (1958). The child's learning of English morphology. *Word, 14,* 150–177. [Research on learning language rules.]

Collis, G.M. & Schaffer, H.R. (1975). Synchronisation of visual attention in mother-infant pairs. *Journal of Child Psychology & Psychiatry, 16,* 315–320. [Research on mothers and babies looking at things together.]

Freeman, N.H. (1976). Do children draw men with arms coming out of the head? *Nature, 254,* 416–417. [Experimental research on young children.]

McGarrigle, J. & Donaldson, M. (1974). Conservation accidents. *Cognition, 3,* 341–350. [The social setting affects children's conservation abilities.]

Richards, M.P.M. (ed.) (1974). *The Integration of a Child into a Social World.* Cambridge: Cambridge University Press. ['New-look' research on early social development.]

Smith, P.K. (ed.) (1984). *Play in Animals and Humans.* Oxford: Basil Blackwell. [A review of theories and research on play.]

Stern, D. (1977). *The First Relationship: Infant and Mother.* London: Fontana. [Studies of synchronization between infant and mother.]

Taylor, A. (1986). Sex roles and ageing. In D.J. Hargreaves & A.M. Colley (eds), *The Psychology of Sex Roles.* London: Harper & Row. [Do sex roles 'blur' in later life?]

CHILDREN'S DRAWINGS

Drawings (c) – (f) display 'intellectual realism': they reveal 'what children think, and not what they see'. Ask a child aged between 3 and 8 years to draw a person with clothes on, a pond with trees around it, and a house with a sun and a bird, and see if you can find any evidence of intellectual realism. You may also be able to devise other subjects for drawing which will illustrate this feature.

(a)

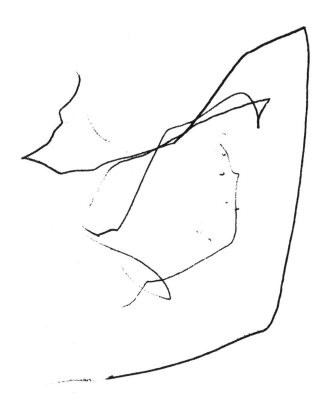

CONSERVATION OF VOLUME

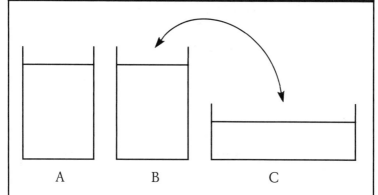

A   B   C

1. Take two identical clear glass tumblers, A and B, and fill them with orange juice to the same height. Ask the child: 'Is there more juice in this one' (point to A) 'or more juice in this one' (point to B) 'or is there the same amount in each?' Record the child's answers by writing them down, or by tape recording the question-and-answer session.

2. Pour the juice from B into C – a differently-shaped clear glass vessel, for example, a shallow dish – and repeat (1) with C in place of B.

3. Pour the juice from C back into B, and repeat (1).

Try (1) – (3) with a 5-year-old, a 7-year-old and a 9-year-old.

Do your results support Piaget's theory of conservation? (See text.)

7. *Psychological Problems*

▽ *Anxiety and related problems; phobias; agoraphobia.*
▽ *Sources of phobias and anxiety.*
▽ *The treatment of fear and anxiety; systematic desensitization; implosion.*
▽ *Sexual problems.*
▽ *Causes of sexual dysfunction.*
▽ *Treatment approaches to sexual problems.*
▽ *Psychological aspects of physical ill-health.*
▽ *Personality and health problems; Type A and coronary heart disease.*
▽ *Cancer and the mind.*

Throughout this book we have been trying to show ways in which psychologists have attempted to understand and explain particular aspects of human experience and behaviour. Some areas of psychology are explicitly concerned with applying psychological theories to the problems and distress that arise in everyday life. Clinical psychology, for example, is about the application of psychological theories and methods in psychiatric, medical and related settings. The range of clinical psychology is now great, encompassing the fields of mental handicap, behaviour problems in childhood, the difficulties of the elderly, the effects of brain damage, delinquency and antisocial behaviour, as well as mental disorders such as depression and schizophrenia. It is not possible in a short chapter to give an overview of this work. What we shall try to do is to give a flavour of the psychological approach by picking out three areas. The problem areas we have chosen are those of anxiety, sexual dysfunction and psychological aspects of physical ill-health. Clinical psychologists were not the first to tackle these problems but they have brought new perspectives to bear on them. Psychology's contribution has often been to test and evaluate the theories that have been put forward to explain particular difficulties and also to systematically evaluate the effectiveness of interventions or treatments.

ANXIETY AND RELATED PROBLEMS

Let us start by considering one particular case in detail.

« Ms J. is a 23-year-old nurse. She was referred for help with a problem which had developed over the preceding year. Prior to this she had few serious psychological difficulties. She had been brought up in a conventional middle-class home along with a brother and sister. She had always viewed herself as the 'nervous' and 'emotional' member of the family but never considered herself as having any major problems. A year prior to her referral she had been working a series of night shifts at a general hospital. When alone on the ward during the night a patient to whom she was very attached died. She was upset at the time but not unduly so. Two weeks later, while working on the ward at night, she was telephoned from home and told that her father was seriously ill. He died a few days later. Over the ensuing weeks bouts of anxiety would arise if she was working alone on a night shift. She would feel dizzy, her legs would shake and she had a feeling of desperately wanting to leave the ward. On occasions she actually left the ward at night when these 'panics' came on. She eventually gave up night shifts but her fear generalized to some degree to working during the day. She was then unable to go to work. Even the thought of work upset her. She was concerned to re-establish her normal work pattern as she was planning to marry and needed the income. »

Phobias

Problems of fear and anxiety, of the kind just described, formed the bread-and-butter work of many clinical psychologists in the 1960s and early 1970s, particularly for psychologists of the behavioural school. Today, even though the range of problems tackled is much wider, fear and anxiety are still a common reason for consulting a clinical psychologist. The problem just described is an example of a *phobic disorder:* the degree of fear experienced is out of all proportion to the objective threat the feared situation poses and is of such an intensity as to restrict and impair the individual's daily life. Phobias are fairly common. One American survey found that more than seven per cent of the population reported a mildly disabling phobia but that severe, crippling phobias were found in only two persons in every thousand. A range of phobias can be found in the community, including fears of illness, injury, storms, animals (rats, mice, spiders, cars, dogs, etc.), heights and crowds. The most commonly treated one is agoraphobia.

Agoraphobia

Agoraphobia begins most commonly between the ages of 18 and 35 and is found predominantly in women. Fear-arousing situations include being away from home, being in crowds, being confined, travelling on trains or buses, and even going shopping. As with other phobias, the feared situation is often avoided and the person's life becomes very restricted as a result. Agoraphobics often experience a state best described as 'panic' in the feared situation. Their heart may thump; they may feel dizzy, sweat or experience a range of other unpleasant sensations. Panic symptoms like these can seem like a real physical disorder such as heart disease and sufferers may even believe they will pass out or die.

Panic disorders of this sort are usually distinguished from *generalized anxiety disorders* in terms of the duration of the anxiety experience. For panic disorder the anxiety is sudden and limited in duration. For generalized anxiety disorder the feeling of apprehension is present over a long period of time and is unrelated to the perception of any specific danger.

THE COMPLEX NATURE OF FEAR AND ANXIETY

Psychologists and doctors have made a number of contributions to our understanding of conditions of this sort. An important beginning has been to reveal the complexity of fear and anxiety. Anxiety seems to involve four systems which interrelate in a complex and, as yet, poorly understood way: a cognitive/verbal system, a physiological system, a subjective/emotional system, and a behavioural system. In some instances of anxiety all four systems are activated. The person perceives and expects danger (cognitive), he or she sweats, trembles and feels dizzy (physiological), feels anxious and frightened (subjective), and avoids the threatening situation (behavioural). But it is possible that these systems can become desynchronized. The person may show all features, except the cognitive perception of a particular threat (as in generalized anxiety, where the person does not perceive any particular danger). It is also possible to be fearful without marked physical changes, and vice versa. Equally the person may experience the cognitive, physiological and subjective aspects of anxiety in a particular situation and yet not avoid it. The clear implication of all this is that treatments may need to tackle these many different aspects of the problem if they are to be effective.

SOURCES OF PHOBIAS AND ANXIETY

There have been many attempts in psychology to explain how phobias are acquired. Indeed, two of the most famous case histories in the history of psychology were presented as attempts to study and explain phobias in a young child.

Little Hans

Sigmund Freud published in 1909 a case history entitled 'The analysis of a phobia in a five-year-old boy'. This became known as the 'Little Hans' case after the name of the boy concerned. Little Hans had developed a fear of horses and of going out. The phobia was explained by Freud in terms of the Oedipus complex. The problems with this interpretation are many. For a discussion of these and of the general looseness of the inferences made about the boy the reader is referred to a brief account of the case in a book by Rosenham and Seligman (see *References*).

Little Albert

In 1920 John Watson, the American behaviourist, reported on an equally famous boy, 'Little Albert'. Watson reported an attempt to establish a phobia in an 11-month-old boy by classical conditioning, that is, learning through the temporal association of two events (discussed in detail in Chapter 9). Briefly, Watson tried to condition fear to a white rat. Whenever a white rat was placed in front of Albert a loud noise was made by hitting a hammer on a metal bar close by. It was known that Albert was frightened of loud noises. After a number of pairings of rat and noise Albert became frightened of the rat and subsequently generalized his fear to rabbits, cotton wool and other similar things.

It is almost certainly true that phobias *can* be acquired through classical conditioning of this sort and the phobias produced can appear irrational to someone not familiar with the conditioning history.

Learning and unlearning

One of the authors of this book has a young daughter who, for some time as a baby, became upset and cried if the word 'hot' was said in the course of conversation. This puzzled many visitors to the house, though it had a simple conditioning explanation – in the preceding months she was at the stage where she spent much time exploring the house and its corners. She would often be spotted about to put a hand on something that might burn, such as a hot radiator; she would be warned: 'Don't touch that, it's *hot*', typically just at the moment when she did in fact touch it. 'Hot', then, became a conditioned stimulus signalling pain.

Some clinical cases of phobia can be shown to be based on conditioning experiences of this sort. The case of Ms J. seems to be explainable in this way. Ms J.'s avoidance of the feared situation (the ward at night) prevents her 'unlearning' her fear reaction. She gives herself no opportunity to learn that she can be on the ward at night without anything tragic happening. In many, perhaps most, clinical cases, however, conditioning experience of this sort cannot be found in the person's history. What the other routes to a phobia might be, are not yet clear.

Passing on fear

Social modelling may be an important factor. It can be demonstrated in laboratory studies that young monkeys with no experience of snakes can develop a strong fear by observing their parents react with fear to a snake. It is not difficult to see how agoraphobic reactions, phobic fear of illness, or a range of other fears could be acquired by humans in this way. Parents may teach fears by direct modelling and such learning may be accentuated by the parents' and child's capacity to encode such experiences in a verbal way. A fear of mice or spiders can run in the family.

Phobias can make good sense

Recently, it has been argued that the assertion that phobias can be acquired by conditioning needs considerable qualification. The conditioning of phobias is highly selective. Only *some* objects and situations are easily linked with fear while others are not. Martin Seligman and others have pointed out that the objects or situations most feared by phobic people are the ones that *were* dangerous in the early stages of human history. The argument goes that evolution will have selected for those individuals who would readily associate particular dangerous situations with fear. People and other animals who quickly learned to be afraid of heights, or strangers or separation would have reproductive advantages over those without this capacity. Learning of this sort is referred to as *biologically prepared*. People do not readily acquire phobic reactions to electric plugs or guns because such objects have appeared too recently in human culture for them to have featured in natural selection. Clearly, we are primed to develop only particular kinds of fears or phobias. What other factors, apart from biological preparedness, promote the acquisition of particular fears is, as yet, largely unknown.

Who is vulnerable?

Conditioning theories have been relatively unsuccessful in accounting for more complex phobias such as agoraphobia or for generalized, non-specific, anxiety states. For agoraphobia, there is rarely an obvious traumatic conditioning event that can be pointed to. A theory of the origin of agoraphobia, therefore, will need to look at a broader range of influences, such as the ones proposed by a team of British researchers, Andrew Mathews, Michael Gelder and Derek Johnston. These workers suggest that there are three *vulnerability factors* which predispose the person to develop agoraphobic symptoms.

1. The early family environment. Families in which there is instability, overprotectiveness or lack of parental care may increase the tendency to be dependent on others and to avoid difficult situations.

2. A general 'anxious' temperament (possibly influenced by genetics).

3. Exposure to general stress in the environment.

The likely sequence for the development of the disorder is as follows. The anxiety-prone person with a 'bad' family background is exposed to stress (conflicts, domestic crises, and so on) which induces a high level of anxiety and physical arousal. When the person then finds him or herself in an overstimulating environment (for instance, a crowded shopping centre or store in the case of agoraphobia), the physical arousal is increased and, eventually, the person experiences a full-blown panic in that situation. An additional factor then determines whether the person becomes agoraphobic or develops a generalized anxiety state. The person will become agoraphobic if he or she attributes the panic experienced to the external situation (the crowded place) rather than internally. The person now sees the panic as caused by the setting and learns to avoid it in future. Once the agoraphobic habit has been produced it will be maintained and confirmed if staying at home is rewarded by family and friends and if the person now avoids going out from fear of having another panic attack. It may be that the panic attack itself is now feared as much as the crowded street or shop.

Looking for danger

This account, of course, does not fully explain why some people are anxiety prone in the first place nor why only some individuals are made anxious by life stresses. One promising line of recent research suggests tht anxious people 'selectively process' information relating to personal danger. It is as if the anxious person is attuned to threats in the environment in a way that the non-anxious person is not. The 'dangers' in this case may be social (for example, rejection) as well as physical (for example, illness). Andrew Mathews has suggested that the anxious person may be locked in a 'cognitive-anxiety loop'. Cognitions or thoughts about danger cause a state of anxiety. The state of anxiety, in turn, activates 'danger schemata'. In everyday terms, perceived danger produces anxiety which makes the person even more aware of thoughts and memories relating to danger. Such a loop produces an escalation of distress until a state of panic is reached.

THE TREATMENT OF FEAR AND ANXIETY

The treatment of phobias has been one of the success stories of modern clinical psychology. A very large number of studies have

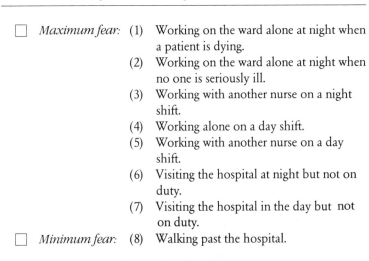

Table 7.1: Hierarchy of fear-inducing situations for Ms J.

☐ *Maximum fear:* (1) Working on the ward alone at night when a patient is dying.
(2) Working on the ward alone at night when no one is seriously ill.
(3) Working with another nurse on a night shift.
(4) Working alone on a day shift.
(5) Working with another nurse on a day shift.
(6) Visiting the hospital at night but not on duty.
(7) Visiting the hospital in the day but not on duty.
☐ *Minimum fear:* (8) Walking past the hospital.

been conducted in the last 30 years evaluating the effectiveness of various therapeutic approaches. With considerable consistency the research points to the effectiveness of *exposure to the feared situation* in reducing phobic reactions. There have been several variants of exposure treatment which have been popular for a time.

Systematic desensitization

In the 1950s Joseph Wolpe developed *systematic densensitization* as a treatment for phobias. The technique has three components. First, the client is trained in *deep muscle relaxation,* to produce a physical state that is incompatible with the experience of anxiety. Second, the client is helped to devise a *hierarchy* of fear-inducing situations. At the top of the hierarchy are situations of maximum fear; at the bottom situations of low fear. An actual hierarchy for Ms J., the nurse, is shown in *Table 7.1.*

Finally the client is asked to imagine each scene, starting at the bottom of the hierarchy, while deeply relaxed. When the fear diminishes the client moves up the hierarchy until the most frightening scene can be imagined without fear. This simple method proved to be effective with a number of simple phobias. Subsequent experiments showed that the relaxation was not essential for this method to be effective.

Implosion

A variation on this particular technique is to use *implosion.* Here the client is immediately induced to imagine the worst possible situation and to experience it fully, without graduated exposure. It is now widely accepted that for systematic desensitization and implosion to work, they need to be accompanied by real life exposure to the feared situation. Graduated exposure is the approach most likely to be effective with Ms J. as it is with most agoraphobics. In most cases the method produces significant changes which are maintained over time, although clients are often left with residual difficulties even at the end of treatment. Why exposure works and how the effect is to be explained remain matters of debate within clinical psychology. It is unlikely that it can be explained in mechanical conditioning terms. It is more likely to be the client's thoughts, expectations and general appraisal of him or herself and the situation, that are changed in the course of 'facing up' to feared situations.

Psychological treatments for generalized anxiety, where there is no indentifiable trigger, are rather less advanced. Effective therapies await a greater understanding of the psychological processes involved. As with many other problems, the attention of contemporary clinicians and researchers is increasingly focused on the role of higher-level 'cognitive' activities in the causation and cure of these anxieties.

SEXUAL PROBLEMS

Sexual problems are a widely acknowledged cause of distress. They can be categorized into three types: the *hypophilias,* the *paraphilias* and the *gender dysphorias.* The hypophilias are typically problems of inadequate responsiveness. An inability to become sexually aroused, for example, would count as an instance of hypophilia. The paraphilias refer to variations from what is considered 'normal' in choice of sexual partner or sexual object. Fetishism, for example, can be considered as a paraphilia, as can homosexuality, though in recent years there has been an increasing awareness that a homosexual preference is not inherently a 'problem' (as noted in Chapter 3), though it may be made so for the individual by social stigma. Gender and dysphoria refers to a subjective sense of discomfort with and alienation from one's ascribed gender. The transsexual (who is most frequently a genetic male) considers himself to be a female trapped in a male body and is a clear and extreme example of such a dysphoria. We will concern ourselves here mainly with the problems of sexual inadequacy, the hypophilias.

A number of aspects of the sexual response can become problematic for people. Psychologists have often distinguished four aspects. A person may have an inadequacy of sexual *interest,* of sexual *arousal,* of *orgasm* or of sexual *pleasure.* The issue of at what point behaviour becomes inadequate is a thorny one. In general it is not possible to apply an absolute standard. What is deemed to be inadequate by one person may be seen as adequate by the next. Equally our notions of what is adequate are highly dependent on the era and culture in which we live.

There are major difficulties in finding out how many people experience sexual problems. The surveys done are often of groups which are untypical of the general population and it becomes difficult to generalize from the results obtained. One study of normal married couples estimated that over 60 per cent of women and 40 per cent of men experienced sexual dysfunction. Nevertheless most of the couples viewed their sexual relationship as satisfactory. This may reflect a healthy tendency to view at least some dysfunctions as 'normal'. Of those presenting to sex problem clinics, the most common problem for men is 'erectile impotence' (an inability to achieve or maintain an erection) and for women 'general unresponsiveness' (an inability to become aroused by, or enjoy, sex).

CAUSES OF SEXUAL DYSFUNCTION

Sexual responses are complex and depend on the integrity of anatomical, physiological, hormonal, social and psychological aspects of the person. It follows that a wide range of physical and psychological factors can disrupt sexual functioning. It is unlikely that most dysfunctions can be accounted for in terms of physical abnormalities but there are a number of diseases which can cause sexual difficulties. Metabolic disturbances, arterial disease, arthritic disorders, neurological abnormalities, myocardial infarction, diabetes mellitus and a range of other conditions can all contribute to the emergence of problems, as can the temporary effects of drugs and alcohol. For most people with sexual difficulties the major causal factors are of a psychological nature. Derek Jehu, a British psychologist who has written at length about sexual problems, distinguishes *historical causes* and *contemporary causes.*

Early experiences

Historical causes are causes within the earlier experiences of the person. Such experiences may take the form of long-term social conditioning associating sexual arousal and behaviour with negative emotions such as fear, guilt, threat or pain. Learning of this sort may occur within highly restrictive families which equate sexuality with immorality. While highly repressive familial attitudes are now probably less common than they were, excessively prohibitive homes of this sort appear to be found more frequently in the backgrounds of those presenting with sexual difficulties. If such conditioning does occur it is not surprising that some individuals find it difficult to undo the effects when, after adolescence, they acquire a sexual partner or marry. It speaks for the strength and adaptability of the sex drive that many persons from highly restrictive backgrounds do escape sexual problems in adulthood. Why some individuals exposed to such conditioning remain permanently affected while others do not is far from understood.

Sexual trauma may also be important. William Masters, Virginia Johnson and other clinicians have pointed to the experience of *traumatic failure* in early sexual encounters. The nature of the attributions made for such failures are likely to be important. An early sexual 'failure' realistically attributed to inexperience or to the difficult circumstances of the sexual encounter may be far less damaging than the internal attribution 'I am no good at sex' as an explanation of why the failure occurred.

It is plausible that sexual victimization experiences in childhood play some role in causing sexual difficulties in women. Sexual abuse by an adult in childhood is common in North America and Britain and research suggests that such experiences can be damaging in terms of adult social and sexual functioning.

Here and now problems

Amongst the contemporary conditions which make dysfunction more likely are the presence of inadequate sexual information in the couple and general non-sexual difficulties in the relationship. Most treatment programmes include an attempt to increase the level of sexual knowledge of dysfunctional couples, as active misinformation is found to be common. Much of the information imparted stresses the *normality* of behaviour which may be interpreted by the clients as indicating abnormality. It may be reassuring and therapeutic to learn, for example, that it is normal for males to show some decline in sexual responsiveness with age.

The presence of anxiety in the sexual context itself is widely believed to be a cause of dysfunction. Two features of anxiety are the phenomena of 'fear of failure' and 'spectatoring'. The previous experience of a sexual 'failure' may induce performance anxiety in subsequent attempts at sex, the person being plagued with the question 'will it happen again?'. The effect of such a fear is to focus attention on the sexual response itself. The person is constantly monitoring his or her reactions: becoming a spectator rather than a participant in the situation. It is only in very recent years that these common clinical ideas have been tested in a systematic fashion in research studies.

David Barlow, in the United States, has conducted a number of studies of the effects of what he calls 'cognitive interference' and anxiety on how dysfunctional and non-dysfunctional people respond to sexual stimulation. Barlow has put forward a model of how dysfunction arises. He suggests that what distinguishes people with or without problems is the psychological reaction to sexual situations in which a *demand* for sexual performance is perceived. A responsive partner, for example, may create a perceived demand and expectation that the person will 'perform'. Whereas this demand produces a positive emotional reaction in functional people and a focusing of attention on erotic aspects of the situation, in the dysfunctional person there is a negative emotional reaction, followed by a tendency to underestimate his or her level of arousal and to overestimate his or her lack of control over sexual arousal. What follows is that the dysfunctional person then focuses more and more attention on very non-erotic aspects of the situation, namely on the negative consequences of not 'performing adequately'. What this theory suggests, then, is that the dysfunctional person stops him or herself from responding sexually because attention is focused on the consequences of failing rather than on erotic aspects of the situation. The person worried about his or her reactions, in effect, makes a self-fulfilling prophecy of failure.

TREATMENT APPROACHES TO SEXUAL PROBLEMS

The treatment programmes devised to help people who are dysfunctional typically attempt to 'undo' the myriad influences that caused and maintain the problem. Many of the treatment techniques available today have their roots in the earlier, influential programmes of William Masters, Virginia Johnson and Helen Singer Kaplan. A number of researchers have reported high success rates for particular types of dysfunction. Joseph Lo Piccolo and colleagues in the United States, for example, have reported success with a 'sexual skills learning model' approach to the sexual problems of women. Whilst therapies of this sort are rightly regarded as one of the more successful areas of psychological therapy, there remain important questions for future research. It is likely that different types of dysfunction will require different treatment approaches. It is also still unclear where therapies do work, *why* they work and which component of the complex treatments offered is the crucial one.

PSYCHOLOGICAL ASPECTS OF PHYSICAL ILL-HEALTH

It is very easy to assume that the benefits of applying psychological ideas will be mainly in the areas of mental distress. While it is true that in the past psychologists have seen their work as most relevant to problems of anxiety or depression or other forms of mental disturbance, times are changing. One of the most exciting and fast-expanding areas in recent years has been the extension of psychological thinking to problems of physical ill-health. What such work obliges us to do is to break down the distinction between mind and body and to become aware that *psyche* and *soma* interact in subtle and complex ways. Increasingly it is recognized that psychological factors play some role in the causation of physical disease and that disease, in turn, poses major problems of a psychological nature for the individual. Body changes in ill-health occur in a context of thought, feeling and behaviour from which they cannot be extracted.

Behaviour and illness

Whether psychological states have a proven role in *causing* ill-health has been the subject of debate for some time. An alternative way of phrasing this question is to ask whether some diseases have a definite *psychosomatic* component. We are not talking here about malingering or about the hypochondriac who feels ill with no physical basis, but about serious, even life-threatening conditions which may have been brought about in part by psychological influences.

There are three forms of influence that have been studied in detail. The first is perhaps the most obvious. Much ill-health and disease is demonstrably the result of *problem behaviour.* The pattern of disease has changed dramatically in the past 80 years. Advances in medication, immunology and in social conditions have virtually eliminated deaths from tuberculosis, influenza, measles and similar conditions, but this reduction has been accompanied by increases in cardio-vascular disease, lung cancer, drug and alcohol abuse and alcohol-related accidental deaths. Increasingly, *how individuals behave* affects the likelihood of their becoming ill. Smoking, alcohol abuse, lack of care in diet and careless driving are all known risk behaviours and changing such behaviours is ultimately a psychological/social rather than a medical problem.

Stress

The second psychological influence that has received research attention is a rather less tangible one – that of life stress. Stress is difficult to define but two sorts of life events have received particular attention: the experience of *loss* and of *life change.* Many practising doctors have noted how the onset of illness in patients often seems to be preceded by loss experiences such as separation and bereavement. A common suggestion is that loss experiences induce a state of hopelessness and 'giving up' in vulnerable people and that this psychological state produces biological changes which make people susceptible to particular diseases.

Life change

Two American researchers, Thomas Holmes and Richard Rahe, introduced the notion that it is the experience of *life change* that affects health adversely. They devised a list of events that would require change of lifestyle and gave each event a weighting or score so that an individual can add up the amount of life change experienced over a period such as a year. The prediction was that high life change would predict the onset of disease. This prediction has been tested in two ways, firstly *retrospectively* by comparing the previous life change of people who are currently ill with those of similar people who are well; and *prospectively* by, for example, categorizing people now in terms of whether they have recently experienced high, medium or low amounts of life change and attempting to predict who will become ill in the future. There have now been many attempts to perform tests of this sort and many have provided some support for the theory, though we shall point out some difficulties with this sort of research later.

One particular form of loss/life change has been shown to have a particularly powerful effect on health – the experience of bereavement. Losing a close family member through death has been shown to raise the levels of morbidity (sickness) and mortality (death) in surviving relatives. How this effect occurs is still mysterious. Does the person's grief in some way affect his or her biology, as suggested by the phrase 'dying of a broken heart', or is the important mechanism more mundane – that the bereaved neglect themselves, or drink more alcohol?

Not everyone exposed to major life change becomes ill and this has led psychologists to look more carefully at what occurs. A major loss or change may not be *perceived* as stressful by some individuals because they see themselves as being able to *cope*. For some 'hardy personalities', as they have been called, change is a challenge to be welcomed, rather than a threat. The person most likely to be adversely affected by life changes is the person who has failed to develop coping strategies, who lapses into helplessness and who, in addition, fails to find adequate *social support* from friends and relatives through the time of crisis.

What causes what?

Research of the sort we have just been discussing has filtered through into the public's consciousness in recent years. It seems to be commonplace now to hear people ascribe their physical health problems to 'stress' or 'having too much on'. It is useful to be aware though of some of the methodological problems that bedevil the professional researcher in this area. Much of the work on loss and life events is based on sick people retrospectively recalling more stressful events in the past year than do a comparison group of well people. Might this correlation simply reflect the tendency of ill people to be in a low mood and to selectively recall stressful events? Or could it be that, rather than life events causing illness, the early stages of the illness existed undetected *prior to* the life events and caused them to happen? It is not difficult to see, for example, how the early stages of heart disease might cause people to be less effective at work and even to lose a job. This loss would then appear to have caused a subsequent heart attack.

Another possibility is that life stress changes *health behaviour* rather than the person's biology itself. The effect of stress may be to make people more attentive to symptoms they normally ignore, more likely to interpret such symptoms as serious, and more likely to seek medical help for them. In research the investigator is often dependent on measuring what the person says and does in relation to his or her health rather than being able to assess biological factors directly. It is possible, therefore, that the apparent link between life stress and illness may sometimes be due to a stress changing how people behave. Exercise 7.1 is designed to help you explore stressful events in your own life and the ways in which you react to them.

PERSONALITY AND HEALTH PROBLEMS

Those who treat physical illness and those who suffer from it have often speculated that particular diseases have associated 'typical personalities'. The implicit assumption is that certain personalities tend to develop particular conditions. It may be thought, for example, that people with high blood pressure are irrascible or that asthmatics are anxious. Many hunches of this sort have either never been directly tested scientifically or, if they have been, they have been found not to be supported by the evidence.

Type A and coronary heart disease

There is one major exception to this general rule. Evidence has accumulated for some time that a particular personality type may be prone to develop coronary heart disease. The coronary-prone type has been described as the 'Type A' personality. The particular traits involved include intense striving for achievement, competitiveness, overcommitment to work, time urgency, impatience and hostility. American research has studied middle-aged men prior to their having heart disease and shown that Type As were twice as likely to have a heart attack. This association was independent of other known risk factors such as smoking, high blood pressure and high cholesterol. Findings of this sort have led to the development of treatment programmes to help Type As change their unhealthy approach to life.

What is Type A?

This area of psychosomatic research, however, also has its problems.

It is not entirely clear, as yet, how *culture-specific* the Type A–heart disease link is. Will the link be as strong or as reliable in other countries as it has been in the United States? The whole concept of a 'type' of this sort has also been much criticized. It can be argued that the Type A personality traits are a cluster of different behaviours which are not necessarily strongly associated with each other. In addition many psychologists feel it is unrealistic to describe a dichotomous, either/ or typology. In general, most personality characteristics are better described in dimensional terms and it might be more reasonable, therefore, to describe individuals in terms of where they appear on the Type A continuum rather than to describe them as either Type A or not. In spite of many criticisms of this sort it seems likely that there is some real substance to this particular theory and that research attempting to understand how this configuration of traits produces heart disease will continue.

CANCER AND THE MIND

The psychological aspects of cancer (neoplastic disease) have been much discussed in the media in recent years, particularly in relation to 'alternative medicine' treatment for sufferers. Of particular interest has been the question whether there are any reliable psychological pre-cursors to the development of particular cancers. Sporadically, research studies have found that cancer sufferers differ from non-cancer patients on particular dimensions. There have been reports, for example, that men with lung cancer have 'restricted outlets for emo-tional discharge' and that 'suppression of anger' is more common in women with breast cancer. Interesting though such findings are, there are real problems in knowing whether what is being picked up is a *reaction to* the development of the disease rather than a precursor of it.

There is rather more firm evidence that once a cancer has developed the physical outcome of the disease depends, in part, on the psychological coping style of the sufferer. In one study a favourable outcome after the development of breast cancer was more common in those women who had shown a fighting spirit ('it won't beat me') or denial ('perhaps it isn't cancer after all') than in those who showed either stoic acceptance or helplessness/hopelessness. Find-ings of this sort would certainly be consistent with other research in psychology which shows that 'helplessness' is a very damaging state for the person, both in terms of physical and mental health.

Cancer, more than many diseases, also *causes* major psychological problems. The diagnosis itself may have a major impact on psychological well-being and this may be exacerbated by the side-effects of treatment and by the physical changes that accompany the development of the disease. However, as with many other life crises, what has struck some researchers is the variation in how individuals respond to the same physical diagnosis or condition. Certainly, problems of anxiety and depression are common in people with life-threatening disease but it is also remarkable how well many maintain their psychological well-being in the face of great adversity. Studies of people in such circumstances reveal that three mechanisms may help people cope.

When threatened by a cancer diagnosis the person may engage in a *search for meaning*. An attempt is made to find a *cause* for the development of the disease ('Was it stress, diet or just bad luck?'). Secondly, an attempt is made to *regain control and mastery* by finding ways of apparently controlling the future. The person might, for example, decide to change his or her lifestyle or diet in some way so as to prevent a recurrence. Finally, comfort is found by *maintaining self-esteem through social comparison* of oneself with others who are 'even worse off than me'. What this work suggests is that potentially traumatic life events need not be devastating. People can survive psychologically by actually trying to make sense of and control their situation rather than being a helpless victim.

The existence of these ways of coping, clearly, may have implications for how people deal with other major threats, apart from the threat of physical illness. Understanding how people repond to these extreme forms of adversity may also throw some light on how people cope, or fail to cope, with the general problems of everyday life.

Recommended Reading

Agras, S. (1985). *Panic: Facing Fears, Phobias and Anxiety.* New York: W.H. Freeman.

Bancroft, J. (1983). *Human Sexuality and its Problems.* Edinburgh: Churchill Livingstone.

Rosenhan, D.L. & Seligman, M.E.P. (1984). *Abnormal Psychology.* New York: W.W. Norton.

References

Agras, W.S., Sylvester, D. & Oliveau, D. (1969). The epidemiology of common fears and phobias. *Comprehensive Psychiatry, 10,* 151–156. [Considers the frequency of various common phobias in the population.]

Bancroft, J. (1983). *Human Sexuality and its Problems.* Edinburgh: Churchill Livingstone. [Includes a good review and discussion of the prevalence of sexual dysfunction.]

Barlow, D.H. (1986). Causes of sexual dysfunction: the role of anxiety and cognitive interference. *Journal of Consulting & Clinical Psychology, 54,* 140–148. [Describes the cognitive interference theory of the causation of sexual difficulty.]

Holmes, T.H. & Rahe, R.H. (1967). The social readjustment rating scale. *Journal of Psychosomatic Research, 11,* 213–218. [The original work on assessing life change is reported.]

Jehu, D. (1984). Sexual inadequacy. In K. Howells (ed.), *The Psychology of Sexual Diversity.* Oxford: Basil Blackwell. [Jehu's account looks at the causes of sexual dysfunction.]

Kaplan, H.S. (1981). *The New Sex Therapy: Active Treatment of Sexual Dysfunctions.* New York: Brunner/Mazel. [The Kaplan programme is considered in this text.]

Lo Piccolo, J. & Stork, W.E. (1986). Treatment of sexual dysfunction. *Journal of Consulting & Clinical Psychology, 54,* 158–167. [Gives an account of the effectiveness of therapeutic techniques for sexual problems.]

Masters, W. & Johnson, V. (1970). *Human Sexual Inadequacy.* Boston: Little, Brown. [The Masters and Johnson programme is considered in detail.]

Mathews, A.M., Gelder, M.G. & Jonston, D.W. (1981). *Agoraphobia: Nature and Treatment.* London: Tavistock. [A comprehensive account of the treatment of agoraphobia.]

Rosenhan, D.L. & Seligman, M.E.P. (1984). *Abnormal psychology.* New York: W.W. Norton. [Includes accounts of 'Little Hans' and 'Little Albert'.]

Rosenman, R.H. Brand, R.J., Jenkins, C.D., Friedman, M., Straus, R. & Wurm, M. (1975). Coronary heart disease in the western collaborative group study: final follow-up experience at $8^{1/2}$ years. *Journal of the American Medical Association, 233,* 872–877. [One study into the relationship between Type A behaviour and heart disease.]

Seligman, M.E.P. (1970). On the generality of the laws of learning. *Psychological Review, 77,* 406–418. [Discusses prepared learning.]

Taylor, S.E. (1983). Adjustment to threatening events: a theory of cognitive adaptation. *American Psychologist, November,* 1161–1173. [Describes psychological reactions to cancer.]

Wolpe, J. (1958). *Psychotherapy by Reciprocal Inhibition.* Stanford: Stanford University Press. [A detailed look at systematic densensitization.]

REACTIONS TO STRESSFUL LIFE EVENTS

It may be useful to consider your own reactions to stressful life events. Here is a list of life events which are generally stressful:

☐ Death of a spouse

☐ Death of a close family member or friend

☐ Major personal illness or injury

☐ Major illness or injury of close family member

☐ Major change in closeness of family members

☐ Engagement

☐ Marriage

☐ The break-up of a close relationship

☐ A family member leaving home

☐ Gaining a new family member

☐ Major change in financial status

☐ Changed work situation (conditions, hours, responsibility)

☐ New job

☐ Being made redundant

☐ Retirement from work

☐ Change of residency

Have any of these happened to you in the last two or three years?
How did you react psychologically to them?
Were you, in fact, 'stressed' by them?
How did the stress show itself?
Were there health problems as a result of the stress?
Overall, did you cope well or badly?
What would have helped you to cope better?

It can be helpful to do an exercise of this sort with a group of other people, so that you can compare reactions.

8. *Your View of the World: Perception and Memory*

Our world is a constant source of stimulation with events of all kinds occurring every second: a noise, a sight, a touch against our skins. The way we monitor what is happening around us is termed *perception,* and we have five perceptual senses – sight, hearing, smell, touch, and taste. Of all our many physical and psychological abilities and skills, perception is, as we shall see, the most vital.

PERCEPTION IS VITAL TO LIFE

Why is perception so important? Imagine that you have no perception of any kind: you can't see the people around you; you can't hear music; there is no feeling over your body; your food might be fresh or it may be rotten; you are unable to smell when the danger of a hidden fire threatens. With the total loss of all senses not only would the pleasures of life disappear, you would also be helpless against any peril to your life. Clearly, then, we must be able to perceive events around us, and to do this we need a system of detection.

160

All our senses, our detection systems, operate in basically the same way. An event, or *stimulus,* such as a sound, or a light, occurs and comes into contact with our body. If the stimulus is strong enough it will activate the appropriate receptor – the ear or the eye in this case. Having detected the stimulus, the receptor then passes the information on to the centre of operations, the brain. This transmission of information is carried out by the passage of minute electrical pulses through the central nervous system (CNS). Having reached the higher centres of the brain, the message is recognized and we become aware of, we perceive, what has happened.

Whilst all the senses are important, in humans certain senses have become more highly specialized than others and so we rely on them to a much greater degree. The loss of the sense of smell, unpleasant as that might be, is not so great a handicap as deafness. In species other than man the position might be different: a hunting animal which relies on scent to detect its food would suffer a much greater impairment should it lose its sense of smell rather than its hearing. It is, however, generally true that of all our senses vision is the most vital. Therefore we will pay special attention to seeing both as an example of how the senses operate, and as deserving of examination in its own right.

THE VISUAL SYSTEM

The receptor in the visual system is, of course, the eye, which contains cells sensitive to light energy. These light-sensitive cells are at the back of the eye and form the *retina:* rather like a film in a camera, the cells in the retina react to and record the presence of light. The retina contains two particular types of light sensitive cells, called *rods* and *cones.*

Rods and cones

It is estimated that more than six million cones and 100 million rods are contained in the retina. The distinction between rods and cones is rather like the difference between black and white and colour film for cameras. The rods 'see' only in black, white, and shades of grey and, being highly sensitive, need less light to function. Cones, on the other hand, are able to 'see' colour but need much more light to do so. In effect, cones are for daytime vision, and rods are for twilight or night vision. It is because of this difference that when we are out at night objects lose their colour: we are seeing through rods, not cones. Having to switch from 'cone vision' to 'rod vision' can cause problems as many car drivers will testify. At twilight, when the quality of natural light fades, colour disappears and other cars or pedestrians crossing the road are 'lost' as they merge into a general murky grey world, only to be seen at the last moment.

The physical working of the visual system is shown in *Figure 8.1*. After passing through the retina, and being converted to the appropriate type of electrical pulse, the light moves through the optic nerves to a point just behind the eye called the *optic chiasma:* at this point the optic nerves from the right and left eyes cross. The effect of this crossing means that objects in the right visual field are passed to the left side of the brain, whilst objects in the left visual field progress to the right side of the brain.

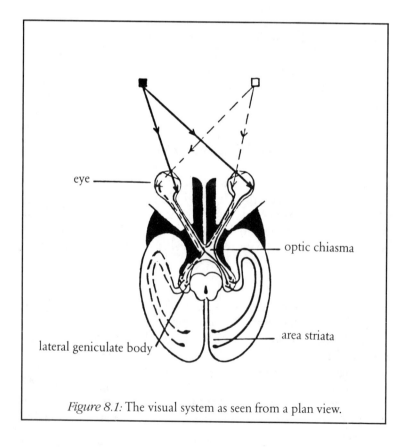

Figure 8.1: The visual system as seen from a plan view.

From the optic chiasma the pulses continue their journey to the *lateral geniculate body* from where they are passed on to the brain's cortex where specialist cells are waiting to 'de-code' the messages. The specialist cells which perform the de-coding operation for vision are at the rear of the brain, in the region called the *area striata*. This is why a bump on the back of the head can sometimes cause us literally to see stars.

The brain cells in the *area striata* are sensitive to signals which represent different sizes, colours, and movements; the total combined action of these cells is to gather and 'translate' the pulses to an understandable form. Our knowledge of how this process occurs is limited. However, a glimmer of the complexities involved can be gained from reading the pioneering work in this field by the researchers David Hubel and Torston Wiesel at the Harvard Medical School in America.

THE PSYCHOLOGY OF PERCEPTION

Up to this point we have looked at the physical workings of the visual system, but there is another dimension to perception, concerned not so much with physiology, but rather with the way that we use our senses to understand and interact with our world – the psychology of perception. Our senses exist to give us information about our environment but it is not enough that they simply say whether or not an event has occurred; much finer distinctions are needed. For example, I might say I have heard a noise, but how loud was the noise? Was it a high or low pitch? Perhaps it was a voice or the sound of an engine? Similarly, most of us can not only tell red from green, blue from yellow, but also with the addition of 'brightness' can tell light blue from dark blue, and even shades of light blue.

SEEING SHAPES

As well as perception of brightness and colour, the ability to see *shape* is important. When we look at an object we see it against some background and the object, or 'figure', stands out against the 'ground'. This 'figure–ground' effect is central to perception, and is essential in allowing us to select what in the whole of the world about us we particularly want information about.

Figures against a background

Most of the time we can easily pick out exactly what we want to attend to, but sometimes this is more difficult. Consider walking into a strange room in dim light. First you might be aware that something is standing in the corner, but several seconds may pass before you make sense of the shape so that it can be perceived as, say, a table or chair. Look at *Figure 8.2*. Concentrate on the black as the foreground figure and on the white as the background. What do you see? Now reverse the process: black as background and white as figure. What do you see now? In both cases the stimulus is the same but the switch between figure and ground causes us to perceive different things.

Camouflage

Sometimes it is advantageous that figure and ground merge: the zebra's stripes, the cheetah's spots, and the markings on many species of butterfly evolved to help the species blend into the background to avoid detection.

Figure 8.2: Concentrate first on the black areas as the foreground figure and the white area as background. What do you see? Now concentrate on the white area as the figure. What do you see?

Perceiving is an active process

Figure–ground effects are not found only with visual stimuli: an ornithologist can hear birdsong against other background noises; the music lover will be able to distinguish the violins against the rest of the orchestra; whilst the gourmet can taste the subtlety of herbs and spices against the background of meat or vegetable. The crucial point here is that whilst we might all be receiving a similar sensory input, the experience of that input may be very different for different people. Perception is not a static process but very much an active one as we select, interpret, and attempt to understand what is happening around us.

Most of the time we are able to use our visual system to give us accurate information about our world. However, there are special cases where the visual system makes errors. The most common example of this is the *illusion.*

VISUAL ILLUSIONS

Look at *Figure 8.3,* the well-known *arrow illusion* (or the Müller-Lyer illusion to use the correct name). The figure with the fins pointing outwards looks longer than the one with the fins pointing inwards although, of course, both lines are exactly the same length. The effect is not confined to fins: the second illusion, the *railway lines* (or *Ponzo*) *illusion* is another example. Whilst both vertical lines are the same length, the top line looks longer than the bottom. No matter which way you turn the book the effect remains.

Whilst illusions are amusing, they may also have an important role in helping us understand more about how perception works. Indeed, as research has shown that other animals are also deceived in this way, there must be something very fundamental about the nature of illusions. However, whilst many theories have been advanced to explain illusions, the most promising combines two facets of our visual perception – *perspective* and *size constancy.*

Look again at the arrow illusion and concentrate on the arrow to the left. Could it be the corner of a room? Now look at the arrow on the right. Could it be the edge of a building near to us? The corner seems furthest away, the edge of the building closer. Similarly with the railway lines, our sense of perspective shows them receding into the distance.

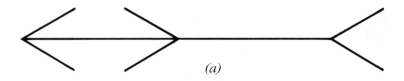

(a)

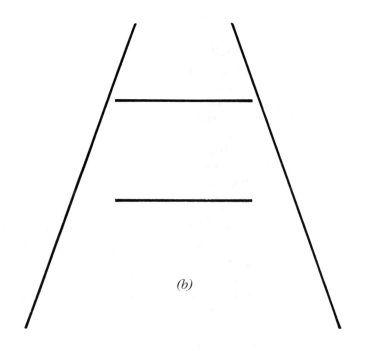

(b)

Figure 8.3: (a) The Müller-Lyer illusion; *(b)* The Ponzo illusion

There is a problem, however, in that if perspective is operating, why does the arrow which should be *furthest* away, and the vertical line which should be furthest away, appear *closer?* Part of the answer may lie in the phenomenon of *size constancy.* We know that the further away an object is, the smaller the image it makes on our retina. As we perceive an object as being further away, so our visual system compensates by increasing the apparent size of what we see. This phenomenon is called size constancy. To compensate for distance we see objects as larger than they should be on the basis of the size of image they produce on the retina. Test this for yourself with Exercise 8.1.

With illusions these two processes may lead to confusion: perspective tells us to look for distance, and in so doing we automatically compensate for distance by enlarging the line which should be, perspective tells us, furthest away. With the illusions shown, both the vertical lines of arrows and the horizontal 'sleepers' of the railway lines are, of course, exactly the same length. In most situations we would have a multitude of other perceptual cues to check our perception against, but with these figures no such checks are available and so we make errors.

Susceptibility to illusions may be a product of learning. The Zulu culture, for example, is based on curves: rounded huts, rounded doors, and even farmland is ploughed in curves – a true 'circular culture' unlike our own which is based on straight lines. Zulus are not misled by illusions of the type in *Figure 8.3.* This indicates that our experience of illusions may be a product of our learning from the environment.

PERCEIVING MOVEMENT

Up to this point we have concentrated on perception of stationary objects. However, our world is not a static one; movement occurs continually and we must be able to perceive it.

The physical processes of seeing movement can be likened to running your fingernail down your arm. As your nail moves, it traces a pattern of sensation as successive sensory tactile receptors are stimulated. So as an image moves across our visual field a pattern of sensation is formed across the visual receptors in the eye's retina. This is, of course, an immensely intricate procedure. Consider the difference between perception of an object moving across your field of vision, and moving your head to look around you. In the first instance, you see the object as moving, yet in the second case the world remains stationary. Clearly our perceptual system can distinguish between the two, integrating information from the eyes with sensations from neck and eye muscles, to say that it is your body, not the world, which is moving.

Auto-kinetic effect

Movement can also be illusory. Try this simple test. Sit in a darkened room, staring at a single spot of light such as a pencil torch. After a few seconds the light will appear to dance around in an erratic manner. This is called the *auto-kinetic effect* (and was used by Muzafer Sherif in his experiment on conformity described on page 89). The eyes have no 'framework' within which to focus and slight eye muscle tremor causes loss of fixation and so apparent movement of the light.

Another example comes from the fact that we tend to assume that of any two objects the smaller one will be moving and the larger will be stationary. Thus on a clear night the moon appears still in the sky, yet when large thin clouds pass in front of the moon it seems to fly across the sky whilst the clouds remain stationary.

There is evidence to suggest that humans, like other animals, are born with some functioning perceptual abilities, including the ability to discriminate colour, size, and visual direction. Indeed, an infant only ten minutes old will correctly move its head in the direction of a noise. However, it is also clear that some perceptual skills have to be learned; very young babies, for example, have a limited ability to follow movement. The eye–muscle co-ordination needed to perceive movement has to be practised and shaped-up through trial and error. Other more elaborate perceptual discriminations require yet more learning; successful wine-tasting, for example, needs far more than taste buds. In considering such learned abilities we turn to the study of the influences of other people on perception.

SOCIAL INFLUENCES ON PERCEPTION

Alongside learning through trial and error, as in the baby example, social learning can have a powerful effect on the way we perceive our world.

Stereotypes

A classic example illustrating the influence of social factors on perception is an experiment conducted in 1947 by Gordon Allport and Leo Postman, two American researchers. People were shown for a short period of time a picture of an interior of a tube train. A number of passengers were seated whilst in the centre of the picture a black man was arguing with a white man. The white man held an open razor in his hand. When asked to describe the picture, approximately half of those taking part in the experiment said that they had seen the black man holding the razor. It seems that on the bais of racial stereotypes some (white) people *expected* to see the black person as the aggressor, and so reported seeing not what was actually there but what they thought should have been there.

Another example is the research first carried out in the late 1940s and early 1950s examining the notion of perceptual defence, of which the most cited is that of Elliott McGinnies.

Perceptual defence

A typical procedure is to show a person a series of words at a very fast speed. The person's task, as the same word is flashed on the screen at slower and slower speeds, is to say what the word is as soon as she or he is able to see it. Of the words shown, some are neutral whilst others are 'taboo' words, most commonly with some sexual meaning. As the words are shown, a measure of galvanic skin response (that is, changes in the electrical conductivity of the skin) is recorded as an indication of emotional reaction.

It was found that typically people were slower to recognize the taboo words than the neutral words. However, the interesting finding came with emotional response. As might be expected, the taboo words caused a greater emotional response than the neutral words, but in many cases the emotional response, measured by sensitive monitoring of the physical reflexes, was found *before* the person reported seeing the word. It was as though the word had been seen but, because of its taboo qualities, was blocked from awareness.

More recent studies, however, have failed to replicate these results. This may well reflect the change from the 1950s to the present day in the emotional loading attached to certain words. Books, magazines, television, and films have all changed in their use of language over the past two or three decades, making us more familiar with, and perhaps less sensitive to, such words.

In conclusion, we can study perception from many perspectives: the physical, biological workings of our sensory systems, the processing and organization of perceived information in the central nervous system, and the psychology of perception from the point of view of learning to use it, and the social influences which affect it. Perception is, then, of fundamental importance, yet it is only part of all our many abilities and skills. Not only must we be able to perceive what is happening around us, we must be able to keep that information for future reference. This ability to store details of what we have perceived is, of course, *memory;* and it is to the workings of memory that we now turn our attention.

MEMORY

As we perceive events in the world around us so we require some system for dealing with the incoming information. The system which carries out this task we call memory. It has been suggested that memory consists of three stages: the first is the placing of the information into a store, this is called *encoding;* the second stage is the holding of the information, termed *storage;* and finally there is the ability to have access to the store, termed *retrieval.*

ENCODING INFORMATION IN MEMORY

The process of encoding is the transformation of a physical event – say a sight or a smell – into a form, or *code* suitable for memory to hold. How encoding occurs is not fully understood, but it can be thought of as the link between perception and memory. When information enters any of our sensory systems a perfect representation of the stimulus, the sight, sound, etc., can be held for a fraction of a second. In the visual system it is thought that this brief sensory memory, or *iconic memory,* is dependent upon both the retina and some part of the brain. The parallel system for auditory input is called *echoic memory.*

ATTENTION

The classic experiments in this field were conducted in 1960 by George Sperling. It was discovered that the holding of information in iconic memory is not under voluntary control, and that the sensory memory fades, or *decays*, very rapidly – in about 500 milliseconds. After this period of decay only a small proportion of what entered the system is retained for storage. What information is retained is that which has been selected through means of *attention*. During the encoding process attention may be directed towards a number of properties of the stimulus.

Take for example the word CAMEL. It is likely that several features of this word will have impressed themselves upon you. It is in black letters; it is in upper case; it has five letters. As well as these physical characteristics the word has certain semantic features: it is an animal, it has a hump, it comes from certain parts of the world. You may have other associations with the word, such as having seen a camel at the zoo, or perhaps even ridden one. Thus your encoding of the word CAMEL takes place not on just one, but on many dimensions. It is possible that during encoding we may not be aware of all the dimensions being used: in other words, in some instances, the process may be automatic.

Attention is clearly of importance at the encoding stage. We can choose to direct our attention towards a particular event, say a television programme, with the result that we will encode more of it than if it were on but we 'were not really watching'. Whilst we can exercise some control over our attention, it is also influenced by a number of other factors such as previous learning or our mood. When feeling threatened, for example, we may notice personal comments to which we would not pay attention when feeling safe or friendly.

The 'cocktail party effect'

However, we do attend to a vast range of stimuli which are filtered out before we are even aware of them. The 'cocktail party effect' provides a good example: against the unintelligible background noise and conversation we will pick out our own name if it is spoken. Our attention has not been directed at every conversation in the room, but a continual monitoring process has alerted us to any external stimulus to which we might need to respond. The rest of the hubbub is allowed to decay from sensory memory without alerting us.

STORAGE IN MEMORY

The information which does not decay from sensory memory, that was selected out through attention, passes into storage. It is useful to conceive of memory storage as comprising two stages, *short-term memory* (STM) and *long-term memory* (LTM).

The magical number 7, plus or minus 2

STM is the part of the memory system which holds information for short periods of time. When we look up a new telephone number and remember it whilst dialling we are using STM. One of the main features of STM is that it has a very limited capacity. So uniform are the experimental findings on this that George Miller has used the phrase 'the magical number seven, plus or minus two' to describe the capabilities of STM. Most adults have a STM capacity – or 'memory span' – of between five and nine items, be these numbers, letters, words, names, ideas, or whatever.

Chunking

It is possible, however, to boost the amount of information held in STM by a strategy called *chunking*. Look, just for a second, at this string of letters RA–CGBI–TVU–SA and now close the page and recall as many as you can. You probably found it difficult to recall all the letters. Suppose we rearrange the spacing so that the string now reads RAC–GB–ITV–USA. Now close the book and see if your memory has improved. The ten letters have been reduced to four units, well within our capabilities.

Rehearsal

Information held in STM is quickly lost. How soon after making the telephone call do you forget the number? Minutes at the most. And so if we want to retain the information we have to employ some strategy to enable it to pass from STM into LTM. Two explanations for this process have been put forward. The first is consistent with the model of memory proposed by Richard Atkinson and Richard Shiffrin in 1968 as shown in *Figure 8.4* and relies on the notion of *rehearsal*. The information in LTM is rehearsed by strategies such as repeating the items, or by forming associations between the new material and material already held in LTM. With sufficient rehearsal the material in

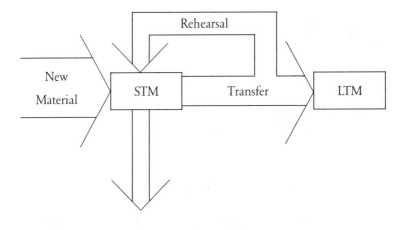

Figure 8.4: The 'rehearsal' model of STM and LTM. *(After Atkinson & Shiffrin, 1968.)*

STM is transferred to LTM where it becomes a more permanent memory.

An alternative view, suggested in 1972 by Fergus Craik and Robert Lockhart, places primary importance not on rehearsal but on *depth of processing*. They propose that any stimulus is analysed in stages of varying sophistication. These stages move from low levels of analysis such as shape and brightness, to higher levels which may involve meaning or connections to other items in memory. Craik and Lockhart proposed that the depth of processing determines how durable a memory becomes. Higher levels of processing give more durable memories.

Organizing memories

By whatever means, we are able to pass information from short-term storage to long-term storage. Having achieved this, how then do we store the memories? It would obviously be highly inefficient to have to scan everything in LTM every time we wanted to remember something; we must have some system of organization.

Endel Tulving suggested the broad distinction between *episodic memory,* remembering specific events and incidents, and *semantic memory,* which is remembering knowledge of various types.

Remembering what you had for dinner yesterday is exercising episodic memory, whilst recalling the capital of Holland is testing semantic memory.

A further refinement to the theory of organization within memory was suggested by Alan Collins and Ross Quillian. They proposed a network of concepts, such that from a general level the concepts give access to much more specific, detailed information. *Figure 8.5* shows how part of a network might look for the concept 'animal'.

RETRIEVAL FROM MEMORY

Retrieval from STM requires a search through the short-term store for the item we want. This takes place at great speed, occurring in just thousandths of a second. We know, however, that information can be lost from STM: how often have you looked up a telephone number only to forget it before completing dialling? Research has clearly shown that we best remember the first and last items which went into STM: it is the middle ones which we naturally lose. Then, if we are distracted by someone talking, or perhaps looking at more numbers before dialling, we continue to remember the first items but lose the later ones as well as the middle ones. As STM is of limited capacity ($7\pm$ 2, remember), when it becomes full, new information displaces existing material. The longer the material has been in storage the better its chances of survival, which may explain why elderly people can clearly recall their childhood but cannot remember what happened yesterday.

You may recall that previously, using the example of the word CAMEL, it was suggested that information is encoded into LTM along a number of dimensions. It follows then that in order to retrieve from LTM we need a *cue* linked to a dimension of encoding to evoke the memory. Thus our memory may be 'jogged' by any number of cues: a song on the radio may evoke memories of people we have known; a smell, perhaps perfume or food, may bring back thoughts of a previous experience; a new author may 'remind' us of one we already know by their style; the word CAMEL may now remind you of this book.

Where did you learn it?

Researchers, like Alan Baddeley, have carried out studies to

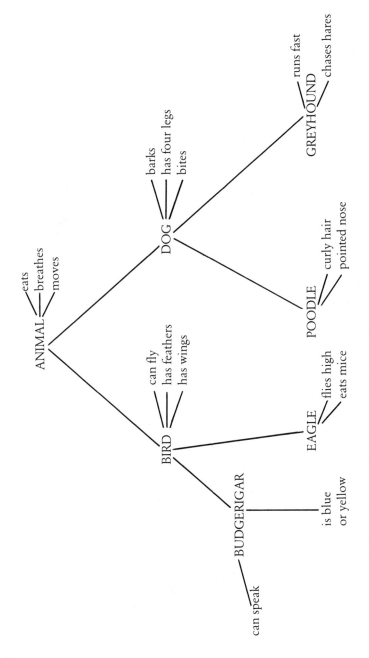

Figure 8.5: A sample from the network of concepts for 'animal'.

demonstrate that successful memory can depend on the presence of contextual cues. In an experiment with divers, Baddeley and his colleague found that words the divers learned underwater were best recalled underwater, and words learned on land were best recalled on land.

Were you sober at the time?

As well as environmental context, the person's own internal state at the time of encoding may also be important for later retrieval. This phenomenon of *state dependent memory* has been shown in a number of studies. In one such study it was found that heavy drinkers who hid money or alcohol when drunk could not remember where it was when sober. However, when drunk again they remembered where the money or drink was concealed. This effect has been found with a wide range of other drugs as well as alcohol.

Recall

In using LTM we might be trying either to recall some information, or we may be attempting to recognize some object placed before us. The weight of experimental evidence shows that recognition is superior to recall. Indeed, so good are our powers of recognition that it makes little difference whether or not contextual cues are reproduced; the memory will be highly accurate regardless.

In the case of recall we need cues to find the memory; the better the cues the better the chances of successful retrieval. With recognition a multitude of cues are presented so that we do not have such problems with accessing the memory. Of course once we have access we must then decide whether the memory is correct for the occasion. Therefore even if access is made easy there is no guarantee that our decision will be the right one: we all make errors of recall and recognition.

Remembering faces

Studies of recognition memory have found that memory for pictures is better than for words, sentences, or patterns, and memory for faces has been shown to be particularly good. Hayden Ellis provides a thorough review of the important variables in remembering faces, and this topic is of special importance when considering eyewitness memory. Investigation of eyewitness memory has been extensive over the last decade and a good summary is provided by Elizabeth Loftus. The accuracy of recognition, as well as recall, has been shown to be adversely affected by such factors as perceiving violence, the complexity of the incident, and the type of questioning used to elicit memory responses. Thus one of the main thrusts of this research has been to point to the gap between memory in the experimental laboratory and in real life. Good memory performance under optimum conditions does not mean that the same level of ability will be found outside the laboratory. Caution must be exercised before we make rules such as 'facial memory is good therefore eyewitness identification will be mostly correct', when, in fact, this is not always the case.

Two ways in which you can improve your own memory are shown in Exercises 8.2 and 8.3.

FORGETTING

Whilst we use our memory successfully time and time again there are occasions when it lets us down. How many students have found that, when most needed in an examination, the vital fact was 'gone'? We have all experienced the frustration of not being able to 'place a face', or putting something in a safe place then not remembering where. Forgetting occurs in a variety of ways and, in this final section, we shall see what psychology has discovered about failure of memory.

The forgetting curve

A typical memory curve is shown in *Figure 8.6:* forgetting is rapid at first but gradullay slows down. There are two explanations for this pattern of memory loss. The first is that as time goes by the memory simply decays; the second is that subsequent learning and experience interfere with existing memories. The weight of experimental evidence favours the interference theory. Not only does subsequent learning interfere with memory – *retroactive-interference* – but existing memories can also cause confusion and forgetting when we try to remember new material – *proactive interference.*

Alongside interference there is, as already discussed, the need to provide contextual cues and personal states to assist memory. In some instances the context or state at encoding or at recall can be so extreme that recollection is very difficult. Crime victims and survivors of

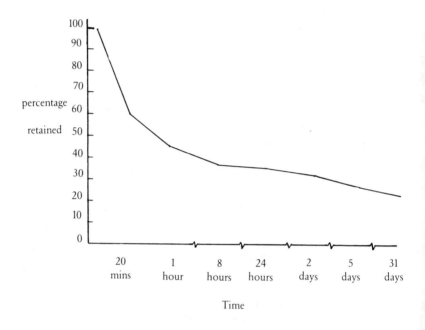

Figure 8.6: A typical forgetting curve.

disasters may well be unable to recall what happened to them. The student sitting the examination may be gripped by panic and thoughts of impending failure, making it impossible to recall all those well-learned facts (ironically when the examination is finished often everything comes flooding back). The emotions or arousal at both encoding and retrieval acted to block access to the memory, a phenomenon which might be thought of as repression in Freudian terms. In most cases the memory loss will be selective, but in extreme cases it can be complete, resulting in total amnesia. Fortunately total amnesia usually lasts only a day or two.

In total our facilities of perception and memory generally function smoothly and in synchrony to enable us to be aware of and respond to our environment and its demands. In the next chapter these processes are taken one stage further with a look at our ability to learn and to think.

Recommended Reading

Baddeley, A. (1982). *Your Memory: A User's Guide.* Harmondsworth: Penguin.

Bruce, V. & Green, P. (1985). *Visual Perception: Physiology, Psychology and Ecology.* London: Lawrence Erlbaum Associates.

Gregory, R.L. (1966). *Eye and Brain.* London: Weidenfeld & Nicolson.

Loftus, E.F. (1979). *Eyewitness Testimony.* Cambridge, Massachusetts: Harvard University Press.

Vernon, M.D. (1971). *The Psychology of Perception,* 2nd ed. Harmondsworth: Penguin.

Zechmeister, E.G. & Nyberg, S.E. (1982). *Human Memory: an Introduction to Research and Theory.* Monterey, California: Brooks/Cole.

References

Allport, G.W. & Postman, L.J. (1947). *The Psychology of Rumour.* New York: Henry Hold. [Social expectation and memory.]

Atkinson, R.C. & Shiffrin, R.M. (1968). Human memory: a proposed system, and its control processes. In K.W. Spence (ed.), *The Psychology of Learning and Motivation: Advances in Research and Theory, Vol.2.* New York: Academic Press. [The influential 'rehearsal' model of memory.]

Collins, A.M. & Quillian, M.R. (1972). Experiments on semantic memory and language comprehension. In L.W. Gregg (ed.), *Cognition in Learning and Memory.* New York: Wiley. [Oragnization of concepts in memory.]

Craik, F.I.M. & Lockhart, R.S. (1972). Levels of processing: a framework for memory research. *Journal of Verbal Learning and Verbal Behaviour, 11,* 671–684. [The alternative depth of processing model of memory.]

Ellis, H.D. (1975). Recognizing faces. *British Journal of Psychology, 66,* 409–426. Research on face recognition.]

Godden, D.R. & Baddeley, A.D. (1975). Context-dependent memory in two natural environments: on land and underwater. *British Journal of Psychology, 66,* 325–331. [Context effects on recall accuracy.]

Hubel, D.H. (1963). The visual cortex. *Scientific American, 209,* 54–62. [Research into the organization of perception within the brain.]

McGinnies, E. (1949). Emotionality and perceptual defence. *Psychological Review, 56,* 244–251. [Recognition, or lack of it, for taboo words.]

Miller, G.A. (1956). The magical number seven plus or minus two: some limits on our capacity for processing information. *Psychological Review, 63,* 81–97. [The capacity of storage in STM.]

Sperling, G. (1960). The information available in brief visual presentations. *Psychological Monographs, 74.* Whole no. 498. [Sensory and iconic memory.]

Tulving, E. (1972). Episodic and semantic memory. In E. Tulving & W. Donaldson (eds), *Organization of Memory.* New York: Academic Press. [The distinction between memories for knowledge and events.]

A DEMONSTRATION OF SIZE CONSTANCY

This is a very simple example of the extent to which we compensate for the size of an object as it recedes from us.

INSTRUCTIONS: Hold your arms out directly in front of you, at right angles to your body and parallel to each other. Lift up each hand such that each palm faces away from you – imagine that your hands are touching the vertical face of a wall, with each hand wholly in contact with it.

☐ Now move one hand, keeping its position exactly as before, towards you and hold it at the level of your other elbow but keeping its position a chest's breadth from that elbow. Look back and forth between both hands. They probably look more or less the same size with the nearer one just a little larger.

☐ Now allow the hand closer to you to move so that its outline overlaps slightly that of your other hand and align the base of the near hand with that of the far hand.

☐ Observe both your hands. Notice that suddenly you become aware that the distant hand seems very much smaller. In fact, it is approximately half the size of the hand held at elbow level.

The illusion that both are hands of approximately the same size – a fact which we all know well – cannot be maintained once the two retinal images overlap. The compensation for size which you made whilst the hands were not overlapping, but were at different distances from you, cannot be maintained once a direct comparison of retinal images is forced on you.

ORGANIZATION AND MEMORY

☐ Ask five friends to look at *List A* for one minute (hiding *List B*).

☐ Then remove the list and ask them to recall as many words as they can within three minutes.

☐ Calculate their average score.

☐ Now repeat the procedure using *List B* and another set of friends.

☐ Compare the average recall of the two groups.

☐ Does presentation in an ordered form lead to better recall?

List A	*List B*
Slate	Metal
Granite	Copper
Copper	Gold
Steel	Iron
Iron	Lead
Gold	Silver
Jewel	Alloy
Silver	Brass
Sapphire	Bronze
Diamond	Steel
Metal	Jewel
Limestone	Diamond
Ruby	Emerald
Brass	Ruby
Stone	Sapphire
Marble	Stone
Alloy	Granite
Bronze	Limestone
Lead	Marble
Emerald	Slate

CAN MEMORY BE IMPROVED?

INSTRUCTIONS: Read *List A* aloud to a friend, once only, and ask him or her to recall it. Keep a note of the number of correct responses.

☐   Now ask your friend to learn thoroughly this sequence:

One = bun	Two = shoe	Three = tree
Four = door	Five = hive	Six = sticks
Seven = heaven	Eight = gate	Nine = wine
Ten = hen		

☐   Now read *List B* having instructed your friend to imagine the learned word as you go down the list. So if the first word was 'dog', your friend might imagine a dog eating a bun.

☐   Complete the list and test your friend's recall.

Has memory improved through using this aid?

List A	*List B*
Flag	Head
Save	Cool
Crock	Whiff
Rancher	Trigger
Utter	Faint
Window	Request
Yolk	Talc
Shell	Single
Season	Castle
Cloud	Pylon

9. *Learning and Thinking*

▽ *Learning by association.*
▽ *Learning by consequences.*
▽ *Reinforcement and punishment.*
▽ *Learning by observation.*
▽ *Thinking.*

▽ *Imagery.*
▽ *Concepts.*
▽ *Creative thinking.*
▽ *Problem solving.*

In the previous chapter we considered the workings of memory, suggesting that the ability to use memory is of crucial importance in our lives. When we can use memory accurately and reliably we say that the material in question – names, faces, facts, skills, etc. – has been *learnt*. In everyday usage the word learning is generally taken to refer to the acquisition of new knowledge or skills. In psychology the term is used in a broader sense to include any change in behaviour that occurs as a result of *experience* rather than *maturation*. A change in the type of music you enjoy might well be described as being due to learning about classical music for instance.

Thus memory and learning are two sides of the same coin: one presupposes the other; we cannot learn without memory and memory holds what is learnt. How does material come to be learnt? There are three theories of particular importance which help to answer this question. We will examine each in turn.

LEARNING BY ASSOCIATION

It was the Russian physiologist and Nobel Prize winner, Ivan Pavlov, who first described learning by association. When studying the canine digestive system Pavlov noticed something unusual; as all dog owners know, their pets salivate at the sight of food, but Pavlov saw his dogs salivating when no food was present. Careful observation revealed that certain cues, such as the sight of the food dish, made the dogs behave as if food were present. Could this phenomenon be reproduced experimentally?

The starting point in Pavlov's experiments was the naturally occurring salivation. This salivation Pavlov called an unconditioned response (UCR) which follows an unconditioned stimulus (UCS), the food. The term unconditioned, meaning not needing to be learnt, indicates that the action occurs naturally, as a reflex. Other examples of unconditioned responses include blinking at a very bright light, or jumping at a loud noise.

During the first phase of Pavlov's experiment a bell was sounded, then after a few seconds food was presented so that the dog salivated and ate. This procedure, linking bell and food, was repeated a number of times. In the second phase the bell was sounded but no food was given; it was found that the dog now salivated in response to the bell alone. Whenever the bell was sounded the dog salivated and continued to do so even though no food was given. The bell had become a conditioned stimulus (CS) with the power to elicit salivation not as a natural response, but as a conditioned response (CR). The process is illustrated in *Figure 9.1.* To distinguish this type of conditioning from other methods (see next section) Pavlov's procedures are termed CLASSICAL CONDITIONING.

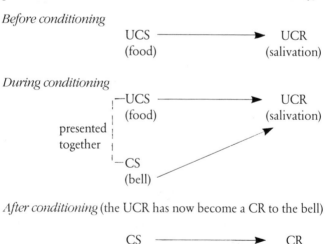

Before conditioning

UCS ⟶ UCR
(food)　(salivation)

During conditioning

┌─UCS ⟶ UCR
│　(food)　(salivation)
presented │
together │
└─CS
　(bell)

After conditioning (the UCR has now become a CR to the bell)

CS ⟶ CR
(bell)　(salivation)

Figure 9.1: Steps in classical conditioning illustrated using Pavlov's experiment.

Generalization versus discrimination

Further studies of classical conditioning revealed a number of other interesting features. A conditioned response can also be elicited by things that are *similar* to the original conditioned stimulus, like a different bell of similar tone. This extension of the range of stimuli which can produce the conditioned response is called *stimulus generalization.* If, however, the animal fails to respond to another bell, too different from the original, the opposite to generalization has occurred, that is *discrimination.* Further, if the dog is continually exposed to the sound of the bell without food ever appearing, it salivates less and less, and eventually the CR is *extinguished.*

Watson's Behaviourism

The idea that behaviour could be learnt rather than being the result of some biological or neurological event, or a symptom of some psychodynamic force, was to revolutionize the study of psychology. The American psychologist, John Watson, took Pavlov's findings as the basis by which to understand all human activity and his article in 1913, 'Psychology as the behaviourist views it', laid the foundation for decades of further study. Simply, Watson argued that we are born with certain innate stimulus-response (S–R) reflexes. Through the process of classical conditioning more and more complex behaviours are learnt to produce our full behavioural repertoire. We know now that Watson's theories are too simplistic and an S–R model of human activity cannot provide all the ansers. However, in deeming that behaviour (rather than introspection, for example) was the proper subject matter of psychology, Watson shaped the work of following generations of psychologists.

Whilst learning by association does not explain all learning, it does occur, as we all know. As a simple example: play a piece of music which you haven't listened to for a long time. Whilst it is playing see what memories you experience: people, places, emotions, conversations, images, may all trickle back to awareness. The music is linked with the events in memory and now becomes a stimulus to elicit the associated responses learnt in your past.

Once bitten . . .

Classical conditioning has also been used to explain why we develop certain fears. (See pages 143 – 145 on phobias.) Consider a child bitten by a brown dog: the fear and pain from the bite may well be linked with all brown dogs so that the next time one is seen the child becomes anxious and fearful. Further, the child may become afraid not only of brown dogs, but black dogs also, of brown cats, or animals with four legs, and so on. In other words, the learnt fear may generalize to animals with similar attributes to the original brown dog. Over a period of time dogs will come and go without biting the child, so the fear gradually subsides as the child grows older: we would say the fear has *extinguished*. However, in some cases fears do not extinguish; they last for a lifetime. To explain this we need to look at another type of learning – learning by reward and punishment.

LEARNING BY CONSEQUENCES

It is difficult to see how all our actions are responses to a conditioned stimulus associated with a physiological reflex. In 1913 Edward Thorndike suggested that perhaps some of our behaviours are learnt by trial-and-error in which the person (or animal in Thorndike's studies) gradually learns that certain actions produce certain outcomes. Thorndike called this INSTRUMENTAL LEARNING, because the person learns that his or her own behaviour is instrumental in gaining rewards or avoiding unpleasantness. From this position various schools of thought evolved within behaviourism, but by far the most influential has been that of radical behaviourism as developed by the American psychologist Burrhus Skinner.

Burrhus Skinner

Skinner argued that two types of behaviour exist: RESPONDENT BEHAVIOUR is like that described by Pavlov; OPERANT BEHAVIOUR – that behaviour which operates on the environment – is analogous to Thorndike's instrumental behaviour. The distinction may be thought of as the former being *elicited* by a conditioned stimulus, whilst the latter is *emitted* by the person with some aim to be achieved. In describing operant learning Skinner, arguably, has made the single most important contribution to the field of psychology.

Skinner's operant conditioning

As was the fashion of the time, Skinner's early experiments were carried out with animals such as squirrels, pigeons and rats. In a typical experiment the rat would be placed in a closed box – now known as a

Skinner Box – and carefully observed. Typically the rat explores its environment, walking and sniffing as rats do. At one end of the box is a bar which, if pressed, releases food into a small container. Eventually the rat's explorations take it close to the bar, and when this occurs the experimenter arranges for a pellet of food to be automatically dropped into the box. The rat is now attracted to that part of the box. As it explores further it touches the bar; again food is delivered. Now the rat returns to the bar, this time paying it great attention. Whilst exploring the bar the rat will probably place its front paws on the bar causing it to depress. As this happens the machinery goes into operation and food is delivered. After eating, the rat returns to the bar to press once more; again food is delivered. Thus through a gradual process of reward for approximations to the desired behaviour to finally rewarding the 'correct' behaviour (bar-pressing) the animal has learnt how to produce a certain consequence: the delivery of food. The behaviour has been *shaped up* by reinforcement, with food as the reinforcer in this example. We can see everyday examples of the use of reinforcers in the use of sweets to increase 'good' behaviour in children and the use of money to increase the productivity of the worker.

A great deal of research has been carried out into the effects on behaviour of varying the amount of reinforcement, the type of reinforcer, and the rate (or schedule) at which reinforcement is presented. If you would like to try out a simple exercise on the effects of reinforcement see Exercise 9.1.

The process of operant learning can be refined even further by introducing a signal to indicate whether or not a behaviour will be rewarded. The experimenter might arrange things so that food will follow a bar press only when a light is on in the box. The rat would quickly learn that it was only worthwhile pressing when the light was on; in other words, the rat has learnt to *discriminate* when the behaviour should be produced. This relationship between signal (the light), behaviour (bar press), and outcome (food) is called a *three-term contingency*.

REINFORCEMENT AND PUNISHMENT

In the example of the rat pressing the lever the outcome was pleasant, from the rat's point of view, and so the behaviour was repeated. We said that the rat had learnt by reinforcement. But what if a particular act leads to an unpleasant consequence? Suppose the rat's bar press had led to a mild electric shock in the floor of the Skinner Box, then the bar press is less likely to be repeated. Here the rat has learnt what *not* to do. This type of learning, the opposite to learning by reinforcement, is called punishment. The rule, in operant learning, is that if the frequency of a behaviour is holding steady or increasing it is being reinforced; if a behaviour is decreasing in frequency it is being punished. Further, we can distinguish between two types of reinforcement and punishment.

Take the example of a school teacher faced with a pupil who is not doing enough work. The teacher wishes to increase the amount of work, or in operant terms, wants to reinforce working. The teacher has two strategies available: extra work may be rewarded by some treat, say more recreation time; alternatively, if the child produces more work then something the child dislikes, extra homework for instance, will be taken away. Both strategies will increase work – hence the work is being reinforced – but in one case by giving something rewarding, in the other by removing something aversive. In the first case the teacher is using *positive* reinforcement, and in the second case *negative* reinforcement.

Old habits

The notion of negative reinforcement helps to explain why some fears last for a long time. We mentioned earlier that a fear, such as being afraid of dogs, could be acquired through learning by association; such a fear can then be maintained by negative reinforcement. If the person continually avoids the feared object, such as dogs from our example, then this behaviour is serving the function of removing something unpleasant, that is, the possibility of feeling frightened. The fearful behaviour is thus being negatively reinforced and it may well persist for a long time.

Let us now suppose that our unfortunate school teacher is faced with another pupil who continually shouts and interrupts in class. Unlike the work, this is behaviour which the teacher wants to eliminate (or punish, in operant terms). The teacher might arrange for the unwanted behaviour to have unpleasant consequences, such as being given extra work, or being kept in after school. Alternatively, the teacher might arrange for the disruption to lead to the loss of something pleasant such as a place in the school games team. Both strategies should reduce, or punish, the unwanted behaviour; one by direct, unpleasant action – positive punishment – the other by removing something pleasant. It is important to note that the term punishment has a specific technical meaning here; it simply refers to the effect of the consequence on the frequency of the behaviour. Punishment, in this sense, does not mean physical pain or distressing aversive events.

Chaining simple behaviours

This system of learning by reinforcement and punishment has been extended to attempt to explain all learning other than respondent learning. Most of our behaviour is much more complicated than bar pressing, so how is that achieved? We can see, if we analyse more sophisticated behaviours, that they are composed of a number of simpler 'bits' of behaviour strung together. For example, in teaching a child how to get dressed we begin with basics such as reinforcing putting arms in sleeves, then doing-up buttons, through to reinforcing tying shoelaces. This linking together of simple behaviours through reinforcement to form a new more complex behaviour – 'getting dressed' in the example – is called *chaining*. Eventually, of course, it is only the 'whole' behaviour which receives the reward.

Private behaviours

Modern-day behaviourists apply this view of learning to understanding all behaviour (except respondent learning). One of the charges often laid against behaviourists is that they deny, or at least ignore, thoughts, feelings, emotions, and other inner processes. However, behaviourists probably spend more time debating 'private events', as Skinner puts it, than most other psychologists. In *About Behaviourism*, (1974) Skinner attempts to show how such human abilities as perception, dreaming, and thought can be fitted into behavioural theory. Derek Blackman, a leading British behaviourist, provides a clear statement of the position of the contemporary operant learning theorist. Exercise 9.2 shows how behaviour analysis can be applied to complex behaviour.

LEARNING BY OBSERVATION

One of the basic tenets of operant learning is that the consequences of a behaviour must be experienced for learning to take place. In other words, acquisition of a behaviour depends on direct reinforcement. Whilst a number of psychologists had suggested that learning might occur without reinforcement, it was the American psychologist Albert Bandura who formulated the idea of OBSERVATIONAL LEARNING. Indeed, observational learning was to become the keystone of Bandura's influential *social learning theory.*

Doing as others do

Bandura argued that for much of our life we are surrounded by other people displaying a huge variety of behaviours, all of which we are free to observe. Through observation we select and learn a multitude of behaviours; note, not by carrying out the behaviour and experiencing the consequences, but simply by watching how other people, or *models,* behave.

The most celebrated demonstration of observational learning was reported by Bandura and his colleagues in 1961. Nursery school children watched one of two adult models: one adult played with a set of small toys, ignoring a large inflated Bobo doll also in the room; the other adult acted violently towards the doll, punching it, hitting it with a mallet and shouting 'Kick him' and 'Hit it in the nose'. Afterwards the children were allowed to play with the doll. The children who had not seen the violent model acted in a normal way towards the doll. However the children who observed the violent behaviour acted in a similar way, hitting the doll and shouting similar phrases. The children had learnt through observation and imitated the modelled behaviour. Later, Bandura showed that the process can also work in reverse. Children who observed a model being chastised for aggressive behaviour were *less* likely to imitate the model's actions.

Bandura described four stages in the process.

1. We can only learn through observation if we pay *attention* to the model's actions. However, the way we focus our attention is not random; we particularly observe models whom we see as attractive, or successful, or have high status, or whom we know from previous observation. Thus if we were advising a cricketer on the art of batting, we are more likely to suggest paying attention to Ian Botham's style than to that of a batsman in the local park.

2. Having observed the model we must remember what happened. This is the *retention* stage. Bandura suggests that we store both a visual image, to be later viewed in our 'mind's eye', and a verbal description of the model's actions. Hence our cricketer might try to visualize Ian Botham hitting sixes, whilst describing the action as 'Botham has an orthodox stance, a loose grip with the bottom hand, appears relaxed, and hits hard through the line of the ball'.

3.   In the third stage, *motor reproduction*, the stored images and verbal descriptions are translated into action – we attempt to reproduce, or imitate, what has been observed. Thus our cricketer will practise batting like Ian Botham. Needless to say, the first attempts will not match the behaviour of the model. A great deal of time and effort, depending on the complexity of the behaviour, will be needed to bring one's own actions into line with the model's. However, given even a great amount of practice there is no guarantee of success. Ian Botham may well possess attributes that cannot be learnt: his physical size and strength, his quickness of reactions, and excellent motor co-ordination. So practise in the 'Botham style' may not produce another Botham, but it may well improve our cricketer's batting. Essential to this improvement is some feedback on the accuracy of reproduction. Such as watching one's own performance, or having another person say how accurate the imitation is.

4.   Finally, whether we continue to do what has been observed depends on our *motivation*. The motivation provides the spur for observational learning to continue. Bandura suggests that there are three aspects to motivation – external reinforcement, vicarious reinforcement, and self-reinforcement.

External reinforcement is analogous to learning by consequences. Thus, if our cricketer scores more runs, wins more matches, and is praised by team-mates, the new batting style is likely to be retained. A series of low scores may mean a new model is sought. (This incorporating of the principles of reinforcement and punishment shows how social learning theory is an extension of operant behaviourism rather than a competing set of ideas.)

Vicarious reinforcement is observing the modelled behaviour working (that is, being reinforced) for *other* people. Thus our cricketer might see team-mates scoring more runs the 'Botham-way' and so he vicariously experiences their success. This, in turn, motivates him to use that style.

Self-reinforcement refers to a sense of pride, achievement, a meeting of personal standards in one's own performance. Our cricketer may not only score more runs (external reinforcement) but he also feels a personal satisfaction with the improved performance. In total, if the behaviour is successful the reinforcement systems will motivate the individual towards repeating those actions; next time the

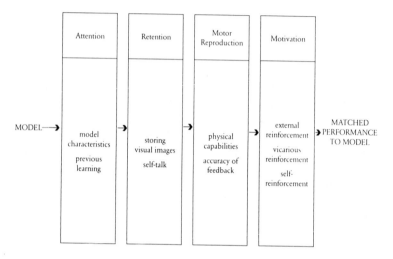

Figure 9.2: Learning by observation (after Bandura, 1977).

person *expects* the behaviour to be successful. If not successful then reinforcement is lacking and the behaviour is less likely to be repeated; we say the person lacks the motivation to act in that particular way. The scheme of learning by observation is shown in *Figure 9.2.*

The study of learning has led to many practical as well as theoretical advances. Education, particularly individually-paced instruction, as with computer-assisted learning, owes much to operant theory. The study of observational learning has alerted us to the potential effects of television for modelling behaviour which might be later imitated as we saw in Chapter 4.

Perhaps the greatest impact has been in the field of clinical psychology where therapies based on the principles of learning by association, through consequences, and by observation have grown and developed over the last 30 years. These therapies, usually called behaviour therapies or behaviour modification, have proved highly beneficial for people suffering a variety of disorders. Indeed, such is their effectiveness that behaviour therapies are now being used not only by psychologists but also by other professionals such as psychiatrists, nurses, social workers and teachers.

THINKING AND THE NATURE OF THOUGHT

In everyday use the word 'thinking' assumes a variety of meanings. Examples include 'I'm trying to think where I put it', in which thinking is synonymous with remembering, and 'Think what you are doing!', where thinking means pay attention. Yet again, a person may say 'I think this or that about the Government'; in which case an opinion or belief is being expressed. If you ask what your friend is doing staring into space, apparently daydreaming, she or he might say, 'Just thinking'. This richness of usage is the starting point for the study of thinking. We must ask what is thought and what are the processes involved in thinking.

The way in which thought is explained depends very much on your theoretical position. Sigmund Freud, for example, distinguished between two types of thought: rational, conscious thought of which we are aware, and non-logical thought occurring at an unconscious level. Other theorists such as Jean Piaget (see page 121) invoke the notion of *schema* – internal representations of physical or psychological activities. Thus babies are said to possess several innate schemata for basic actions such as grasping, crying, sucking and gazing. As the child matures so these basic schemata are elaborated and joined to form more complex cognitive structures (or operations in Piaget's terms). Jerome Bruner similarly suggests that we hold cognitive 'models' of the world constructed through the use of images and symbols such as language. There is also the view, expressed by Frederic Bartlett among others, that thinking is a form of skilled behaviour. Indeed, Burrhus Skinner argues that 'thinking is behaving', with the behaviour occurring at a covert rather than overt level. We also know that damage to certain parts ot the brain impairs ability to think. We should not therefore neglect a physiological component to thought.

However, regardless of our theoretical model, we must still decide what it is that constitutes thought. Two strong candidates emerge – imagery and language.

IMAGERY, LANGUAGE AND THOUGHT

What colour is your front door? In answering this you probably looked in your 'mind's eye' at a picture of your door. We can form images with all our senses; we can 'hear' music, or 'smell' bacon cooking by conjuring up the right image.

Strong and weak imagers

The ability to form and control images is not the same in everyone; some people are strong imagers whilst others have only weak imagery. For those with strong imagery, the images can play an important part in thinking. Albert Einstein said that he evolved his scientific formulations in 'more or less clear images' which could later be reproduced or combined as he thought. Similarly Friedrich Kekulé solved a problem in chemistry when, in a dream, an image formed which showed him the chemical structure (of benzene) which he had sought for some time.

It is possible that in answering the question about the colour of your front door you did not use an image. The words 'your front door' may have a colour associated with them as part of their meaning; symbolic thought, language in this case, provided the answer – an image was not needed. The benefits of symbolic thought will become clear when we discuss concepts.

The exact relationship between language and thought is uncertain and at least three views prevail. The first is that thought is dependent upon language; it is vocabulary and grammar that determine thought. For example, the Hopi Indians have exactly the same word for insect, aeroplane, and air pilot. However, we do not know whether using the same word means that the objects are seen, or thought of, in the same way.

The second view is the opposite, that is, that language is dependent upon thought. This view is seen clearly in Piaget's theory in which as the child's ability to think develops, so language is acquired to further the process of thought. Thus, for Piaget, a pre-linguistic child who sees an action and imitates it is already thinking; language, when it develops, is a tool to assist the process of thinking.

The third view, proposed by the Russian psychologist Lev Vygotsky, is that language and thought are independent. Thinking has the purpose of re-structuring a situation to give it meaning; language is used to communicate. Thus 'cat' has the meaning of a furry animal; to say 'I wish that all cats were friendly' is to communicate something about cats. However, the two abilities do have some degree of overlap: this overlap we call 'verbal thought'. There are, Vygotsky argues, aspects of language such as reciting a poem by heart which are not thinking; and areas of thinking such as imagery and mathematical symbols which are not language.

In total there is no ready answer to what constitutes 'thought'.

Imagery, symbols and language provide some clues, but there is the complicated matter of 'thinking about thinking'. How do we do this? We know we are 'aware' of thinking, but how does the awareness work? The debate has been running since the time of Aristotle and there is no sign of a conclusion. (This topic in relation to other animals is considered in Chapter 11.)

THE PROCESS OF THOUGHT

As thinking is a private experience, investigators have to rely on a person's description of what they are thinking. Introspection, as it is called, was one of the earliest methods used in psychology as we noted in the Introduction. Wilhelm Wundt founded his *Psychologisches Institut* in 1879 in Leipzig with the aim of studying consciousness through introspection. The great difficulty with the method is that it is impossible to check the accuracy of introspection; and also if some thinking takes place outside of awareness, introspection will not reveal it. These problems turned investigators to the study of the results of thought, rather than thought itself. We shall look at several lines of investigation.

CONCEPTS

In the previous chapter we looked at the memory network for 'animal'. This network consists of grouping various attributes, shared by animals, into a single category or *concept*. We hold a vast number of concepts for a range of objects, events, people, and abstract ideas. The great benefit of this is that they allow quick communication: if you say the words 'chair' or 'truth' or 'countryside' most people will understand what you mean; there is no need to describe things in detail. Concepts are of two types. With a classical concept every instance must conform to the rule: all 'husbands' are adult, male and married. Probabilistic concepts, on the other hand, only allow inferences to be made: thus for the concept of 'bird', you might say that 'birds fly', which is *probably* true, but as certain birds do not fly, the statement is not invariably correct. Most of the concepts we use in everyday life are probabilistic; there are usually exceptions to the rule.

One of the processes of thinking is the combining of concepts. To state that 'Skinner is a psychologist' is to use a single concept, psychologist. However, to say 'Skinner is a psychologist who studies behaviour', is to combine the concepts of psychologist, study, and behaviour to give a new meaning.

Not all concepts are verbal, some are held in images. The concept of 'middle C' exists as an image which I can 'hear'. By combining this auditory image with those of other notes I can produce a tune 'in my head'.

CREATIVE THINKING

The ability to combine concepts to produce a new concept is an example of creative thought. In a sense, most things we do are creative as no two thoughts or actions are identical, but creativity is generally reserved for ideas which are original in that they are markedly dissimilar from what already exists. And, the creation must be recognized as such by other people; we often hear the comment that a creative person was 'ahead of their time'.

As we shall see in Chapter 10 a number of tests of creativity have been devised. Some of the main types are shown in *Table 9.1*. Tests such as these have been used in studies attempting to describe the creative person. Although this is not to say that creative people are always producing new ideas. Some very creative people produce only a few ideas, but they are of tremendous impact. It is quality not quantity that counts. In this sense, there is little evidence that tests of creativity can predict who will produce ideas of quality.

The nature of the creative process has puzzled psychologists for many years, and the early analysis by Graham Wallas in 1926 has been as useful as any since. Wallas suggested that there are four stages in creative thinking – preparation, incubation, illumination, and verification. Three of these stages are self-evident: one must begin by thinking about the problem (preparation); a solution will eventually emerge (illumination); and this has to be verified in practice (verification). However, the notion of incubation is less obvious. This refers to a process leading to illumination which occurs during a rest period when the problem is not being actively considered. In other words, the idea of incubation indicates that problem-solving can take place *outside* conscious awareness. For this reason incubation is difficult to investigate and so its workings, or indeed its existence, remain uncertain. However, this is not to deny that sometimes the solution to a problem suddenly 'appears' or 'comes to mind' when we

Table 9.1: Tests of creativity

☐	Circles	Using a circle as a starting point, draw as many pictures as possible.
☐	Common problems	Think of problems in a common situation such as making the bed.
☐	Consequences	List what would happen in unlikely situations such as all the traffic lights being stuck on red.
☐	Incomplete figures	Make a drawing using a few given lines.
☐	Product improvement	Make as many improvements as possible to a product such as a child's toy or a dishwasher.
☐	Remote associations	Find a fourth word associated with three words, e.g. rat – blue – cottage.
☐	Unusual uses	Think of as many uses as possible for a common object.

least expect it. In the following section we discuss a number of famous examples of this phenomenon.

PROBLEM SOLVING

We cannot always solve problems by tackling them directly. We often need to take a sideways look at a problem: what Edward De Bono calls lateral thinking. Early psychologists such as Wolfgang Köhler argued that successful problem solving depended on *insight:* a sudden awareness of the solution – as doubtless preceded Archimedes' shout of 'Eureka!' – as it bursts into consciousness. Try the problem in

┌─────────────── Exercise 9.3 ───────────────┐

A PROBLEM NEEDING INSIGHT

PROBLEM

The pilot of an aeroplane is flying a solo test mission carrying a new type of bomb. In front of him are two buttons, marked 'A' and 'B'. Button A locks the bomb doors, sealing the bomb inside the plane; button B opens the doors releasing the bomb. Midway through the mission, flying at 5,000 feet, the pilot receives the message from ground control to 'press button A'. The bomb is not to be dropped. The pilot, such is the anxiety, mishears the message and presses button B. The mechanism works perfectly, the bomb doors swing open, the holding apparatus is released, the bomb (which is there) is free to fall. The bomb does not leave the aeroplane. Why?

The answer is given on page 200.

└──┘

Exercise 9.3. There is no catch, when you see the solution you will experience insight.

In Kohler's experiments, chimpanzees had to reach pieces of fruit outside their cage. Two sticks were available, neither long enough to reach the fruit. The solution, which some chimps discovered, was to join the two sticks. Kohler argued that mental restructuring of the situation allowed insight to occur. However, the process of gaining insight is helped by experience: chimps allowed to play with sticks before facing the problem solved it much more quickly.

When faced with a problem we draw not only on experience, but also on our powers of reasoning. We attempt to spell out the consequences of a particular action: 'If I drive to Newcastle, setting off at 9 a.m., and stop just once for petrol, I'll be there in time for the meeting'. In this way we can, we hope, arrive at a solution logically. In generating solutions to some problems we need to test our ideas; for this we need negative as well as positive information. Try this simple problem. Ask a friend what is the rule for the series '2, 4, 6'. The rule is simply 'ascending numbers'. Most people will say '8, 10, 12', '14, 16, 18';

then say the rule is 'numbers rising by two'. Few people seek to disconfirm their idea by saying, for example, '7, 8, 9' which would conform to the rule but disprove their initial idea of it.

PERCEPTION, MEMORY, LEARNING AND THINKING

In this and in the previous chapter we have looked at the basic abilities of perception, memory, and learning. We have seen how these abilities are enhanced by thinking. It should be clear that these abilities are not independent, but function to provide an integrated whole. Memory and learning permit the organism to go beyond merely reacting to what it perceives. They enable it to develop and change as a result of experience. In humans thinking about and learning from the past not only frees us from the present but helps us shape our future.

Recommended Reading

Davey, G. (ed.) (1981). *Applications of Conditioning Theory*. London: Methuen.

Evans, J.St.B.T. (1983). *Thinking and Reasoning*. London: Routledge & Kegan Paul.

Hill, W.F. (4th ed. 1985). *Learning: a Survey of Psychological Interpretations*, London: Harper & Row.

Radford, J. & Burton, A. (1974). *Thinking: Its Nature and Development*. Chichester: John Wiley & Sons.

References

Bandura, A. (1965). Influence of models' reinforcement contingencies on the acquisition of imitative responses. *Journal of Personality & Social Psychology, 1*. 589–595. [Deals with observational learning.]

Bandura, A. (1977). *Social Learning Theory*. Englewood Cliffs, New Jersey: Prentice-Hall. [A detailed look at learning by observation and imitation. Including discussion of the four stages in observational learning.]

Bandura, A., Ross, D. & Ross, S. (1961). Transmission of aggression through imitation of aggressive models. *Journal of Abnormal & Social Psychology, 63*. 575–582. [Nursery school children and the learning of aggression.]

Blackman, D. (1980). Images of man in contemporary behaviourism. In A.J. Chapman and D.M. Jones (eds), *Models of Man*. Leicester: The British Psychological Society. [A discussion of tne place of behaviourism in contemporary psychology.]

Kohler, W. (1925). *The Mentality of Apes*. New York: Harcourt Brace Jovanovich. [Deals with insight; describes chimp experiment.]

Pavlov, I.P. (1927). *Conditioned Reflexes*. New York: Oxford University Press. [Learning by association: classical conditioning.]

Skinner, B.F. (1974). *About Behaviourism.* London: Jonathan Cape. [Considers behaviourism and looks at how perception, dreaming and thought can be fitted into behavioural theory.]

Thorndike, E.L. (1913). *The Psychology of Learning.* New York: Teachers College. [A discussion of learning, and deals with trial-and-error as one important aspect.]

Torrance, E.P. (1967). The Minnesota studies of creative behaviour: national and international extensions. *Journal of Creative Behaviour, 1,* 137–154. [Detailed studies of measures of creativity.]

Wallas, G. (1926). *The Art of Thought.* New York: Harcourt. [Describes the stages in creative thinking, and considers many aspects of thinking.]

Watson, J.B. (1913). Psychology as the behaviourist views it. *Psychological Review, 20,* 158–177. [Presents the S–R model of human activity.]

Solution to problem in Exercise 9.3

The aeroplane is flying upside down.

Exercise 9.1

THE POWER OF REINFORCEMENT

Among the wide variety of reinforcers it is known that social rewards, such as praise and attention, are very powerful in influencing behaviour. To demonstrate this try a simple experiment.

Ask a friend to sit and talk to you for five minutes about what she or he has done today. All you have to do, without telling your friend in advance, is nod and say 'Good, I see' whenever he or she uses someone's name or a pronoun such as 'I' or 'she'. Whilst your friend is talking, and you are delivering social reinforcement, have a second friend keep count of the number of names and pronouns spoken. Count over one-minute intervals and plot the results on a bar chart. You should find a pattern of results similar to that shown below.

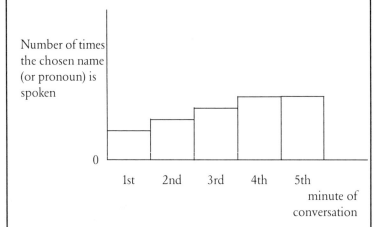

After five minutes explain to your friend what is happening. It is very unlikely that she or he will have realized what was going on. Nevertheless, despite this lack of awareness, behaviour was changed through the power of reinforcement.

You can perhaps appreciate why many psychologists argue that reinforcing consequences are the most powerful determinants of our behaviour.

UNDERSTANDING YOUR ACTIONS – APPLIED BEHAVIOUR ANALYSIS

This example shows how we can understand behaviour by analysing both its antecedent setting conditions and its consequences. The behaviour is the writing of this book. When you have grasped the principle, analyse your behaviour of reading it.

ANTECEDENTS:

> authors all trained in psychology
>
> authors all working at the same university (originally)
>
> authors all experienced teachers
>
> the idea for the book
>
> a lot of meetings
>
> negotiations with publisher
>
> signing contract to write it

BEHAVIOUR:

> putting pen to paper

CONSEQUENCES:

Positive	*Negative*
the book appearing – peer esteem; career prospects enhanced	late nights writing
helping people to learn about psychology	revision of draft
being paid for writing (only just!)	checking proofs

By virtue of this book appearing the positive consequences outweigh the negative. Had it been the other way round you would not be reading this.

The A : B : C analysis can be applied to any behaviour. Try analysing why you get angry, what makes you happy, what things interest you.

10. *Measurement and You*

Psychometrics is the name given to psychologists' attempts to measure, or quantify, different aspects of our behaviour. The emphasis upon measurement has always been strong in psychology, though the lead was given by the British biologist Sir Francis Galton. Galton set up an 'anthropometric laboratory' at the International Exposition of 1884, in which visitors could receive a thorough analysis of their physical and psychological functions – vision and hearing, reaction times, and muscular strength – for the sum of threepence. The laboratory remained in operation for a while at London's South Kensington Museum, enabling Galton to build up a body of data on *individual differences* between people.

STANFORD–BINET TEST

The development of psychological testing since those early days has been shaped by practical requirements rather than by theoretical concerns. In 1904, for example, the French government set up a commission to look at the particular problems faced by subnormal children attending Paris schools, and Alfred Binet was called in to devise a variety of sensory and perceptual tests which could be used to assess these deficiencies, so that programmes could be devised to remedy them. The result was what has now become the *Stanford-Binet* intelligence test, which has been used very extensively with children all over the world.

ARMY ALPHA AND BETA TESTS

In a similar way, the development of the well known *Army Alpha* and *Army Beta* intelligence tests was in response to a pressing practical need. When the USA entered the First World War, it was necessary to assign the vast numbers of new recruits to different types of service, and to make other administrative decisions about them, by screening them rapidly for intellectual level. These Army tests served as an early model for other group tests of intelligence, of which there are nowadays very many.

PSYCHOLOGICAL TESTING TODAY

The number and variety of contemporary psychological tests available today is vast, and psychological as well as educational testing is routinely carried out on a large scale, especially in the USA. Nearly all of us have taken a psychological test at some point in our lives. In fact tests are one of the ways in which members of the general public are most likely to come into direct contact with professional psychology.

From disrepute . . .

The popularity of tests and testing has changed over time. In the 1960s, for example, the whole ideology behind testing was seen as elitist, competitive, and socially divisive. The British '11-plus' examination provides some justification for this view. On the basis of written tests lasting no longer than a few hours, children were classified as either having passed or failed, and this determined the course of their secondary education (as well, in many cases, as their future career). The obvious undesirability of labelling children as failures at this early age, along with the introduction of comprehensive secondary education, eventually led to the abolition of the 11-plus. This outcome is somewhat paradoxical in that tests were originally devised in order to benefit those who were disadvantaged in society.

... to favour

The 1980s have seen a marked revival of interest in evaluation and assessment. Tests are fashionable once again. In the USA, the concept of *competency-based* education is based on the explicit and continuous monitoring of the child's progress by means of routine, regular testing; in fact the testing itself forms part of the instruction in some cases. In Great Britain, there are calls for a return to the teaching of basic skills of numeracy and literacy, and for their assessment by means of standard tests, perhaps as a reaction against the educational experiments of the 1960s.

Of course, the tests are neither good nor bad in themselves. We need to take account of the setting in which they are given, and of the uses to which they are put. Let's examine some of these.

USES OF TESTS

A psychological test is simply a refined form of observation. By asking people standardized questions under similar conditions, we hope to get samples of behaviour which can be compared from one person to the next. As far as possible, we also try to obtain *objective* assessments of people's behaviour rather than relying on our own subjective interpretations (though this is not always a straightforward affair, as we shall see later). The three main areas of application are in clinical, in educational, and in industrial work.

Clinical

Clinical psychologists work with people who are unable to cope. They rely upon tests to help them to pinpoint the nature of a particular person's problems. They might want to assess the precise intellectual deficits shown by people with head injuries from a car crash, for example, or to analyse the moods and emotions of people with depression, or to assess the personalities of people with hallucinations and delusions. In each case, psychological tests may enable them to make a more accurate diagnosis of the current problem, and also possibly to predict what the likely outcome of treatment might be.

Educational

Educational psychologists are concerned with the diagnosis and treatment of behavioural problems shown by children at school. These might include learning difficulties, emotional problems, social anxieties, and so on. Here again, tests are used to provide basic background information about pupils' particular strengths and weaknesses, and this information is used in working out remedial strategies.

Industrial

The industrial psychologist uses tests in making decisions about people at work. One of the main applications is in vocational guidance counselling. Test results can help in deciding which careers might be suitable for the undecided school leaver, for example. They also help in making personnel selection and guidance decisions within the work environment: in fitting people into jobs, and in tailoring jobs to suit people.

POTENTIAL ABUSES OF TESTS

In all of these applications, tests are essentially tools that are used by the psychologist, and the correct interpretation of the results requires skill and training. For this reason, the availability of tests is (by and large) restricted to qualified users, and the qualifying procedures are under the aegis of professional bodies such as The British Psychological Society and the American Psychological Association. These bodies also publish technical and ethical guidelines for the construction and use of tests. In the UK, anyone who wants to purchase a test is asked for details of his or her psychological qualifications, and is the then graded accordingly. Less experienced users have access only to those tests requiring little technical expertise, such as those which might easily be administered with the help of the manual alone. They are not qualified to obtain those tests, for example, whose use requires the interpretative skills of the experienced clinician.

Misinterpreting

The reason for this kind of restriction is that tests are very easy to abuse and misinterpret. The knowledge that a child scored 85 on a particular IQ test, for example, would be treated with great caution by an educational psychologist. This score is only a very rough indicator of general ability. It is subject to many sources of error, and it leaves out a great deal of information about the underlying *profile* of the child's particular strengths and weaknesses. The psychologist would also recognize that whilst a high IQ score undoubtedly does tell us that a child possesses some kind of ability, whatever that might be, a low score does not necessarily tell us that the child does not. An off day, a lack of willingness to comply with test instructions, tiredness, boredom and many others factors can all give rise to a low score.

In the mind of the unqualified layperson, however, these scores can easily take on a spurious air of scientific objectivity. A worried parent might easily regard an IQ score as a kind of precise, objective characteristic like height or weight. Because of the anxiety that this kind of misunderstanding might cause, not to mention the harmful misuses that might be made of confidential test scores were they to fall into the wrong hands, it is up to psychologists to make sure that their data remain confidential. This is all the more important at a time when there is public concern about who does and who does not have access to the large amounts of personal information that are held on centralized computer files.

VARIETIES OF PSYCHOLOGICAL TEST

Perhaps the most comprehensive guide to the vast range of psychological tests currently available is the *Mental Measurements Yearbook,* edited by Oscar Buros. The 8th edition, which was published in 1978, contains details and independent reviews of well over 1000 tests. A comprehensive British guide, *Tests in Education,* has also recently been published by Philip Levy and Harvey Goldstein. In this section we will try to convey a broad picture of this field by outlining the main types of test that psychologists use. In the rest of the chapter, we will look at two of the best-known types of ability test in more detail, that is, at tests of intelligence and creativity.

Typical versus maximum performance

One very broad distinction we can make is between tests of *maximum performance* and tests of *typical performance.* Those of the first type are designed to measure people's ability to work at their limit, when they are trying as hard as possible to succeed on a task. Two of the most common types are tests of *ability* and of *attainment*. Tests of typical performance, on the other hand, are used to gain an impression of how people typically behave rather than how they perform 'at their peak'; the two main types of these are tests of *personality*, and of *interests and attitudes*.

Individual versus group

1. There are four other ways of classifying these basic types of test. We speak of *group tests* or *individual tests*, which is self-explanatory. In the interests of time-saving and efficiency, large-scale tests of ability and achievement are likely to be administered to groups of people, whereas diagnostic and clinical tests are most often given on an individual basis.

Specific versus general

2. Second, tests can be described as being either *general* or *specific*. A test of general intelligence or personality would fall into the first category, whereas a test of musical ability, or an inventory to measure social anxiety, would fall into the second.

Self- versus other-reports

3. Third, some tests use *self-reports*. These contrast with those based on *other-reports*, such as ratings of the test subject by peers, supervisors, teachers, or other expert referees.

Pencil-and-paper versus performance

4. Finally, it is useful to make the distinction between *pencil-and-paper* and *performance* tests. The first type involve the subject in writing, or in other types of form-filling, and consequently require a certain level of basic literacy. Performance tests, on the other hand, are specifically designed to eliminate this requirement. It would be impossible to test very young children or retarded subjects on pencil-and-paper measures, for example, and so performance tests would be used. These might involve the manipulation of toys, coloured blocks, or pictures. Subjects' responses would be spoken, physically acted or indicated rather than being written down.

TESTS OF ABILITY AND ATTAINMENT

'Pure' ability

Ability (or aptitude) tests are designed to measure people's capabilities as independently as possible from their experience or learning about the tasks in question. The most obvious example of this is to be found in measures of general intelligence (see Exercise 10.1). An adult's overall score on the *Wechsler Adult Intelligence Scale* (WAIS), or a child's total score on the *Stanford-Binet test*, or on the *Wechsler Intelligence Scale for Children* (WISC), is supposed to reflect the 'pure' intelligence of that person regardless of learning, experience, or good or bad teaching. In practice, this is well-nigh impossible. Any test score is bound to be influenced at least to some degree by the subject's previous experiences of similar tasks, and IQ tests simply strive to keep these influences to a minimum.

Attainment

Tests of attainment (or achievement), on the other hand, are specifically designed to measure learning. School examinations provide a good example. When you take an examination in history, algebra or French, your examiners want to find out how much of your course of instruction has sunk in, and how well you have understood that material. Of course, this is also affected by your general ability in the subject. Scores on an exam paper are not pure measures of learning any more than scores on an ability test are pure measures of ability. However, attainment tests are geared to the assessment of particular courses of instruction. They cover the syllabuses and objectives of these courses as accurately and comprehensively as possible.

TESTS OF PERSONALITY, INTERESTS AND ATTITUDES

Self-reports

As we said earlier, *personality tests* are designed to assess what the person is typically like. Probably the best-known ones are *self-report* inventories, such as the *Eysenck Personality Questionnaire* (EPQ) or the *Minnesota Multiphasic Personality Inventory* (MMPI), in which people are asked to give 'yes' or 'no' answers to questions such as, 'Are you mostly quiet when you are with other people?' or 'Do you always practise what you preach?' On the basis of their answers, subjects obtain scores on personality *dimensions,* such as extraversion – introversion (see pp. 41 – 44), and these scores can then be used to make direct comparisons between individuals. The questionnaire items are stringently selected so as to give very pure measures of the personality dimensions in question. This is often done by using the technique of *factor analysis,* which statistically identifies the main dimensions in the whole network of relationships between individual test items.

Projective tests

Another well-known method of personality assessment is by the use of *projective tests.* Most people have heard of the *Rorschach Inkblots Test,* in which subjects are questioned systematically about their perceptions and interpretations of a series of visually ambiguous, symmetical grey/black and coloured inkblots. These responses are used by the tester as a basis for personality assessment.

A number of different approaches are used in projective testing. These include the *Thematic Apperception Test* (TAT), in which the subject creates a story about what is going on in a series of pictures showing human figures in different situations; open-ended word association; sentence completion tasks; and projective doll play in which children are asked to make up stories about a set of dolls placed before them which might, for example, represent their immediate family members. All of these techniques rely on the skills of the tester in making what are essentially subjective judgements about the responses. This subjectivity is clearly a disadvantage in comparison with the more objective techniques of the self-report inventories, but the advantage is that the person's responses are less constrained by the format of the test, and are therefore more likely to convey their real feelings and attitudes.

Tests of interests and attitudes

Tests of interests and attitudes are designed to map out a comprehensive picture of the subject's expressed preferences for different activities, such as work activities, hobbies, and other leisure pursuits, and they tend also to be based on self-reports. The *Strong Vocational Interest Blank* (SVIB), for example, is used in careers counselling. Subjects' statements about their interests and hobbies are compared with the typical profiles obtained by a wide variety of different occupational groups, and these comparisons can then be used to guide undecided subjects towards an appropriate career choice. The well-known *Allport-Vernon-Lindzey Scale of Values* takes a rather more general approach. Subjects are asked to answer 45 questions such as, 'If you had some time to spend in a waiting room and there were only two magazines to choose from, would you prefer: (a) *SCIENTIFIC AGE* (b) *ARTS AND DECORATIONS?*' Their total responses to a number of such questions give rise to a profile of values on six scales, namely the *theoretical, economic, aesthetic, social, political* and *religious.*

MEASURING INTELLIGENCE

We all have an idea of what is meant by describing someone as 'intelligent' or 'unintelligent', and most people have heard of, and quite possibly taken, an intelligence (IQ) test. In spite of people's familiarity with the idea, and in spite of the vast amount of IQ testing that is routinely carried out, you might be surprised to hear that the problem of defining and measuring intelligence is still one that psychologists have not yet managed to solve. In a famous symposium reported in the *Journal of Educational Psychology* in 1921, 14 eminent experts were asked to explain their understanding of the meaning of intelligence – and 14 quite different views emerged. These included:

☐ 'the ability to give responses that are true or factual'

☐ 'the ability to carry on abstract thinking'

☐ 'the ability to adjust oneself to the environment'

☐ 'the ability to learn or profit by experience'. . . . and so on.

We are still not a great deal nearer agreement, over 60 years later.

One of the main stumbling blocks is that 'intelligence' is often conceived in the abstract, as a kind of general property that can be defined independently of the activity in which it is displayed. Many psychologists would now argue that intelligence can only be defined in relation to particular activities. You may be very intelligent in the way you plan your finances, or in reading a railway timetable, yet you may, at the same time, be very unintelligent in the way in which you go about building a garden shed, or mending your car. The trouble is that certain types of activity, in Western society, are seen as requiring more general intelligence than others. Intelligence tends to be defined in terms of one's ability to perform the skills valued by the educational system: the ability to read, write, compute, speak foreign languages, and so on.

This is very apparent when we examine the contents of a typical IQ test. Exercise 10.1 shows 12 examples from Part 1 of the 1968 revision of the *AH4*, a well-known IQ test designed by Alice Heim for use with the general adult population. It is easy to see that the abilities required to do well on these 12 questions are those which are cultivated in the school system: logical reasoning, knowing the precise meanings of words, being good with numbers, and so on. The test obviously does not measure intelligence of the type that is needed in getting on well with other people or in doing practical jobs, for instance; and this leads to a circular argument. Intelligence is defined in terms of abilities that are needed for scholastic success, but the validity of intelligence tests is often assessed in terms of their ability to predict that success. You might say (only half-jokingly) that the safest operational definition is that 'intelligence is what intelligence tests measure'.

On the face of it, this would seem to be a very unsatisfactory basis for a test, but practitioners would argue that we can put IQ tests to many practical uses even if we don't fully understand the nature of what we are measuring. We can tell the time without understanding how the clock works, for example, and demonstrate the properties of electric currents without understanding the fundamental nature of electricity.

Information processing

Some of the more recent attempts to understand intelligence *are* now in fact beginning to move away from this circular, *operational* definition, in trying to pin down the *processes* involved in intelligence. Robert Sternberg has recently proposed a theory which adopts an *information processing* approach to intelligence. Intelligent behaviour is broken down into computer-like operations and strategies, and this may well provide a very useful way of side-stepping the conceptual problems of the test approach. In the meantime, tests will continue to be administered in increasing numbers.

Compared to the average

We have already mentioned the *Stanford-Binet* and the *WISC* tests, which are two of the best-known individual IQ tests for children. Both of these include performance alongside verbal tests and, in each case, a child's IQ is calculated by comparing his or her score on the test with an *age norm,* that is, with the score that other children of the same age, on average, obtain. Binet introduced the idea of the child's 'mental age', which is where his or her score falls in relation to the test's age norms. If the child's mental age is higher than his or her chronological age, the IQ score will be higher than average, and lower than average if these are the other way round. The average – where a child's mental age is the same as the chronological age – is usually set at IQ=100.

British Ability Scales

In Great Britain, these two well-known tests are being superseded by the *British Ability Scales* (BAS), the first edition of which was published in 1979. These Scales are the product of a big research project based at the University of Manchester, which used educational psychologists all over the country to pilot the tests on a massive and comprehensive sample of schoolchildren. There are 12 separate scales on the test, including some innovative features such as divergent or 'creativity' tests (see next section), and Piagetian developmental tasks (see pp. 126 – 129).

Group tests of intelligence are those which many of us are likely to have encountered in our school careers: the Moray House and NFER tests have been widely used on British children. In North America, the *Lorge-Thorndike* tests, the *School and College Ability Tests* (SCAT) and the *Miller Analogies Test* are amongst the better-known measures of general intelligence.

RELIABILITY AND VALIDITY

Scores on all of these tests are subject to many sources of error. If the person is having an off day, or happens to be very familiar (or unfamiliar) with some of the test items, or if there is a noisy road outside the test room, then the test score will not give an accurate reading of his or her true ability. Because of this, testers try to assess the *reliability* of different tests. One way of doing this, is to give the test to a group of people on two separate occasions, to see how closely the two sets of scores agree. This is known as *test-retest reliability.*

Another way of looking at reliability is to assess the *internal consistency* of the test. We can compare how well scores on half of the items agree with those on the other half, for example. A good test should be reliable over time, and also be internally consistent.

The other vital property of a test, which is, in a way, even more important than reliability, is its *validity* – the extent to which it measures what it is supposed to measure. Validity is usually assessed by comparing scores on the test with those on some external *criterion* measure. Tests of musical ability, for example, which might involve making pitch judgements, analysing chords, memorizing melodies, and so on, are sometimes used in guiding children towards an appropriate musical career. Such tests might be validated by comparing test scores with assessments of real-life musical abilities, such as the ability to play an instrument, to sing or to improvise. The tests would be regarded as valid if they gave an accurate prediction of real-life musical ability.

This brings us back to the particular problems involved in measuring intelligence. How can we assess the validity of an IQ test by comparing test and criterion scores when we cannot agree on a definition of intelligence, that is, on what the criterion should be? There is no way round this problem, unless we adopt a view of the nature of intelligence which is radically different from that which is implicit in IQ tests.

MEASURING CREATIVITY

Before reading further, try to answer the questions in Exercise 10.2.

Some common answers to the first 'Uses for objects' item, are that a brick might be used as a doorstop, as a hammer, as a weapon, or 'to stand on if short'. These questions require you to use your imagination, and to generate plenty of ideas. This ability has been called *divergent thinking* – your thinking branches out, or diverges, from a given starting point. This is rather like the idea of 'lateral thinking', popularized by Edward de Bono. De Bono's 'creative problem solving' techniques, which involve lateral thinking, reputedly save a great deal of money for industries which adopt them because they are said to generate new ideas and to increase job satisfaction. In contrast, the thinking skills that were required in Exercise 10.1 are problem solving or *convergent* skills: you are required to *con*verge on the one correct solution to a problem.

Convergent and divergent thinking have sometimes been equated with 'intelligence' and 'creativity' respectively. Is this equation realistic?

Convergent versus divergent thinking

The study of creativity arose from a general dissatisfaction with the concept of giftedness that was implicit in educational selection procedures, such as the 11-plus examination system in Great Britain. This examination, in one of its versions, had three separate papers – in English, in arithmetic, and in what was called 'intelligence'. This last paper was a conventional test of convergent thinking.

Writers such as Joy Guilford, who delivered his presidential address to the American Psychological Association on the subject of 'Creativity' in 1950, had begun to realize that there might be a whole realm of *creative* abilities which were not being tapped by traditional examination procedures. If these abilities were independent of convergent intelligence, and if they were important in children's development and education, their omission was presumably a serious one. Many of the child-centred, informal teaching methods that were being developed around this time put creative abilities in a very central position.

Jacob Getzels and Philip Jackson carried out a pioneering and controversial study in 1962 which looked at the relationship between intelligence and creativity in a sample of 533 Chicago schoolchildren. They identified a 'high creative' group who had high scores on what they called 'creativity tests' but low scores on IQ tests, and a 'high intelligence' group whose scores were biased in the opposite direction. Getzels and Jackson's provocative finding was that these two subgroups performed equally well on measures of educational success, which seemed to indicate that creative abilities were just as important as intelligence in school attainment.

Unfortunately, this study was riddled with problems of methodology and experimental design, and so the results are inconclusive. Nevertheless it served to stimulate an immense amount of further research, which has confirmed the importance of creative thinking abilities. Creativity has now become an established and respectable part of psychometrics, and divergent thinking tests are a recognized part of general ability tests (as in the *British Ability Scales*). Though there is still a certain amount of disagreement, it is probably reasonable to conclude that convergent and divergent thinking are generally regarded as distinct abilities in their own right; that they are both parts of general intelligence, showing positive correlations under certain testing conditions but not under others, and that both can be used to predict educational success.

CREATIVITY AND PERSONALITY

The British psychologist Liam Hudson made an interesting new contribution to this field when he looked at the relationships between intelligence and creativity in arts as compared with science subjects. In his book *Contrary Imaginations,* Hudson used the labels 'converger' and 'diverger' to refer to *people,* that is, to styles of personality, rather than merely to patterns of thinking ability. Investigating British school boys aged 11–18, he discovered that 'divergers' (good at divergent and relatively poor at convergent thinking) are likely to be drawn towards arts subjects such as languages or history, whereas 'convergers' are more likely to go in for science subjects such as physics or engineering. 'All-rounders', who score high on both types of test, are likely to go in for 'intermediate' subjects such as biology, or social sciences.

Convergers and divergers

In a subsequent book, *Frames of Mind,* Hudson went further in his explorations of the personalities of the diverger and the converger. He found that the diverger is more likely to be disrepectful of authority, to be emotionally open, and to be flexible with regard to sex roles. These patterns of personality seem to be learnt culturally, in the sense that society 'channels' people down pathways with labels such as 'artist' and 'scientist' from a fairly early age. Early biases in thinking style are elaborated by social forces into a whole network of behavioural styles, and patterns of interests and attitudes. The differences between convergers and divergers are charmingly encapsulated in the auto-biographical statements that Hudson asked his subjects to make in one study. Part of a typical converger's statement ran as follows:

" . . . *10-15 years. Going into a C form (3C) I started well. Captained the school 3rd form cricket XI and got into the 3rd form rugby team at scrum half. In the fourth form I worked harder and was promoted to 5A (from 4C2) but in doing so lost my cricket captaincy due to a slight argument with the cricket master who had insisted that I play for a draw when a win was still possible. We almost lost. In the 5th form had a good school year . . .* **"**

Compare this with the response of an extreme diverger to exactly the same task:

 “ . . . *I like friends, lots of them. I like people. I like parties. I like jazz, modern and trad. I like King Oliver, Bechet, Shelley Manne . . . I like New Orleans, and Mississippi style real hot. I love sketching. I prefer drawing portraits, preferably girls. I dislike Modern Art. I am at heart liberal. I like films. I love B.B. She sends me. I shall marry when I am 26. I hope to have a girl and a boy. I adore girls . . .* **”**

The difference speaks for itself.

Now if we can reliably establish the link between convergent thinking and science on the one hand, and divergent thinking and the arts on the other, their equation with intelligence and creativity respectively raises something of a problem, since it seems to imply that artists tend to be unintelligent and scientists uncreative. Of course this cannot be true, and the problem arises because of the confusion between the *potential* for creativity, which divergent tests are supposed to measure, and *real-life* creativity, which is of course displayed in the works of scientists as well as of artists. We might hazard a guess that both convergent *and* divergent thinking skills are involved in creative work in both domains. When we prepare for a piece of creative work by gathering together materials, doing background reading, and mulling over the problems, it is very likely that divergent abilities will be brought into play. Once the ideas are crystallized and the course of the work is set, whether it be an essay, a picture, a musical composition or a piece of scientific research, convergent skills are called into operation in formalizing, or realizing it: in working out the final details. In other words, divergent tests do not measure creativity, but they might well give psychologists clues about some of the processes that are involved in it.

This is probably typical of the whole enterprise of psychological testing. Human beings are such complex, ever-changing creatures that it is impossible to measure them in the same way that the properties of physical objects can be measured, and we must also remember that it is the human beings themselves who are doing the measuring. To put this another way, we could say that psychologists must be careful not to model their measurement procedures too closely upon those of the natural sciences. So long as we keep a clear idea of what they *cannot* do, there is no doubt that psychological tests have many valuable practical uses.

Recommended Reading

Anastasi, A. (1982). *Psychological Testing,* 5th ed. New York: Macmillan.
Heim, A. (1970). *Intelligence and Personality.* Harmondsworth: Penguin.
Kline, P. (1976). *Psychological Testing.* London: Malaby.
Shelley, D. & Cohen, D. (1986). *Testing Psychological Tests.* London:
Croom Helm.

References

British Psychological Society Professional Affairs Board, (1980). Technical recommendations for psychological tests. *Bulletin of The British Psychological Society,* 33, 161–164. [Official statement by the BPS.]
Buros, O.K. (1978) (ed.). *The VIII Mental Measurement Yearbook.* New Jersey: Gryphon Press. [The standard reference guide to psychological tests, which includes independent reviews of each one.]
Getzels, J.W. & Jackson, P.W. (1962). *Creativity and Intelligence.* New York: John Wiley. [A pioneering, though heavily criticized research study.]
Guilford, J.P. (1950). Creativity. *American Psychologist, 5,* 444–454. [Guilford presidential address to the American Psychological Association.]
Hudson, L. (1966). *Contrary Imaginations.* Harmondsworth: Pelican. [Research on 'convergers' and 'divergers'.]
Hudson, L. (1968). *Frames of Mind.* Harmondsworth: Pelican. [Further exploration of the character of 'convergers' and 'divergers'.]
Kline, P. (1983). *Personality: Measurement and Theory.* London: Hutchinson. [A very readable introductory text on personality.]
Levy, P. & Goldstein, H. (1984). *Tests in Education: A Book of Critical Reviews.* London: Academic Press. [A comprehensive guide to tests.]
Sternberg, R.J. (1985). *Human Abilities: An Information-Processing Approach.* New York: W.H. Freeman. [A cognitive psychological approach to the IQ question.]
Thorndike, E.L. et al. (1921). Intelligence and its measurement. *Journal of Educational Psychology, 12,* 123f. [A report of the famous 1921 symposium on defining intelligence.]
Vernon, P.E. (1979). *Intelligence: Heredity and Environment.* San Francisco: W.H. Freeman. [A sensible, thorough and well-balanced text book.]

PART OF THE AH4 IQ TEST

AH4
QUESTION BOOK
(1968 REVISION)

AH4

INSTRUCTIONS

Below are some examples of the test. Do them now.
Write your answers on the answer sheet. Write the *number*, not the word.
Some of the examples are already done for you.

DO NOT WRITE ANYTHING ON THIS PAPER
PART I. EXAMPLES

Q1	1, 2, 3, 4, 5, 6, 7, 8, 9. Write down the largest of these figures.	Q1
Q2	1, 2, 3, 4, 5, 6, 7, 8, 9. Write down the middle one of these figures.	Q2
Q3	*Late* means the opposite of . . . $\quad$ 1 $\qquad$ 2 $\qquad$ 3 $\qquad$ 4 $\qquad$ 5 appointment, early, behind, postponed, immediate.	Q3
Q4	$\qquad\qquad\qquad$ 1 $\quad$ 2 $\quad$ 3 $\quad$ 4 $\quad$ 5 *Big* means the opposite of . . . tall, large, place, small, high.	Q4
Q5	1, 4, 7, 10, 13 . . . What number comes next?	Q5
Q6	2, 4, 8, 16, 32 . . . What number comes next?	Q6
Q7	*Fish* is to *swim* as *bird* is to . . . $\quad$ 1 $\quad$ 2 $\quad$ 3 $\qquad$ 4 $\qquad$ 5 man, fly, walk, aeroplane, sparrow.	Q7
Q8	$\qquad\qquad\qquad$ 1 $\quad$ 2 $\quad$ 3 $\quad$ 4 $\quad$ 5 *Low* is to *high* as *bad* is to . . . evil, red, try, good, right.	Q8
Q9	Here are three figures: 325. Add the largest two figures together and divide the total by the smallest figure.	Q9
Q10	Here are three figures: 594. Subtract the smallest figure from the biggest and multiply the result by the figure printed immediately before the biggest figure.	Q10
Q11	*Young* means the same as . . . $\quad$ 1 $\qquad$ 2 $\qquad$ 3 $\qquad$ 4 $\qquad$ 5 youthful, ancient, vigorous, hot, baby.	Q11
Q12	$\qquad\qquad\qquad$ 1 $\quad$ 2 $\quad$ 3 $\quad$ 4 *Gift* means the same as . . . parcel, toy, birthday, buy, present.	Q12

If there is anything you do not understand, please ask the tester *now*.
DO NOT TURN OVER UNTIL YOU ARE TOLD TO DO SO.

A TEST OF CREATIVITY

USES FOR OBJECTS

1. How many uses can you think of for a brick?
2. How many uses can you think of for a paper clip?
3. How many uses can you think of for a blanket?
4. How many uses can you think of for a jam jar?

PATTERN MEANINGS

Think of all the things that each of these patterns might be:

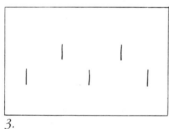

1.

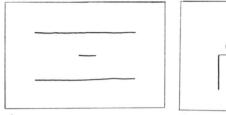

2.

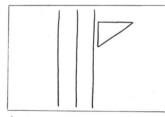

3.

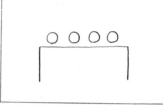

4.

SIMILARITIES

Think of all the ways in which the following pairs of objects are alike:

1. An apple and a pear.
2. A radio and a telephone.
3. A violin and a piano.
4. A cat and a mouse.

11. You – The Human Animal

Humans are animals. Today most of us accept this, and yet it is a relatively new idea, new enough for us often to set ourselves apart in phrases such as 'man and animals' or 'humans and animals'. It was Darwin who was the major influence on our thinking about the 'human/animal' relationship. In *The Descent of Man* he put forward the view that we evolved from other animals and were not a distinct and separate creation. This view is now as much a part of our everyday thinking as that the world is round rather than flat. But the nature of 'the difference' between us and other animals is still very much discussed.

Before reading further you might like to pause and think about your answers to the questions in Exercise 11.1, which deal with some commonly held views about the differences between humans and other animals. The thinking on this subject has centred around a number of topics: that we are the peak of evolution – the best thing to have been invented so far; that our special qualities include having a language, being thinking, intelligent creatures, conscious of our actions, and showing intentional behaviour.

HUMANS AND OTHER ANIMALS COMPARED

Read the following statements. Do you agree with them? Tick 'yes' or 'no', as appropriate.

☐ Humans are the peak of evolution.   Yes   No

☐ Humans are capable of intelligent
behaviour, other animals are not.   Yes   No

☐ Humans can think about abstract
problems, other animals cannot.   Yes   No

☐ Non-human animals have no mental life.   Yes   No

☐ Language is unique to humans.   Yes   No

☐ Communication in non-human animals is
unlearned.   Yes   No

☐ Only humans have a sense of themselves – a
self-awareness.   Yes   No

☐ Non-human animals cannot show intention
in their behaviour as can humans.   Yes   No

☐ Communication in non-human animals is
straightforward. Only humans can lie
about their thoughts and feelings.   Yes   No

☐ Humans are more sensitive than other
creatures, and are more aware of the
world around them.   Yes   No

☐ Non-human animals cannot feel pain to the
extent that humans can.   Yes   No

☐ Any 'relationship' that a human has with
another animal is on an entirely different
level to that of a human – human relationship.   Yes   No

There is no universal agreement on the views outlined in this list – many are, as yet, a matter of debate.

This chapter explores some of these issues. We shall look at the research evidence on areas of difference. The unique and special characteristics which other animals have, and which we lack, will also be highlighted. The ethical issues involved in using other animals will be discussed, and finally we shall look at our relationships with other animals.

IS LANGUAGE UNIQUE TO HUMANS?

Language has been said to be the essence of humanity, but what is meant by the term 'language'? It is not easy to define because it has many characteristics. *The Shorter Oxford Dictionary* mentions 'speech' and 'words and methods of combining them in the expression of thought' in its definition. Psychologists have tried to tease out the various qualities of language.

- [ ] Language is symbolic and the symbols are arbitrary.
- [ ] It enables us to communicate about things remote in time and space.
- [ ] Language is learned and is passed on by tradition.
- [ ] Language enables us to express our thoughts honestly or to prevaricate.
- [ ] By using language we can reflect on the nature of language itself.

And there are many more qualities; indeed, Charles Hockett and others have identified 16 qualities or 'design features' in language. But if one takes these features one by one, many are found in communication systems among other animals.

Take communication in honey bees. Bees, on returning to the hive, can convey information about the distance and location of a food source, by performing a 'waggle dance'. The dance seems to be symbolic, although some suggest that since the rate of waggling is related to the distance of the food source the relationship is not truly symbolic. In fact different bees have different dialects. For a given distance a German bee waggles more slowly than an Egyptian one.

The ability to communicate about something remote in space is found in other animals. The dog's marking behaviour enables it to convey information when it is no longer present. This 'displacement', as it is called, is also found in the alarm calls of some species, which can indicate whether a predator is in the air or on the ground.

The fact that language is *learned* and *passed on by tradition* is not exclusive to human language either. Chaffinches, for example, learn their local dialect song from other chaffinches in a particular critical period during development. Thus the song is passed from one generation to the next. Fostered birds reared by chaffinches from another locality learn the song of their foster parents; they do not sing like their biological parents.

So some of the qualities of human language are found in communication systems of other species. However there are other qualities over which there is still much debate and these are highlighted next.

CAN OTHER ANIMALS TALK?

In trying to answer this question, attempts have been made to teach other animals our language. The first attempts involved trying to teach chimpanzees to speak. After much effort two or three words could be articulated ('mama', 'cup'), but it became clear that the chimpanzee larynx is simply not designed to produce the range of sounds needed. Since speech is not essential in language communication – deaf people communicate linguistically using signs – later attempts at teaching apes used this and other non-vocal methods.

Washoe and Nim

Washoe and Nim are two chimpanzees, among a number, who became famous during this research. They each learned over 100 signs from Ameslan (American Sign Language) and were able to associate accurately sounds and visual cues, and they could sign appropriately when asked to name these cues. On a few occasions the chimps combined the signs in novel ways. Thus 'water bird' and 'candy drink' were created.

The language quality of 'openness' or the ability to coin new phrases (and new meanings), by making new combinations of words, appeared to have been found. But more careful analysis of the signing of these chimpanzees raised doubts. Records of sign combinations showed that combinations were not produced grammatically (or syntactically). One of Nim's longest utterances, 'give orange me give eat orange me eat orange give me eat orange give me you', shows this clearly. Although children also play with words to some extent and make nonsense phrases, the new phrases generated by the chimps formed such a tiny proportion of their total range of combinations, it was felt that they may have occurred purely by chance. Thus the ability to display 'openness' remains in doubt. Nevertheless these apes showed truly exceptional abilities and were able to learn language to the level of a young child. Chimps could learn to use arbitrary symbols and they could refer to objects not present; indeed their abilities went well beyond what was previously thought possible.

Parrot talk?

But apes are not the only animals to have been the focus of attention as far as language is concerned. Many birds imitate speech and some recent research suggests that at least one parrot may be doing more than just imitating. An African grey parrot has been taught, by his trainer Irene Pepperburg, to name 40 objects. He can answer questions such as 'What shape?' or 'What colour?' by correctly naming one of four shapes and five colours. It appears that this parrot may understand abstract categories. Whatever the explanation, we are left realizing that if 'man is language', then many qualities of language that were once thought to be unique to humans are also present in non-human communication.

CAN OTHER ANIMALS THINK?

Does a mouse think about what it will eat for its next meal? Or, if not a mouse, then what of a parrot or a chimpanzee? Darwin certainly believed that animals possess some powers of reasoning, and recent research supports this.

Donald Griffin, in his book *The Question of Animal Awareness*, suggests that mental experiences are 'the objects and events that are remote in space and time' which we think about, or have in mind. A mental image of a future event in which the 'intender pictures himself as a participant' is what he means by intention, and this is another quality which has often been said to be uniquely human. Human language and thought are often considered to be so closely linked that some would argue that one cannot exist without the other, but studies in other animals make this assumption questionable.

A variety of abstract problems can be solved by non-human animals. Frederick Rohles and James Devine demonstrated that chimpanzees can learn the concept of 'middleness'. They could learn to select the middle one from various numbers of objects arranged in different ways. Children aged between four and six can also solve this type of problem. In a series of studies, carried out in Moscow by Zoe Zorina, crows learned to take food concealed under a row of identical caps, such that on the first trial food was under the first cap, on the second trial it was under the second cap, and so on. Evidently after several trials the 'logic' of the progression of the food's location was learned.

There is suggestive evidence of the use of mental images by other animals from a study of pigeons. Pigeons were taught to discriminate between geometric shapes and their mirror images. They were then required to indicate which of two symbols a sample symbol most resembled. The symbols were presented at a variety of angles, and the pigeons were found to be quicker at selecting the correct response than were humans who were also tested in this way. Humans appear to require some form of mental representation in order to do this task and, if this is so, then does this also apply to pigeons? If not, in what way can this ability in pigeons be explained? At present the best way for us to explain this ability in other animals is to consider it in terms of thinking, but thinking *without* language.

If intention requires imagery, as Donald Griffin believes, then if it can be shown to occur in other animals this too would indicate 'thinking' in these creatures. A number of birds will feign injury. The broken wing display of the sandpiper is one such example, and it is shown by incubating birds as they move away from the nest when a predator threatens. This behaviour has been accounted for in terms of a ritualized display characteristic of a species, but it is possible that intentionality may play a part. Donald Griffin points out that primates and members of the dog family can show intention, because they can learn to 'mislead' in a situation where there is competition for food. If so, then the goal of the behaviour is not what it outwardly appears to be, and evidence for thinking, and one further 'design feature' of human language, will have been found to occur in other animals.

INTELLIGENCE

Reasoning power is often said to be central to the concept of intelligence. Although psychologists argue over the definition of intelligence, problem solving ability is frequently included in any assessment of an individual's intelligence. Experiments comparing problem solving abilities in humans and other animals have been devised. For example, Morton Bitterman used a fish, a reptile, a bird and two mammals – a rat and a monkey – in various learning tasks. He found, that the fish was least successful and the two mammals showed the best performance.

On the face of it this kind of experiment may seem perfectly sensible as a way to compare intelligence in different species but, in reality, it is fraught with problems. Every species is uniquely adapted to a particular environment and way of life. A deep sea fish, for example, is likely to rely much less on eyesight than do birds, and it has probably never encountered a vertical face, such as the wall of a fish tank, in its natural setting. A rat is used to walls and confined spaces – it lives in tunnels and can readily learn routes through a maze to a food source. Psychologists in the past frequently used maze learning tests when comparing learning abilities in different species, but such a test is quite inappropriate for many species. Once we find problems that are appropriate for each species it then becomes hard to equate the degree of difficulty of each problem in any comparison.

The notion that humans are at the top of an evolutionary scale is highly misleading. Evolution is not a simple progression; mammals and birds, for instance, each evolved at the same time from different groups of reptiles. Birds did not evolve before mammals as is often thought. Because each species is uniquely adapted it is not possible to arrange them in a linear hierarchy from least to most intelligent.

If we use the kinds of non-verbal problems that are used in intelligence tests for humans on other mammals we are likely to find that cats and dogs are less competent at solving these problems than are non-human primates. But, since we ourselves are primates, it should be no surprise to find that our adaptations are more like theirs. In our terms, we are undoubtedly the most intelligent, but we may ignore or disregard qualities in other animals simply because we do not share them.

Clever Hans

An example highlights this point. At the turn of this century a retired German mathematics professor had an exceptional horse, so exceptional was he that he was called 'Clever Hans'. Anyone could ask Hans a complicated arithmetical problem and he could miraculously stamp out the correct answer with his hoof. Hans amazed the people who flocked to see him. Could Hans count? For some time it was believed so until one keen observer noted that, at dusk, Hans made mistakes. Careful manipulation of the circumstances in which Hans was questioned showed that if no one present knew the answer then Hans didn't either. Hans' intelligence was in his ability to detect minute changes in his audience as they awaited his answer. As he stamped, when he reached the correct number, he observed a slight increase in tension in his audience and ceased stamping. Hans had learned, not to count, but to observe his audience very closely. He was indeed an amazing horse, but was he intelligent?

TOOL-USE AND CULTURE

Extending the body with a tool, in order to attain a goal, has often been viewed as intelligent behaviour. Human culture has been built on this ability and yet it is not uniquely human. Other primates have been observed using tools. Chimpanzees use twigs to gouge insects from cracks and crevices, and leaves as 'sponges' to soak up drinking water from inaccessible sources. Sea otters use two stones to crack open shellfish – one stone is used as the anvil and the other as hammer. Crows will use a matchstick to aid grooming, and the woodpecker finch uses sticks to find its insect prey.

Some forms of tool-use in non-human animals seem to be passed on by genetic means – the woodpecker finch may be an example of an innate predisposition to tool-use (although not all authorities accept this) – however, other forms of tool-use do *not* appear to be 'built-in' adaptations but are spontaneous solutions to problems confronting particular individuals which are then passed on to others by observation and imitation. This seems closer to our idea of intelligence or reasoning behaviour.

Some delightful examples of cultural traditions have been recorded in Japanese macaques. In a macaque colony, whose diet was supplemented with sweet potatoes, one female was observed to wash the sand from her potatoes in a stream. Soon other macaques imitated her and over some years this new practice was established virtually throughout the population of the area. Another example concerns snowball making. Again this practice was started by *one* monkey and it rapidly spread throughout the population and became a characteristic of their winter behaviour.

Although these examples of tool-use and culture are quite limited in type and range, it is clear that other animals, and in particular other primates, share the ability to solve problems which we believe characterizes intelligent behaviour. Whilst the reasoning abilities of humans may go far beyond what is demonstrable in animals, it is clear that the basis of this behaviour *is* found in these creatures. Probably the major difference between us and other primates is that whilst tool-use is essential for our survival, it has only a minor place in the life of other primates.

WHAT THE HUMAN ANIMAL LACKS

We are very aware of the sights, sounds and smells around us so it is perhaps surprising to learn that our sensory sensitivity is not exceptional in the animal world. Many animals are more aware than we are in one or other sensory modality, and in some creatures there are senses about which we know nothing.

Seeing other colours

Honey bees see a world in colours that are different from ours. They can see ultraviolet, a colour invisible to us, but they are less sensitive to the red end of the spectrum. Honey bees can orient themselves using the polarization patterns of the blue sky, an ability totally lacking in humans.

Long distance smelling

Although we might expect to be able to see another person at a distance of perhaps half a mile the idea that we could smell them at such a distance seems laughable and yet such an ability would be nothing to the male silk moth; it can detect the presence of the female moth, by odour alone, at a distance of several miles. Similar feats of sensitivity exist in the salmon which can identify the tributary of its birth, after travelling across the ocean, by smell alone. It appears that salmon become imprinted on the olfactory characteristics of their native stream and this enables them to relocate those waters quite precisely.

Hearing ultrasounds

Many animals have the ability to hear sounds well outside our audible range – they may also communicate using ultrasonic cries. Rodents for instance make ultrasonic cries which are audible to cats. A pet parrot was recently reported as perplexing its owners by its imitative ability. The owners believed that their television was changing channel by itself until they realized that the bird was imitating the ultrasonic signals of the TV remote control commander. Bats, whales, dolphins and porpoises all have hearing outside our audible range, and they can produce signals which enable them to echolocate obstacles or prey. A bat can locate and catch its insect prey *entirely* by echolocation.

Sensing electricity

Sensitivity to electric fields is another sense beyond our imagining. Electric fish can produce an electric current from special organs and are so sensitive to electric fields that they can locate the objects around them in dark and muddy waters. They can also identify other electric fish species and their own mates by this means.

There are many more examples of this kind but these serve to demonstrate that our perceptual abilities are in some respects quite limited compared to some other animals.

AWARENESS AND CONSCIOUSNESS

Sensitivity to the environment tells us nothing about how *self-aware* other animals are, but experiments have shown animals can be made aware of what they are doing. A rat can be trained to press one of four levers depending on which of four activities it is engaged in when a buzzer is sounded. Thus if the buzzer sounds when it is grooming it can press the 'grooming' lever to receive a food reward.

Using mirrors

Other evidence of self-awareness comes from primate studies. Chimpanzees and orang-utans can look in a mirror and recognize themselves if they have a little time to become used to mirrors. But a cat, dog or rat cannot. Gordon Gallup painted small red patches on lighly anaesthetized chimpanzees in places which could not be seen unaided. These animals looked long and hard at the patches when later they were given mirrors. Chimpanzees will also use mirrors to groom parts of their bodies which they cannot otherwise see.

Consciousness and self-awareness are not thought to be identical. Donald Griffin suggests that consciousness involves the presence of mental images to regulate behaviour. So that evidence of intentional behaviour would in his view be a sign of consciousness. The issue of how other animals feel about themselves is a very difficult field of study. One person cannot really know whether another person's experience is the same as their own. We have evidence however that some non-human primates can recognize themselves and this is perhaps very close to, if not the same as, our own consciousness. Indeed Gallup goes so far as to suggest that if a chimpanzee can contemplate itself, and hence perhaps its own existence, this is not far from the contemplation of its nonexistence or mortality.

ARE HUMANS 'BETTER' THAN OTHER ANIMALS?

In any discussion of the behaviour of humans and other animals, one question that often arises is: do we see excesses of cruelty in other animals which are not found in humans? To say someone behaved 'like an animal' often means that they are cruel, but is there evidence that humans are different from other animals in this respect?

Killing for pleasure

Two examples provide some clues to the answer. A fox in a chicken run may 'kill for pleasure'; it will kill in excess of its needs and may leave many dead chickens in its wake. Male lions taking over a pride by displacing ageing or diseased males may kill most or all the cubs of the pride. Indeed infanticide occurs in many animals in certain circumstances. Can this behaviour be explained? The fox's prey in this example is captive. It cannot escape as a wild animal would be able to. Human intervention in the breeding of fowl has provided an unnaturally dense source of prey, which would rarely if ever be encountered by a fox in a natural setting. In the evolution of prey-catching the fox probably showed this excess killing beyond need, which appears to be wasteful of energy, so rarely that it made no impact on the survival of the species. Whatever the explanation for foxes it must also be said that humans also kill for pleasure in excess of their needs. Hunting and shooting for sport, and the use of other animals for luxury items, serve as examples of this characteristic in us.

Infanticide

Infanticide is explained by sociobiologists as an adaptation which reduces the survival of the genes of competing males, and enables the males showing this behaviour to take over the females and impregnate them. A lioness will care for her cubs for two years: whilst lactating she does not ovulate and so the removal of her young returns her rapidly to a state in which she can be impregnated again.

Infanticide is also found in humans. Violent acts towards children are more common in families where a child is not biologically related to the parent who rears it. Thus like the lion taking over new females, the step-parent joining an existing family is statistically more likely to harm these unrelated offspring than is the natural or biological parent.

Infanticide is also practised as a fertility control and it is sometimes directed towards female infants in societies where the male is valued more highly than the female, and where a female requires a large dowry from her parents before she can be married.

Whatever our views are on the acceptability, morally or legally of these forms of behaviour in humans, we cannot deny that they occur. The claim that such behaviour is animal-like, whilst not recognizing ourselves as animals, is absurd. Such behaviour is one facet of our human nature; it does not distinguish us from other animals. It should be borne in mind however that recognizing that such behaviour may occur is not the same as claiming that it is inevitable. Most of us accept that being rational beings we should be able to learn to control this aspect of human behaviour.

HUMAN USES OF OTHER ANIMALS

Ethical issues involved in using other animals for food and in research cover many areas, two of which are briefly considered. The first issue concerns whether there is any moral justification for placing ourselves before all other animals, and the second issue revolves around the problem of how such animals should be used, if they are used, to ensure that they do not suffer.

The Bible tells Christians that 'man' has 'dominion' over all animals – this view has been used by some Christians to justify using animals in any way they choose. 'Speciesism' is a term coined by Richard Ryder to describe the view that humans are uniquely important in the scheme of things and discrimination against other species is possible simply because they are other species. Ryder suggests that speciesism, like racism or sexism, has no more moral justification than they have.

Another less extreme form of speciesism is 'speciesism with a reason'. Here discrimination is practised because other animals are held either to lack, or possess to a lesser extent, attributes which we have. An example might be that other animals lack consciousness, or feel no pain. The problem here is to justify the reason, for as we have seen, it is hard to differentiate between other animals and humans on clear-cut grounds.

If we accept the use of animals, for instance, for food or research then how can we ensure minimal suffering or distress? Knowing when an animal suffers is not always easy. Guinea pigs are often said to make 'friendly' little pets because they can be easily handled. A guinea pig sitting quietly on a child's knee is probably 'freezing'; it is alarmed and is displaying the characteristic 'immobility response' of these rodents which is shown when a predator is about. Because we do not recognize the meaning of this 'sitting still' we believe the animal to be 'friendly'. We cannot identify suffering by merely searching for signs in other animals of our ways of expressing it. Many animals do not cry out, or produce tears when injured, as we do. We are being anthromorphic if we expect to see such signs. The only way that we can begin to understand other animals is by studying them. If we understand their behaviour and lifestyles then we can, if we believe it to be justified, use them humanely.

There are almost as many views about how we should or should not use animals as there are animal species, and it is clear that a consensus on this issue would be hard to achieve.

RELATIONSHIPS WITH OTHER ANIMALS

Humans can form close associations with other animals as pets. All human societies have tamed and domesticated animals, and this close association between two or more species is not unique. Ant and aphid species benefit by a close association, as do the honey guide (a small bird) and the honey badger. Ants 'farm' aphids for their honeydew (a substance similar to cuckoo spit), whilst the aphid gains protection from predators. The honey guide leads the badger to a nest of bees, the badger opens the nest and then both can feed. Humans and other animals living together often exchange food for protection, or milk, or wool, and the latter need not be harmed by such an association. It is likely that there has been no time in our evolution when humans have not enjoyed other animals as pets and today pets play a large part in life in Western societies.

Pets

Studies of pet owners reveal that people may feel very strongly about their pets. A Swedish survey in 1974 using a random sample of Swedish dog owners, found that 93 per cent agreed that 'the dog gives me love and affection', and 63 per cent agreed that the dog gave them someone 'to lavish love on'. Feelings involved in the pet–owner relationship were very strong indeed. Research by two of us on the relationships that people have with their pets produced some intriguing findings. If you would like to find out more about your relationship with your pets before reading on, complete Exercise 11.2.

The technique described in this Exercise is a modified version of the repertory grid technique (described in Chapter 2). This technique allows the assessment of people's individual perceptions of what is important to them in their relationships with others. In our study we used 30 pet owners and we took six relationships with humans and two with pets for each subject. Just as in Exercise 11.2, each subject compared relationships in threes (or triads); this enabled us to find out what was important to each of our subjects in their relationships. The 'important things' are termed 'personal constructs'. An example might be that one relationship was 'fun' whilst another was 'serious'; thus the construct would be 'fun – serious'. Constructs are very personal and no two people produce the same ones.

In our study, all the people we tested were able to make comparisons between relationships with humans and relationships with other animals. Statistical analysis of the results revealed that for about one third of our subjects the pet(s) were rated as more important on a whole range of constructs when compared with significant human relationships. A dog might be more loved, easier to talk to, or missed more, than a spouse, for example. Not all our subjects described themselves as pet lovers and for these the pets were not rated so highly; they occupied an intermediate position in relation to the human relationship explored.

Over all 30 subjects no constructs emerged which could not be applied to the pets, and all those tested found that they could easily compare relationships with humans and with pets. To put it another way: *the important things in relationships with other people were evidently not dependent on 'higher human attributes'* – according to our study. We may be capable of intellectual discussion but this does not seem to be central in an important human relationship. It follows from this, if our study reflects a general tendency, that the potential of pets to satisfy many of our needs is just as great as that of friends, parents or partners. Obviously much more research is needed but our findings suggest that the important things for humans in their relationships with other humans are not necessarily unique to us as humans, but are very much the qualities that relationships with other animals can provide – if we choose to have a pet. This is not of course the same as saying that people should have pets, or that pets are 'people substitutes'.

A VERY SINGULAR ANIMAL

In conclusion, the human animal is undoubtedly a very singular one, but many qualities that were once thought to be uniquely human do not now appear to be so. Some of the qualities of language are found in other animals and yet our use of language goes far beyond anything that has been observed in other species. Human language is a highly complex communication system: it can be written, spoken, communicated through gestures and, with 'tools', any message can be conveyed around the world, by radio for example, or beyond by satellite.

Our ability to solve problems by thinking or with the use of tools exceeds that shown by other animals. Tool-use has become essential to our survival; it is central to our way of life. Our thinking powers also appear to be beyond those of any other creature. We can reflect on our nature and mortality, the reason why we are here on earth, and the possible existence of an all-powerful deity. Our quest for understanding appears to be greatly in excess of that shown by other animals for, although we may observe curiosity in other animals, as Diane Fossey did in describing a gorilla exploring its own fingers through her binoculars, our need to explore and find out appears to go so very much further. But our ability to solve problems does not mean we have found all the answers.

We are very special animals, but we still have many problems to solve and not least of these is the solution to the problem of our inhumanity to our own kind and to other animals.

Recommended Reading

Dawkins, M.S. (1980). *Animal Suffering: The Science of Animal Welfare.*
London: Chapman & Hall.

Gould, J.L. (1982). *Ethology, the Mechanisms and Evolution of Behaviour.* London: W.W. Norton.

Griffin, D.R. (1976). *A Question of Animal Awareness.* New York: Rockefeller University Press.

McFarland, D. (1985). *Animal Behaviour: Ethology and Evolution.* London: Pitman.

References

Beninger, R.J., Kendall, S.B. & Vanderwof, C.H. (1974). The ability of rats to discriminate their own behaviour. *Canadian Journal of Psychology, 28,* 79–91. [Self-awareness in rats.]

Berryman, J.C. (1981). Animal communication. In A. Colman (ed.), *Cooperation and Competition in Humans and Animals.* Wokingham, England: Van Nostrand Reinhold. [General coverage of communication in non-human animals.]

Berryman, J.C., Howells, K. & Lloyd-Evans, M. (1985). Pet owner attitudes to pets and people: a psychological study. *Veterinary Record,* 117. [Relationships between people and pets.]

Bitterman, M.E. (1965). The evolution of intelligence. *Scientific American.* London: W.H. Freeman. [Intelligence compared in a variety of animals.]

Crocker, J. (1985). Respect of feathered friends. *New Scientist, 1477,* 47–50. [Tool-use in crows and the 'talking' parrot are discussed.]

Dickemann, M. (1985). Human sociobiology: the first decade. *New Scientist, 1477,* 38–42. [Female infanticide in humans.]

Eaton, G.G. (1976). Social order of Japanese macaques. *Scientific American, 235(4),* 96–106. [Cultural transmission in macaques.]

Fossey, D. (1983). *Gorillas in the Mist.* London: Hodder & Stoughton. [A detailed study of gorillas.]

Gallup, G.G. Jr. (1979). Self-awareness in primates. *American Scientist, 67,* 417–421. [Use of mirrors by chimpanzees.]

Holland, V.D. & Delius, J.D. (1983). Rotational invariance in visual pattern recognition by pigeons and humans. *Science, 218,* 804–806. [Pigeons and pattern recognition.]

Rohles, F.H. & Devine, J.V. (1966). Chimpanzee on a problem involving the concept of middleness. *Animal Behaviour, 14,* 159–162. [Chimpanzees and the concept of middleness.]

Ryder, R.D. (1975). *Victims of Science.* London: Davis-Poynter. [Speciesism and animal experimentation considered.]

Thorpe, W.H. (1974). *Animal Nature and Human Nature.* London: Methuen. [Hockett and the qualities of language.]

HUMAN AND PET RELATIONSHIPS COMPARED

This exercise takes some time to complete: allow yourself about one hour.

INSTRUCTIONS: Write down the name, on separate cards, of a person known to you in each of the following categories: *1.* Spouse or girl/boyfriend. *2.* Friend of same sex. *3.* Parent of same sex. *4.* Own child (when under 10 years). Or, if you have no child imagine how he or she would be. *5.* A well-liked child under 10 years of age known to you. *6.* Someone you dislike. *7.* Your present pet. *8.* A former pet.

Shuffle the eight cards and take three at random (a triad).

Think about your relationship with these three; in what important way are two of those relationships different from the third?

Note this 'construct' down giving its opposite pole too (e.g. your Construct No. 1 might be 'easy to talk to' – 'difficult to talk to').

Shuffle the eight cards and repeat this procedure until you have about 10 different constructs.

DO NOT PROCEED UNTIL YOU HAVE COMPLETED THIS.

Now draw a grid of 8 x 10 squares (or however many constructs you found). (See over page.)

Taking one construct at a time, note which pole applies to the individuals (elements) listed. Use '1' for the positive end of the pole (choose the end which you prefer) and '0' for the opposite end. In the example given above you could use '1' for 'easy to talk to' and '0' for 'difficult to talk to').

Fill in the grid, working one construct at a time. If the construct does not apply at all to some elements leave the squares blank.

When the grid is complete you can compare the profile of each of the eight relationships which you have explored.

Who is most like whom?

Is your pet relationship like that which you have with a friend, or a child, or is it unlike all your human relationships?

You will probably discover some interesting similarities and differences in your relationships with others.

You may repeat the whole exercise using different people if you wish.

HUMAN AND PET RELATIONSHIPS COMPARED

ELEMENTS	PERSONAL CONSTRUCTS									
	1	2	3	4	5	6	7	8	9	10
1 LUKE	1	1								
2 MOTHER	1	0								
3 MARY	1	1								
4 LISA	0	0								
5 TOM	1	0								
6 PAUL	0	0								
7 ROVER	1	1								
8 PATCH	0	1								

Constructs 1 and 2 have been filled in on the grid as an example.

12. *Psychological Research Methods and You*

▽   *Experimental, correlational and observational methods.*
▽   *Surveys and tests.*
▽   *The individual in psychology.*
▽   *Longitudinal and cross-sectional studies.*
▽   *Fields of psychology.*
▽   *Psychology and the paranormal.*
▽   *Psychology and YOU.*

If you volunteered to take part in some psychological research what would be expected of you?

Throughout this book you will have noticed that much of what has been said about human behaviour, cognition and emotion has been backed up by psychological research: research which has enabled psychologists to explain some of the underlying causes and mechanisms controlling what we do, think and feel. Over the years our understanding of people has developed and changed and at times one view has been completely superseded by another one: we noted in Chapter 3, for instance, that views on sex differences in intellectual abilities have changed profoundly over the last century, and in Chapter 6 that opposite advice has been given on child rearing at different times.

Repeatable and scientific

All psychologists are trained in research methods and an important feature of these methods is *replication*. If psychologists can repeat a piece of research and reproduce the earlier findings then they are

239

justified in believing that the two sets of results are more than just a chance occurrence. This scientific approach to the study of people and other animals has many advantages, but it also has some limitations: there are some areas of human experience with which this approach cannot deal adequately.

Psychoanalysis

The scientific approach within psychology came, in part, as a reaction to some of the earlier approaches – in particular to that of Sigmund Freud. We noted, in the Introduction, that Freud's psychoanalytic theory explained the basis of human behaviour in terms of instincts housed in an unconscious area of mind. By concentrating on this aspect of the mind Freud's theory, by its very nature, could not be proved or disproved in any scientific sense and, as a result, many psychologists rejected his views as not useful.

Behaviourism

One person whose approach was in total contrast to Freud was John Watson (1875–1958) the main instigator of Behaviourism who was discussed in Chapter 9. Behaviourists are concerned with the stimuli which act on an organism to change or shape its behaviour. The organism is viewed from the outside; its behaviour, the readily observable acts, form the data for this school of psychology. The stimulus–response connection, or S–R connection as it came to be known, is central to this approach. The mind plays no part because it can not be observed directly.

 Watson found that much learning in humans and other animals could be explained in terms of these observable connections, as he showed with 'Little Albert' (in Chapter 7), and he went so far as to say that given the appropriate environment any normal child could be *made* into a lawyer, artist or beggar. In many ways Watson's views were very optimistic – almost anything is possible – whereas for Freud, because the most basic drives were thought to be inbuilt, they formed and shaped the person in ways that could not be escaped.

Psychoanalysis and Behaviourism can be seen as at the two extremes of the influences on psychology. Other theories and schools of psychology have developed which also play an important part in contemporary psychology, but these cannot be detailed here. Nevertheless all the approaches have contributed to the methodology of the discipline and it is to these methods that we now turn our attention. We begin with the *experimental method* described in the Introduction.

EXPERIMENTAL, CORRELATIONAL AND OBSERVATIONAL METHODS

The drug experiment described at the start of the book, on page 7, illustrates one form of a typical experiment in psychology. It was designed to answer a specific question: 'Does a particular drug reduce anxiety in anxious people?' The experiment included an experimental group to whom the drug, the *independent variable,* was administered and a control group who received a placebo in place of the active drug. The independent variable is so called because it is the variable which the psychologist chooses to manipulate. The aspect of behaviour which is measured following the treatment, in this case anxiety, is called the *dependent variable* because it is assumed to be dependent on the treatment which the experimental group receives. A comparison of the anxiety levels in the experimental and control groups enables the psychologist to measure the efficacy of the drug; the experiment has been planned so that the only difference between the groups is the presence or absence of the active drug, and the control group provides a baseline level of response with which the effects of the drug can be compared.

Control groups

A no-drug control group of this kind is not always essential in the design of an experiment of this kind. In some cases the psychologist may simply use two or more dose levels of the drug (or levels of the independent variable) because these also enable a comparison to be made. Psychological experiments are described throughout this book and include: the Purdue University 'touching' experiment in Chapter 1, the 'tedious task' experiment in Chapter 4, and the learning and recall experiment 'underwater' or 'on land' in Chapter 8.

Useful though the experimental method is, it has its limitations. An experiment is only appropriate when we have a specific hypothesis to test. But even with a hypothesis we are not always willing or able to perform experiments. The Milgram experiment supposedly on the effects of punishment on memory (in Chapter 4) is an example of an experiment which today we would *not* be willing to perform because it would be regarded as unethical. And there are other situations in which a hypothesis cannot be tested experimentally.

Correlations

The question 'are females more intelligent than males?' is one such example, because it is not possible to compare two groups of people identical in all but sex. In other words, the *independent variable* of sex cannot be assigned by the psychologist to one group as can the drug in the study outlined earlier. All that can be done is to compare groups of males and females who share a number of similarities (age, class, education, and so on) and compare the results. This is a *correlational study* and one result might be that the males performed at level B and the females performed at level A on a given test of intelligence. Such a finding tells us nothing about whether our biology (in this case sex) determines our performance on intelligence tests. There is a common tendency to confuse correlational findings with causal links between two factors.

'Natural' experiments

Alternatively, a hypothesis might be 'are the frontal lobes of the brain the part which is concerned with self-awareness?' Once again this is an example where an experiment would be considered unethical. But sometimes 'natural' experiments arise which permit a comparison to be made between those with and without a particular part of the brain. Sadly, the 1939–45 war provided many severely brain-damaged people and, by studying these people, neurophysiologists and psychologists came to understand much more about the relationships between parts of the brain, behaviour and experience.

Another example of a 'natural experiment' is found in the research on children who have been orphaned. Much of the research in Chapter 5 on love and attachment arose out of comparing such orphaned children with those who live with their parents.

How objective are the 'facts'?

One problem for psychologists is the nature of the questions asked or hypotheses generated. Ideally they should be objective and not evaluative. But this can be quite difficult to achieve – values are often implicit in what we accept as 'facts'. An example of this problem can be seen in past views of racial differences. About 100 years ago many

British white people accepted as a fact their own superiority over black- and brown-skinned people. The latter were felt to be less intelligent and in need of control by the white people whom they frequently served. So strong was the belief that skin colour and superiority were linked that a naturalist, Thomas Belt, recording the behaviour of the army ant, noted that the 'light coloured officers' kept the 'common dark-coloured workers' in line. The superiority of a light skin evidently extends across the animal kingdom. Such an assumption may seem laughable today but in a society where racism was endemic such views were accepted as objective facts about humans and ants. We have not yet outgrown all such problems.

Feminist psychologists, for instance, have argued that the questions posed in psychology (and other disciplines) are bound to be value-laden in a patriarchal society. Male dominance or superiority is, they suggest, implicit in our view of the sexes, and male and female roles are often assumed to be determined in great part by biology (as we saw in Chapter 3). Thus, for example, since women tend to do most child care, questions about the 'maternal instinct' lack objectivity because implicit in this is an assumption that it is right that women should be maternal. Females lacking such feelings are thought to lack an essential feminine quality whereas males lacking such feelings do not have their masculinity questioned.

Observing

Often a psychologist will begin research without any specific question or hypothesis in mind. She or he may wish to study a particular topic within human behaviour or the behaviour of non-human animals. For instance, an activity such as play in children may be chosen because the psychologist wants to understand more about this activity. The first phase in such a study is observation – the psychologist simply observes the behaviour in as many naturally occurring situations as possible. Once this is done it may then be possible to investigate more rigorously – perhaps by experiment – a particular piece of behaviour. At this point questions may be asked, such as 'does play experience influence children's performance in learning and thinking?' (discussed in Chapter 6).

Observational methods are a vital first stage in research but on their own they can rarely answer our questions about behaviour. The majority of research on non-human animals described in Chapter 11 began with careful observation of the animals in their natural habitats, but after the initial observations we need to control the variables involved, changing one thing at a time, before we can see the individual effect of a given factor on the behaviour under scrutiny. In natural circumstances there are usually too many uncontrolled variables for us to be able to identify how one event influences another.

SURVEYS AND TESTS

Other methods used by psychologists include *surveys* and *tests*. The psychologists may, for example, wish to find out what people do, think or feel in an area in which there are little or no data. The survey includes questions and perhaps interviews. One of the most famous surveys was that by Alfred Kinsey and his co-workers on sexual behaviour mentioned in Chapters 3 and 7. Prior to this little was known about the average person's sexual experiences and this survey was an attempt to find such information at a time when observational methods were considered inappropriate. Since Kinsey other researchers, such as William Masters and Virginia Johnson, have studied sexual behaviour in the laboratory. Volunteers prepared to be subjects have been observed and recorded during sexual activity. Whilst such research may seem to be voyeuristic to some readers it produced a much greater understanding of this aspect of human behaviour. As a result of this research many people who have sexual problems have been helped.

Finding the norm

Charting what is average or 'normal' for humans is one important aspect of psychological research. We all tend to take ourselves as the norm (providing that we are not too obviously different from our peers) and discovering that others' experience may be very unlike our own is important in increasing our understanding of others. The primary purpose of much research on child development, as we saw in Chapter 6, has been to establish what the average child, in a given culture, is capable of at a given age. A parent with little contact with other parents may worry greatly at a child's nightmares, bed-wetting, thumb-sucking or nail-biting, but all these are common at a particular stage in development and are thus quite 'normal'. This knowledge can bring relief to the parent. Normal is not, of course, necessarily 'desirable' or 'good'. Having nightmares is distressing whether or not other children also have them and it should not prevent us from searching for their cause or finding some way to alleviate them.

Tests are conducted in psychology to measure a variety of aspects of human behaviour – personality and intelligence are just two examples, which are considered in Chapters 2 and 10. Tests are carefully constructed so that the aspect of humans in question can be systematically examined in large numbers of people. As we saw in Chapter 10, intelligence tests are made up of a range of questions, or exercises, which people are asked to complete under specified conditions. The variations in the people tested can then be correlated with their test performance. If it is found that children who are educationally disadvantaged do less well on intelligence tests, then such a finding may lead to the suggestion that their education should be changed. If improved education makes for no improvement in the children's performance then other causes need to be investigated.

THE INDIVIDUAL IN PSYCHOLOGY

Many of the psychologist's methods are concerned with the study of subjects who are grouped on the basis of some similarity. But all of us know that we are unique individuals – even identical twins, who may look undistinguishable to others, have different environments and as people they may be very aware of their uniqueness. Much of scientific psychology seems to overlook this individuality; indeed, the Humanistic approach in psychology stresses that science is not the total answer to our understanding of people; rigorous observation and experiment excludes important aspects of the individual's subjective experience. However, one particular approach – the *case study* – makes the individual the focus of attention.

A case study is an individual case history. The life of a person is reconstructed at a given point in time through the memories of that person and others, plus the aid of recorded events (for example, diaries). The clinical psychologist might use this technique to find out whether an earlier life event is a significant factor in the precipitation of a later problem. An example of this type of approach was described for Ms J. in Chapter 7. Personal Construct Theory is also a technique which seeks to explore the subjective experience of the individual. Examples of this can be found in Chapters 2 and 11.

LONGITUDINAL AND CROSS-SECTIONAL STUDIES

A case study is typically retrospective, but another variation on this is to plan a study of individuals over many years by regular interviewing over that period. A *longitudinal study* is designed to do this over 10, 20 or even more years; we saw an example in Chapter 4 in which children's TV viewing and general behaviour was investigated at 9 and 19 years of age. The advantage of this over the case study is that the data are collected by direct interview and the problems of remembering in the case history approach are avoided. Longitudinal studies have the advantage that they provide in-depth data on each individual but they also permit comparison between individuals.

Obviously longitudinal studies are time-consuming and expensive; an alternative way of getting information about changes over time is the *cross-sectional study.* In this, groups of people at different ages, matched on a range of criteria, are tested. For instance 100 people in each group at ages 10, 15, 20, 25, 30, 35 and 40 years, and matched on such factors as education, socio-economic status, and health, might be investigated. Although such a study enables a comparison to be made between people of different ages it can give us no information about change in any one individual over time. The 40-year-old's life experience might be so unlike that of the 10-year-old that differences between the two may be due largely to their being born into very different environments rather than age differences *per se.* These generational differences are known as cohort effects.

One of the most encouraging findings of recent years which arose out of improved research methods and which illustrates the cohort effect was the discovery that intellectual changes with age are much less than was once thought by psychologists. Earlier conclusions that ageing was associated with intellectual decline were based on cross-sectional data. However longitudinal data, by Warner Schaie and others, have shown that performance on intellectual tasks *improves* throughout the major part of adulthood. The earlier finding could be attributed not to age but to cohort effects. This work has transformed our view of adulthood which is now seen as a *developmental* period of life just as is the earlier phase of life. The notion that 'you can't teach an old dog new tricks' is changing. Old dogs and old people are discovering that there is still a lot of learning possible. Today the concept of life-long learning is accepted because psychological research has shown that popular wisdom has underestimated the abilities of older people.

FIELDS OF PSYCHOLOGY

Psychologists usually work within specific areas of psychology each with its own particular methods of study. Physiological psychologists study the brain, nervous system, and other bodily processes to discover how each influences the others. The study of brain-damaged patients mentioned earlier is carried out by them. Experimental psychology and comparative psychology are both fields in which experimental methods are applied to assist in understanding the behaviour of humans and other animals. Traditionally experimental psychology is often used to explain how people respond to external stimuli (as in visual perception) but the use of experimental methods is not confined to this area as the numerous examples throughout this book show.

Human development is the province of developmental psychologists who are concerned with explaining development throughout life. This topic may seem to embrace every aspect of human psychology but in fact personality, cognition and social psychology are generally considered to be separate specialities, though interrelated. Influences in human development shape our personalities, but the latter field has become so specialized and is often concerned with devising methods of personality assessment that the field is generally considered to be a separate one. Cognitive psychologists study how the mind processes the information which is received – processes involved in memory or problem-solving for example. The influence of others on the individual is the concern of social psychologists and, as we saw, a person's behaviour can be greatly changed by the social context within which it occurs.

Clinical psychologists are occupied with people with psychological problems. Their concern ranges from the treatment of relatively minor stresses to the major forms of mental illness such as schizophrenia. Their aims are to diagnose the nature of the illness and to effect its treatment.

Psychologists are also found in many applied fields, for instance educational psychologists who specialize in helping children both in the classroom and in the home. Applied psychologists are active in many other areas of life, from advertising to personnel selection, but essentially their aim is to apply the fast expanding body of knowledge in psychology to people in all walks of life.

PSYCHOLOGY AND THE PARANORMAL

It must be clear to the reader that there are various areas with which psychologists are less well equipped to deal. The work of psychologists typically aims at producing results which are *repeatable* but some events in our lives are single, or one-off occurrences. If you have seen a ghost or had a prophetic dream it is unlikely that you could reproduce the event on demand so that the psychologist could investigate it. Attempts to produce paranormal phenomena such as extra-sensory perception (ESP), telepathy and psychokinesis, in the laboratory, have rarely succeeded and, as yet, psychologists have developed very few successful techniques to investigate these phenomena, or theories to adequately explain them.

While there is evidence that many parapsychological phenomena may be the result of distorted perceptions on the part of the observer, or deception on the part of others, there are enough examples of 'unexplained knowledge' for most psychologists not to dismiss this topic as a bogus area of study.

A recent president of The British Psychological Society, Ralph Hetherington, has drawn the attention of psychologists to the need to investigate paranormal phenomena. In a public lecture he described one well-documented case of premonition experienced by a Mr John A. A. Williams in 1910.

Mr Williams was proprietor of a large slate quarry and one day, whilst travelling by car, he suddenly felt certain that there was soon to be a terrible disaster at the quarry. He drove to the nearest post office and contacted the quarry (by 'a wire') to tell the quarry manager to stop his men from working in the quarry immediately. This the manager did and shortly afterwards all the ground on which the men had been working fell over 300 feet (about 100 metres) to the bottom of the quarry. Without Mr Williams' directive the men would undoubtedly have been killed.

Detailed evidence of this case was gathered and yet no good explanation of John Williams' 'knowledge' has ever been found. Could John Williams have noticed some small sign on a recent visit to the quarry which revealed the quarry's precarious state? The possibility cannot be ignored but amongst all those who have carefully considered this case this explanation seems inadequate. What other explanations are there? If John Williams literally saw no signs of the impending disaster then how did he come to know of it?

Psychologists cannot explain such incidents adequately. This well-documented case is only one of many. Psychologists are beginning to consider how they can research these apparently paranormal phenomena which people report. It may be a long time before we begin to understand just how these things happen but trying to unravel these mysteries is an exciting prospect; perhaps in the years to come we shall have some explanations to offer for some of the extraordinary phenomena that we call the paranormal.

PSYCHOLOGY AND YOU

The impact of psychology on the lives of us all is considerable. Advances in psychological research have enabled us to understand much more about alleviating the distress caused by psychological problems; they have increased our understanding of how the mind works, and how we think and feel; they have highlighted the best conditions for promoting learning and creativity; and they have enabled us to pinpoint some of the causes of human weaknesses and strengths. Much is yet to be understood and there can be no doubt that, in future, we shall enlarge our knowledge. Nevertheless the majority of the explanations which psychologists have to offer look at the similarities between people, the needs, drives, wishes and behaviour patterns which some or all people have in common.

There is, however, at least one area which is never likely to be fully explained by psychologists, and that is: what makes you the unique individual that you are?

Recommended Reading

Boring, E.G. (1957). *A History of Experimental Psychology.* New York: Appleton Century Crofts.

Colman, A.M. (1981). *What is Psychology?* London: Kogan Page.

Thomson, R. (1968). *The Pelican History of Psychology.* Harmondsworth: Penguin.

References

Belt, T. (1888). *The Naturalist in Nicaragua.* London: Edward Bumpus. [Includes descriptions of the behaviour of army ants.]

Hetherington, R. (1983). Sacred cows and white elephants. *Bulletin of The British Psychology Society, 36*, 273–280. [Rare and one-off events.]

Kinsey, A.C., Pomeroy, W.B. & Martin, C.E. (1953). *Sexual Behaviour in the Human Female.* Philadelphia: W.B. Saunders. [One of the first major studies of female sexual behaviour.]

Masters, W.H. & Johnson, V.E. (1966). *Human Sexual Response.* Boston: Little, Brown. [The first major study of human sexual responses.]

Schaie, K.W. (1975). Age changes in adult intelligence. In D.S. Woodruff and J.E. Birren (eds), *Aging: Scientific Perspectives and Social Issues.* New York: Van Nostrand. [Intellectual changes with age.]

Sidgwick, M., Gurney, E., Myers, F.W.H. & Podmore, F. (1962). *Phantasms of the Living: cases of telepathy printed in the Journal of the Society for Psychical Research during thirty five years.* New York: University Books Inc. [Includes the description of a premonition by Mr J.A.A. Williams, on pages 119–123.]

GLOSSARY

Ability tests: tests designed to measure people's maximum performance, independent of their learning.

Adrenal gland: a hormone-producing or endocrine gland situated over the kidneys.

Adrenaline: hormone secreted by the adrenal gland and active in emotional excitement.

Age norms: the average scores obtained on psychological tests by people at given age levels.

Aggregation: A summing together of different instances of behaviour.

Agoraphobia: one of the more common forms of irrational fear or phobia in clinical groups. Strong fear and panic may occur in a range of situations, such as crowds, public places, travelling on trains or buses.

Androgens: a collective term for the hormones produced chiefly by the testes, the chief one of which is testosterone. Responsible for the maintenance and development of many male sexual characteristics.

Androgyny: the combination of masculine and feminine characteristics within an individual male or female.

Area striata: the part of the brain which deals with vision.

Attachment behaviour: behaviour which promotes proximity and physical contact with the object of the attachment.

Attainment tests: tests designed to measure people's progress, or learning, on a given course of instruction.

Attribution: the perception of the *cause* of an event.

Authoritarian personality: a constellation of personality characteristics which characterize people with prejudiced attitudes centering on respect for authority.

Auto-kinetic effect: the apparent movement of a stationary spot of light when seen in complete darkness.

Autonomic nervous system: a system of nerve cells and nerve fibres which control the functions of smooth muscles and glands.

Behaviourism: a school of psychology associated with John B. Watson. It defined psychology as the study of behaviour, and limited the data in psychology to observable activities. Mental events were excluded.

Behaviour modification: therapeutic technique, often involving the use of rewards and punishments, based on operant conditioning.

Catharsis: the purging or release of an emotion through direct or indirect expression (e.g. fantasy expressing).

Central nervous system: the brain and spinal cord.

Cerebral cortex: that part of the brain responsible for many 'higher' human mental activities.

Chromosome: microscopic body found in a cell nucleus containing genes, the individual's hereditary material.

Classical conditioning: the learning of a response through association with a previously neutral stimulus and studied by Pavlov.

Cognition: a person's thoughts, knowledge and ideas about him/herself and the environment.

Cognitive dissonance theory: one of the best-known cognitive consistency theories, which was proposed by Leon Festinger, and which explains how people resolve inconsistencies in their knowledge, beliefs and behaviour.

Cognitive processes: refers to mental activities involving evaluation and appraisal. It can sometimes be used as equivalent to thought.

Consciousness: a state in which an individual is aware of or is 'inside' what is happening. Often used synonymously with awareness but generally thought to be rather more than this.

Conservation: a cognitive advance which Piaget proposed as a central feature of concrete operational thinking, acquired at around the age of seven.

Constructive alternativism: the theory that the world may be construed in very different ways without any one view being 'correct' in an absolute sense.

Control group: a group in an experiment that is not given the treatment whose effect is being studie (see *Experimental group*).

Convergent thinking: the ability to focus on the correct solution to a problem.

Correlational study: a study which is designed to find out the degree of correspondence between two sets of measures.

Dependent variable: the behaviour or response measured in a psychological experiment which is believed to be changed by the independent variable.

Discrimination: the process of learning to differentiate between various stimuli in order to produce the correct response.

Divergent thinking: the ability to generate different ideas from a given proposition, or problem.

Echoic memory: the sensory memory system for sound.

Echolocation: the emission by an animal of high frequency sounds which can be heard and timed by that animal as they are reflected off solid objects in the vicinity. Used by bats for flight in darkness and the location of food.

Ecological approach: a research strategy in developmental psychology which takes account of all the interacting social and environmental influences upon humans.

Egocentrism: the tendency to see the world only from one's own point of view, which Piaget believed was an essential feature of early childhood.

Encoding: the transformation of a sensory input into a form (code) for storage in memory.

Episodic memory: the part of the memory which holds details of people, places and events.

Ethologist: one who researches the behaviour of animals, and who works primarily in their natural habitats rather than the laboratory.

Experimental group: a group in an experiment that is given the treatment whose effect is being studie (see *Control group*).

Extinction: the gradual fading of behaviour when it fails to produce a reinforcing consequence.

Extravert: a psychological type who is more concerned with social life and the external world than with inner experience.

Factor analysis: a statistical technique which reduces a large number of test interrelationships to a small number of factors.

Family therapy: treatments taking the whole family, rather than the individual, as a focus.

Free association: a form of word association in which a subject reports any word which comes to mind in response to a stimulus. Also the reporting of anything that comes to mind without modification.

Gender identity: the concept of oneself as either masculine or feminine.

Gene: transmission of individual hereditary traits, contained in a chromosome.

Generalization: the production of a response by a stimulus similar, but not identical to, the original stimulus when learning took place.

Generalized anxiety disorder: chronic long-term high anxiety. The individual is continually anxious and frightened.

Hermaphrodite: an individual who has both male and female reproductive organs, also applied to individuals in whom there is a contradiction between their external genitals and/or secondary sexual characteristics and various internal structures e.g. gonads.

Hypothalamus: a part of the base of the brain concerned in particular emotions, motivation and sleep.

Iconic memory: the sensory memory system for vision.

Identification: a process of personality development involving taking on the characteristics of other people.

Imprinting: learning that occurs within a limited period early in life (usually in relation to the mother and likened by Lorenz to a pathological fixation); and which is relatively unmodifiable.

Independent variable: the variable in a psychological experiment which is under the control of the psychologist, and is varied by her or him.

Insight: the discovery of the solution to a problem.

Intelligence: a general ability whose definition remains elusive.

Interactionism: the view that both person and situation are important in determining behaviour.

Introvert: a psychological type who is more concerned with the inner life and reflection than with social life and the external world.

IQ tests: tests designed to measure the 'intelligence quotient', i.e. intelligence defined in some operational manner.

Lateral geniculate body: a part of the brain which acts as a relay for visual information from the eye to the visual cortex (area striata).

Long-term memory: the relatively permanent part of the memory system.

Moderator variable (use of): using a second measure in conjunction with a particular score to make a better prediction: for example, the prediction of school achievement from an intelligence test might be improved if a measure of 'motivation' were also used.

Motivation: the readiness to act to achieve certain goals and outcomes.

Motor reproduction: the physical carrying out of behaviours learned through observation.

Mutual gaze: when two people look at each other simultaneously.

Object permanence: the concept that objects still exist when they are out of sight, and which Piaget proposed was acquired in infancy.

Oedipus complex: the Freudian notion that at a certain stage boys experience a conflict between sexual desire for the mother and punishment (castration) by the father, and which derives from a famous Greek myth.

Oestrogen: a sex hormone produced by the ovaries and responsible for the development and maintenance of many female characteristics.

Operant behaviour: any behaviour which, following the established setting conditions, leads to reinforcement.

Optic chiasma: the point in the brain which is a cross-over junction for the optic nerves.

Ovary: the sex gland in the female which produces ova and sex hormones.

Panic disorder: a disorder in which severe fear escalates to a full-blown panic, typically 'out of the blue', rather than in response to any specific feared object or situation.

Paranormal: any psychological phenomenon that cannot be explained by current psychological theories, including telepathy, psychokinesis, poltergeists, clairvoyance and many others.

Parasympathetic nervous system: the cranial and sacral parts of the autonomic nervous system. Active in relaxed or quiescent states of the body.

Perceptual defence: the apparent refusal to see words which might be upsetting or taboo.

Personal construct: an important way in which an individual views his or her world. A pattern or template which the individual uses to make sense of his or her experience (from George Kelly's Personal Construct Theory).

Personal Construct Theory: a theory of the mind put forward by George Kelly.

Pituitary gland: a hormone-producing, or endocrine gland located at the base of the brain. Its secretions influence sexual development, metabolism and growth.

Placebo: an inert substance used in place of an active drug, given to a control group in an experiment.

Positivity bias: the bias towards viewing a situation in such a way as to enhance self-esteem.

Prejudice: negative or hostile attitudes towards groups of people which are based on overgeneralized stereotypes *(see Stereotypes).*

Presumed central tendency: the expectation that others will respond with the average or 'normal' response.

Proactive interference: the interference of items stored in memory with the learning and recall of new items.

Progesterone: a sex hormone produced by the ovaries and responsible for preparing the uterus for pregnancy and the breasts for lactation.

Projective tests: open-ended personality tests whose results rely on the subjective interpretation of the tester.

Psychoanalysis: a method developed by Freud and his followers concerning the treatment of mental and nervous disorders in which the role of the unconscious is emphasized.

Psychometrics: the theory and practice of psychological testing.

Reflex: a physiological reaction, such as eye-blink to a bright light, over which we have no control.

Reinforcement: any outcome of a behaviour which either maintains or increases the frequency of the behaviour.

Reliability: a statistical index of the degree to which a test provides consistent measurements.

Repertory grid: a technique devised by George Kelly to assess personal constructs.

Respondent behaviour: a type of behaviour which, unlike operant behaviour, corresponds to a reflex action.

Reticular activating system (also known as the reticular formation): a network of cells running up through the brain stem. It receives inputs from all sensory pathways and is closely connected to the spinal cord, thalamus and cortex. Thought to play an important role in arousal.

Retina: the part of the eye which is sensitive to light and contains the rods and cones.

Retroactive interference: the interference in memory of items memorized earlier by items subsequently learned.

Rods: elements of the retina for black-and-white vision.

Role taking: the process of imitating and identifying with the behaviour of other people, or role models.

Schedules of reinforcement: the rate at which behaviour produces the reward – the weekly pay packet, for example.

Schema (plural schemata): cognitive structures which are abstract representations of events, people, and relationships from the real physical world.

Schizophrenia: one of the most severe forms of mental disorder, often accompanied by hallucinations and disordered thinking.

Semantic memory: the part of memory which holds knowledge.

Sensory threshold: the level at which low levels of stimulation are first perceived.

Shaping-up: the gradual production of a complex behaviour by initially rewarding more and more accurate approximations to it.

Short-term memory: the part of the memory system taken to be of limited capacity and only able to hold material for relatively short periods of time.

Social comparison: people's constant need to validate their opinions by comparing them with those of others.

Social facilitation: the increase in speed of a response as a result of social stimuli from others engaged in the same behaviour.

Socialization: the process whereby newborns gradually become fully-fledged members of society.

Speciesism: a term used to describe the view that one species is more important than any other. Usually used in relation to humans versus other animals.

State-dependent memory: memory that is formed in a particular biological state – such as when drunk – and so is best recalled when the person is in a similar state.

Stereotypes: generalized sets of beliefs or attitudes about groups of people, which are usually inaccurate.

Symbolism: a major developmental acquisition of the second year of life which enables the child to internally 'represent' objects not immediately present.

Sympathetic nervous system: the part of the autonomic nervous system made up of the ganglionic chain lying outside and parallel to the spinal cord. Active in emotional excitement.

Transsexual: a person with a disorder of sexual identity: for example a transsexual man typically feels himself to be a female trapped in a male body and may want to live as a woman and to have surgery to feminize the body.

Transparencies: non-realistic aspects of young children's drawings where some parts of the scene or objects portrayed are visible through other parts.

Unconditioned response: a behaviour, such as a reflex, which naturally occurs following a given stimulus.

Validity: a statistical index of the degree to which a test measures that which it is supposed to measure.

INDEX